D0898380

PRAISE FOR THE WORKS OF

DAN NEEDLES

Winner of the Stephen Leacock Memorial Medal for Humour

"Needles writes better, with a finer sense of pitch and rhythm, than most of the dramatists whose work we are asked to take seriously." *National Post*

"Like visiting an old friend, but how many people do you know who are actually as entertaining as Walt Wingfield? . . . Comic gold." *Toronto Star*

"I love Wingfield on the stage and on the page— either way it's great entertainment that's family friendly and with a kind message at its heart." James from Summerside, Prince Edward Island

"Skillfully drawn observations on human foibles." *Times Colonist*

"Persephone Township may not be on the map, but it is none-theless in the Canadian psyche." *The Globe and Mail*

Wingfield's
WORLD

The

COMPLETE LETTERS

from

WINGFIELD

FARM

Wingfield's
WORLD

DAN NEEDLES

Vintage Canada

To Heath

(L - R) Dan Needles, actor Rod Beattie and director Doug Beattie strike a Three Musketeers pose at the opening of *Wingfield Unbound*, the fourth play in the series, in front of the Grand Theatre in London, Ontario, in April 1997. (Photo courtesy of Off Broadway)

PREFACE

The first of Walt Wingfield's letters to the editor was published in 1974 in the Shelburne *Free Press and Economist*, a weekly newspaper in Southwestern Ontario. Walt has been writing, on and off, pretty much ever since.

In 1984, the letters to the editor became the basis for a one-man stage play, "Letter from Wingfield Farm," performed by Rod Beattie and directed by his brother Doug, which introduced the story of the stockbroker-turned-farmer to a wider audience. Six more episodes followed over the next twenty-five years, and Walt's adventures in Persephone Township played out in theatres across Canada and the United States.

Over the years, Walt has become an alter ego, not just to this writer but also to my friend Rod, who lives with the characters of the Seventh Line every day on stage. They used to be my friends, but now it seems they spend all their spare time over at Rod's place, shooting pool. Rod and I have both spent a considerable part of our lives inhabiting this peculiar parallel universe of the town of Larkspur and its environs.

The only reason we celebrate decades and centenaries is because of the calculations of some forgotten Byzantine astrologer. Seven has always been a much more significant number for me personally, and it appears the Wingfield saga has come to a resting point after the seventh episode. I thought it was an appropriate time to bring all the letters together in one volume, tracing Walt's story from the day he arrives on the farm, through marriage, fatherhood and a deeper exploration of his adopted community. Walt's years are calculated in roughly the same way we measure dog years; one season in Walt's life works out to be about four seasons of real time for the rest of us.

So, by my convoluted reckoning, this volume stands as the twenty-eighth anniversary edition of the "Letter from Wingfield Farm." Hope you can join us for the celebration. Dogs are welcome!

Chapter One

LETTER FROM

Wingfield

FARM

A NOTE FROM THE EDITOR

There's a lot to read in a weekly newspaper. At first bounce, you wouldn't think there was anything much to say about a town like Larkspur. And yet my staff and I manage to squeeze ten thousand words a week into every issue of the *Free Press and Economist*. Forty thousand words a month. About eight fair-sized novels every year, I guess.

Of course, you couldn't find anyone to publish novels like this. That's because we're dealing with the public side of life in the community; only those sanded and polished and varnished facts that can be printed safely without leading to anything more controversial than a brick through the front office window. Nothing is said about the darker side of Larkspur life . . . although we look hopefully every week in the police report.

No. You have to go to the city papers for the juicy stuff. Nowhere in this slag-heap of words will you find the Larkspur resident unclothed, so to speak . . . although I see the Turnip Festival Queen sure made a stab at it this week.

The closest we come, I suppose, would be Walt Wingfield and his Letters from Wingfield Farm. Generally speaking, if you asked my advice on how to run a weekly newspaper I'd say avoid unsolicited contributions. Every crackpot within fifteen miles wants to get something in the paper. But in my case, some of my best material came to me just that way.

Walt Wingfield is an ex–chairman-of-the-board–turned–farmer. He used to be chairman and chief executive officer of MacFeeters, Bartlett and Hendrie . . . the big brokerage house down on Bay Street. Well, one day about a year ago, he gave up his six-figure income and bought a hundred-acre farm out on the Seventh Concession of Persephone Township. He said he wanted to make a stand, to simplify his life.

He'd taken on a tough job. If you look at a climate-and-soil map for this part of Southern Ontario you'll see a small circular zone marked "4a." That is Persephone Township. "Pursefoan" in the native dialect. It enjoys the same climate and growing conditions as Churchill, Manitoba. It is a land of sand hills, cedar swamp, feldspar outcroppings and about half an inch of topsoil.

The day he arrived in town, Walt stopped by the office to buy a subscription and we had a chat. I could see what he was doing was very important to him. He wanted more of an audience than just his ducks and chickens. He suggested my readers might be interested in a weekly progress report. I listened to him, without telling him yes or no, because I wanted to think about it. He didn't press me for an answer, which surprised me because you know how city people always want to know everything right now.

Then, one day about a week later, I was clearing up at the back after we'd closed and I looked up to see Walt pushing an envelope through the mail-slot. The transformation was remarkable. Gone was the three-piece pin-striped suit and in its place was the "After Dawn" look by Co-op: blue denim bib overalls, a Korean tartan flannelette shirt, brand-new work boots and a green forage hat.

I opened the envelope and found a letter that turned out to be the first in a series of missives that now form a kind of farm diary for Walt's first year out on the Seventh Concession.

⟶ *April 21*

Dear Ed,

I was delighted to meet you on my first day in Larkspur last week and I enjoyed our chat thoroughly. You may remember my telling you I've taken over the old Fisher place at R.R. #1, Larkspur, on the Seventh Concession. I've taken a leave of absence from my firm in Toronto in order to try this experiment in farming, which has long been on my mind.

At my age there isn't really much time left for a man to explore some of the things he might have done or been. I've enjoyed some success in the world of finance, for which I'm grateful, but, still, I have a deep and unswerving conviction that a man may pursue his life and satisfy his wants with far less brouhaha than I have experienced so far. Persephone Township is the place to prove it.

The Fishers had their auction last Saturday. I watched as the neighbourhood descended on the place and picked it clean. After it was over, and the Fishers had driven off to their new place in town, the auctioneer walked over the property with me. His name is Freddy. He's an interesting chap, friendly and outgoing, and seems to be well-regarded as an auctioneer despite a very noticeable stammer, which brings his sales to a complete halt from time to time. He runs a beef and dairy operation on the farm next door; plants corn, grain, potatoes, turnips; does auction sales, some blacksmithing, small auto repairs and real estate. It's what I believe is called mixed farming.

As we walked, Freddy and I talked about the farm and my plans for the summer. Although the sun is warm and some green is starting to show through the dead grass, the ground is still spongy, muddy and wet. We stopped beside an old hay-wagon parked out behind the barn.

"That'll come in handy," I said.

Freddy pushed his eyebrows up and stared at the sky.

"Well, now, Walt, maybe I should have mentioned this before, b-b-but I lent that wagon to old Fisher last summer. You're welcome to the loan of it, if you like."

We walked on.

"What's this? A perfectly serviceable old hay-rake. I'm glad that wasn't sold at the auction."

"Well, now, there again, Walt, that belongs to The Squire across the road. I asked him to take it away before the auction b-b-but. . . ."

I explained that the first thing I was going to need was some cedar posts for a fence.

"By golly, Walt, old Fisher bought some cedar posts off me last fall and n-n-never picked them up. I guess they belong to you now."

"Is there anything else of mine in the neighbourhood?" I asked.

Over the next couple of days I lost the hay-wagon and the rake but I had returned to me: fifty cedar posts, a cream-separator, a cultivator, a set of harrows, five bags of cement, a load of corn and a horse. The horse is a mare named Dolly or something, but I have named her Feedbin since that is where she can most often be found. She's a spirited creature and seems to have been a racehorse at some time or other, because she can turn only to the left. Consequently, I make a perfect spectacle of myself, riding into Larkspur. Freddy has been no help at all about this.

"You'll get used to her," was all he could offer. "Besides, you're not going to be using her much!"

That is where he is wrong, for I propose to teach this horse to pull a plough. As I explained to Freddy, when you drive loud machinery, you miss a great deal of what nature has to offer. You can't hear the rich pageantry of life in the hedgerows if you insist on riding around the fields on a noisy tractor. Of course, Freddy couldn't understand this. But he has been extremely helpful none the less. He put out the word and now all the old horse-drawn implements on the Seventh Concession have been pulled out of driving sheds and left in a pile at my gate. With a few small repairs they'll be as good as new.

I'm not fooling around here. I've never been more serious in my life. I propose to be as good at this farming game as my neighbours, but, at the same time, I plan to preserve some of the old ways. It won't happen overnight, but eventually, the neighbourhood will come to think of me in much the same light as Montaigne and Thoreau were thought of in their communities—gentlemen farmers, rich in barnyard philosophy.

I see myself driving into town in the carriage often enough that they'll feel obliged to put up a hitching post in front of the General Store. Won't that be something?

Yours sincerely,
Walt

Dear Ed,

I struck the first snag in the livestock department while doing chores this morning. One of my new ducks stood apart from the rest of the flock, rocking uneasily back and forth on his heels, as if someone were trying to push him off balance. When I approached he quacked and fell over, struggled to his feet and went back to wobbling precariously back and forth.

All was clearly not well. After chores, I picked him up and started down the lane for the farm across the road. It seemed an excellent opportunity to meet the neighbours for the first time. By giving them an opportunity to show their expertise and offer advice, I hoped to win new friends . . . and cure the duck.

As it turned out I met my neighbour in the road, a man known in the community as The Squire. He is an elderly man, round-shouldered and bent over from many years of hard work. He was wearing a shabby pair of patched hound's-tooth trousers, which might have been fashionable for a few weeks in the 1960s, and a long-sleeved shirt with pink flamingos on it. He was busy snatching handfuls of bird's nest out of the mailbox and arguing with a squadron of blackbirds hovering a few feet above his head.

"Good morning. I'm Walt Wingfield."

He looked up sharply and peered at me as if the morning sun hurt his eyes.

"G'day."

His attention returned to the mailbox. I made another attempt to start conversation.

"I've taken over the old Fisher place. Lovely morning. Have you lived in the area all your life?"

He thought about this for a moment, peered at me again and said, "Not yet."

I laughed politely and carried on. "I seem to be having a problem with this duck. It doesn't seem to be able to keep its balance. A very bad case of the wobbles, you might say."

That got his attention. The Squire straightened up and examined the duck more closely.

"Wobbles?" he said. "You've kept ducks before, have you?"

I hadn't, but as long as he thought so I wasn't going to persuade him otherwise. "So you think it's the wobbles too, do you?" I asked.

"Yep. Wobbles."

"Well, now that we know it's the wobbles, what happens next?"

"They generally die."

"Yes, but isn't there something we could do before it dies?"

"You could hit it over the head and throw it in the ditch. That'd save you carryin' it back to the barn."

"I mean, couldn't we call the vet?"

"You could do that."

"What's the matter? Is that terribly expensive?"

"No, no. If you got time to carry a duck around I reckon you can afford a vet for him."

The Squire turned and shuffled his way back up his lane. Our conversation was apparently over.

"Appreciate the advice, thanks," I called after him.

I picked the duck up and took him back to the house, set him on the verandah and went inside to phone the vet in Larkspur.

The vet dismissed our diagnosis about the wobbles and said that it sounded more like coccidiosis. He told me to separate the sick ones from the rest of the flock and then add four milligrams of sulphur dioxisol to a litre of drinking-water. I wrote all this down and then asked him what to do with the sick one. His manner changed abruptly and became quite patronizing.

"Oh, is this a small child's pet?" he asked.

"No," I said warmly. "I'm trying to raise ducks for a living."

"I see. Well, give it plenty of water, keep it warm and call me tomorrow if there's any change." He rang off before I could question him further.

I went back out to the verandah to my patient. He was lying on his side now, describing wide arcs across the cement with his foot. I ran back inside and phoned Freddy. You have to hold the receiver down when you dial Freddy's number because we're on the same party line. The phone rang and rang and finally stopped after the tenth ring. I lifted the receiver and heard Freddy's bright "Hyello."

"Freddy, do you know anything about ducks? I have a very sick duck here."

"Now, Walt," he said soothingly, "don't you worry about your poultry. Leastways, not until it's lyin' on its side and kickin' at the air like."

"But Freddy, that's exactly what he was doing just a minute ago."

"Is that right? Well, you run back down there and I'll bet you he's quit that by now. They generally give that up after a bit . . ."

"But Freddy. Something's got to be done. I'm really worried."

"Walter!" he said sternly. "Throw that duck out and get some work done. The forenoon's half gone and you should be ploughin'."

I heard a click and realized Freddy had hung up. I went back out to the verandah and found the duck, stretched out and very still. He was dead. I lifted him up gently, took him down to the apple tree beside the barn and buried him there in a short service attended by a few of his friends, the farm's first casualty.

Yours sincerely,
Walt

—— *May 15*

Dear Ed,

Any success I've enjoyed in the world of business has been entirely the result of my habit of setting objectives for myself and my staff. "Fail to plan and plan to fail" is my motto. To keep me on track at the firm, I used a weekly planning calendar that was invented by a successful insurance man years ago. There's room in it for a list of daily things to do, plus what we call the "Dominant" or most important task to be accomplished during the week. I thought it made sense to implement the same system here on the farm because it served me so well at the firm. Besides, I have always believed that a few private-sector principles would go a long way towards improving the farm situation.

Consulting my calendar this morning, I noticed with some satisfaction that the Dominant for week number one—a new fence along the concession road—is done. The Dominant for week number two—a new pig run and a new roof on the driving shed—is also done. However, this week's Dominant—ploughing the top fields—is not done. Now, when this happens, we have a little box at the end of the week that says, "State reason for failure to meet objective." I have noted in this box that Canadian Tire is fresh out of parts for an 1870 chilled-steel Oliver plough, that Feedbin ate her horse collar and that it's been raining since Sunday.

The trick is to stay busy at all times. I decided to drive into Larkspur to ask Ron, the chap who runs the gas station, where I might get a cord of seasoned hardwood for my wood stove.

"Try Delbert Coutts over on the Town Line," said Ron. "You could use the phone in there . . ."

I started into the office.

" . . . only Delbert don't have no phone. . . . She'll take a quart, ma'am."

I got back in the car and headed off up the Town Line, thinking I knew where the Couttses lived but in the end I had to stop and ask my way. The driver of the township road-maintainer obligingly stopped his machine, leaned out of the cab and gave me what passes in this part of the country for directions.

"Now, what you do . . . is you go down the Town Line until you get to the old brick church . . . the one that burned down last summer . . . only you don't turn there. You keep right on goin', and when you get to the bridge at the fifth side-road, well, it's about a half a mile before that. So, when you reach the bridge you've gone too far."

Eventually I found it. Two rows of maples lined the drive to a stately Victorian farmhouse, picturesquely surrounded by rusted-out truck cabs, a few rolls of fence wire, a pile of rails, a couple of dead sheep and about fifteen hounds in full cry. I waded my way through the hounds to the door of the summer kitchen and knocked. I assumed the general din would alert any residents to my arrival. There was no response. I knocked again. The hounds were beginning to eye me suspiciously. Just as I was turning to go a small voice behind me said:

"Yes?"

I turned to see a frail old woman peering at me from behind the screen.

"Oh, pardon my disturbing you. Does Delbert Coutts live here?"

"Who?"

"Delbert Coutts . . . does he live here?"

"Oh yes."

"Is he here, now?"

There was a pause.

"No," she said finally.

"Well, where could I find him?"

This was evidently a tough one. Her eyes dropped to the curling linoleum at her feet. My eyes followed hers and I noticed a pair of sock feet sticking out over the edge of an old couch just inside the door. There was no telling who the feet belonged to, and it sure didn't look like we were going to be introduced.

"He's over at the lot."

"Do you mean the wood-lot?"

"No," she said brightly, and we lapsed into another one of those silences she was so fond of.

"Well, which lot?" I was beginning to get exasperated.

"They're building a house . . . over at the lot." This with a motion of the hair curlers to the southeast.

That was good enough for me. I apologized once again for having disturbed her and waded my way back through the hounds to the car. Sure enough, a little further down the line the frame of a bungalow was rising from a building lot. A man dressed in coveralls sat on the doorstep, having what Freddy calls a carpenter's lunch: a quart sealer of cold tea and a foot-long dill pickle.

"Good morning," I said. "I'm looking for Delbert Coutts."

His response was "Oh yeah," but he didn't say it the way you or I would. He said it in a singsong way, as if I'd said something particularly interesting.

"Ohhhhhhh, yeah?"

"Are you Delbert Coutts?"

"Nope."

I was obviously dealing with a Coutts of some description. Careful use of direct questioning would flush him out.

"Where can I find him?"

"Back at the house."

"Oh no, he isn't. I just came from there."

"Should have been. He was havin' a nap when I left." The sock feet. That clinched it.

"You must be his brother, Alvin."

"Yup."

Finally, I thought, we're getting somewhere.

"I'm looking for cordwood. Maple or beech would suit. I need it in sixteen-inch lengths. Do you have any?"

He studied me thoughtfully for a moment and said, "You got the old Fisher place, don't ya?"

"There's nothing but dead elm on the place and I need something better to burn until the weather warms up."

"Elm burns pretty good."

"I want maple or beech. Do you have any?"

He screwed up his face, shook his head slowly and stared at the ground. I prepared for the worst.

"Yup . . . some."

"I'll give you thirty dollars a cord."

"We been gettin' thirty-five."

"Delivered?"

"Could do."

Now normally, I wouldn't conclude business on such flimsy evidence that the wood did indeed exist, that they had a truck or that there was the slightest chance of seeing it delivered before September first, but I pressed on. I pulled a roll of bills from my pocket and peeled off a ten, a twenty and a five and handed them to him. Judging from the expression on Alvin's face, either he had never seen folding money before or he had no idea that business could be conducted at such breakneck speed. It couldn't be helped. I didn't want to spend the whole of week number four out there.

On my way home I stopped at the gas station to ask Ron what on earth was the matter with those people. He was deep inside the engine of a Dodge pick-up and he listened as I told him my adventures with the several members of the Coutts family. At the end of the story, he emerged from the engine compartment, wiped his hands on a greasy rag and pulled his cap around straight.

"Funny thing about the widow Coutts," he said. "She seems to have gotten mixed up about those boys. Sometimes she can tell them apart same as you or me. Other times . . . heh! Try her now, Willy," he called to his client, who was sitting behind the wheel of the Dodge. The engine turned over in a series of dry heaves, caught and revved up to a rattling crescendo.

"One thing about them Coutts people though, Walt," he shouted over the din. "They sure are good at getting you to figure things out for yourself. Like most folks around here. You'll get used to that, Walt."

An explosion rattled the windows of the garage and a sheet of flame shot up from the truck carburettor.

"Whoooaaaa JEEEZ! Shet her down, Willy!"

I ducked out the side door and went home to wait for my load of wood.

Yours sincerely,

Walt

——— *May 25*

Dear Ed,

As soon as the sun breaks over the hill, the chill leaves the air and the land springs to life. Bees hum in the ancient fruit trees like the Toronto Symphony warming up. This morning I walked out to get the mail along a cordillera of fruit blossoms, drinking the air as if it were the finest champagne. For the first time I realized the extent of my inheritance. Apples, pears, a few black cherries and, right smack in the middle, for no apparent reason, a great big mulberry tree. I was looking at the earliest phase of a mulberry pie.

I tried to imagine how old these trees must be. A hundred years? What stories they could tell about this land and the people who farmed it. I walked in a wide circle through the trees, towards the mailbox, soaking in the first real warmth of spring and thinking how far away from gridlock, fern bars and smog I have come in the last six weeks.

"And this our life, exempt from public haunt
Finds tales in trees, books in the running brooks . . ."
"G'day."

The scratchy old voice startled me and I looked around to

see The Squire, who had been leaning against his mailbox and watching me stumble through the orchard, reciting poetry to myself.

"Good morning," I said.

"Nice fence."

I thanked him for the compliment and showed him what was to come. Within a few days there will be cedar posts and eight-strand wire going all the way down the concession to the corner of the side-road.

"Won't be the same without Fisher's cattle down my lane all summer," said The Squire, with a chuckle. "I may keep a garden this year."

"Well, one thing I can promise you is good fences," I said stoutly.

He squinted critically at my fields and nodded his approval. "Yep. I can see you're takin' a real interest in the place. It's a good farm. Just needs to be brought back a bit. I've often thought how you might make this farm pay."

Now, here was the advice I was looking for and it looked like we were going to hit it off after all. I settled back and prepared for a good chat about crops and the weather.

"You have?"

"Oh, yeah. Now you take this here field. The first thing you want to do is square it off, right back here to the lane." His arm made a chopping gesture right through my orchard.

"Square it off . . . ?"

"Then you get on 'er with a trencher crew and tile 'er up. Three rows to the corner down there. She'll drain like a bath-tub . . ."

"But you don't mean these trees here?"

" . . . then you bulldoze that hedgerow out there right the way back to the road."

"But you can't be suggesting I get rid of the orchard?" I protested.

"Well, of course. You gotta get rid of them old trees."

"But they must be over a hundred years old!"

"I know. It's a dirty job, wrestling with those old brutes. But I'll give you a hand. A couple of days with a chain-saw and a back-hoe and you'll see the back of 'em."

I thanked him politely for his offer of assistance but explained that I planned to keep the orchard.

"What for?" he demanded, a scowl returning to his face.

"Well, there must be some money in apples, don't you think?"

"I expect there's a lot. No one's got any of it out yet."

I felt I was missing something. "I know I'm not going to make a fortune," I said. "But there isn't another apple-grower within five miles of here."

"They're all dead. Starved to death tryin' to grow apples at ten cents a pound. Look here, Mr. Wingfield. You can't make a farm pay by wastin' your time and wastin' your land. But you go ahead. You doctor up them old fruit trees if you like . . ." He turned away to leave, paused and looked back over his shoulder.

"Give you a place to run your ducks, I expect."

And he shuffled away, back up his lane.

I walked back to the house, feeling completely deflated. It had been such a beautiful day and it was spoiled by a grouchy old man who didn't like trees. I banged the garden gate so hard it jumped off its hinges and toppled over onto the paving stones. I looked back up the lane to The Squire's and fumed for a minute. He was walking up the gangway of his barn, towards the open mow, and I could see him framed in the daylight shining through from the east because several barn boards had blown off the far wall. A few pieces of steel were missing off the roof, too. In fact, the whole farmstead had a decaying look about it.

He's certainly managed to disguise his own prosperity. What does he know about making a farm pay, anyway? I looked at the fruit trees again, took a deep breath of perfume and pollen and made a decision.

These trees can stay right where they are.

Yours sincerely,
Walt

———— *June 2*

Dear Ed,

Writers who describe night-time in the country are forever rattling on about the chirping of frogs and the rustle of night wind on leaf. They've obviously never been around here on a night when the moon is full. The sound I most commonly hear is the scream of some unfortunate creature being mugged at the back of my swamp. Last night, the hounds got the scent of a coon or something, chased it around the quarry for about an hour until it made a break across the top of the hill, and then finally treed it up by Freddy's. A stream of lanterns issued from Freddy's, danced across the top of the hill, and the air was shattered by a volley of artillery that sounded like the opening of the spring offensive.

From where I lay, I could practically hear the whisper of little wings as another furry soul wended its way heavenward. I was just managing to get back to sleep when I heard a sharp

"Hyello" from downstairs. Wondering who it could be at that late hour, I got up, stumbled downstairs and opened the door.

There I saw a face peering at me from the other side of the screen, a great, pale, cavernous face with hollow, sunken eyes and a stained roll-yer-own hanging from the lower lip. For a moment I thought someone must have propped a dead man at my door as a horrible practical joke. I felt along the wall for the axe.

"G'day, Walter," said the corpse, only his lips didn't move. Then I realized the voice belonged to another man, out of sight behind the door. It was Freddy, slightly unsteady on his feet, glassy-eyed and grinning cheerfully.

"I was wondering if you m-m-might have a drop of lemonade, Walt," He teetered back on his heels and came forward again. "Jeez, I hope we didn't get you up."

I let them all in. There was Freddy, his two nephews, Willy and Dave, who had to stoop to avoid hitting their heads on the door-frame, and the corpse, who turned out to be Jimmy, the hired man. Hired for what I don't know. He looked to be thirty years past his retirement.

It was only polite to offer them something to drink and, of course, I joined them. I really had no intention of sitting up to all hours, but then, this was the first company I had had for six weeks. I'm a bit fuzzy about how they talked me into it but soon we were all sauntering back up the lane towards Freddy's for a nightcap.

Inside Freddy's kitchen, caps were snapped off beer bottles, chairs tilted back and sleeping hounds nudged aside for more foot room. The house had an odd smell to it: stale beer, kerosene lamps, wood-smoke and dead mice. Willy and Dave look like two straggly Fenians and they laugh like guinea hens at just about anything you say to them. It's a high-pitched laugh that carries for miles and travels through house walls undiminished.

They were talking about some horse they were thinking of taking on the winter racing circuit through the States. To contribute to the conversation I turned to Jimmy and asked him if he had much experience with horses. This produced an immediate effect on the company. Willy and Dave swung their chairs around and made an elaborate display of getting themselves comfortable.

"Tell him about the big bay mare that ran the lights through Larkspur. Heeyah, heeyah!" said Willy.

"No, no!" said Dave. "Tell him about the black trotter that ran away with you and Violet McKeown on the way up the Pine River to church. Heeyah, heeyah!"

Jimmy reached out with his long waxen fingers and delicately brushed the ash off his cigarette into the cuff of his pant leg. "No," he said, in a gentle quavering voice with a trace of an Irish accent. "There's a story in both them harses, but I'll tell yas about the pair of matched Clydes I bought off old Ewing, the year after the war."

"Which war was that, Jimmy?" asked Dave. "The one against the States?"

"No, no, of course not," scoffed Jimmy gently. "The war in '39." Turning to me he continued. "Old Ewing, Walt, he had a hell of a temper. And these harses, ahh, they was a balky pair of brutes. One time they balked real bad on him when he was drawing straw just up the line here. Well, he got off the wagon and he flayed 'em with the lines until his arm damn near wore off. But they wouldn't move. They just quit."

"So what did he do?" I asked.

"He reached up and he pulled an armful of straw from off the wagon and he threw it down there right underneath the harses. And then he set fire to it, so he did. Well, the harses jumped ahead, about ten feet. Then they quit again. Then the wagon caught fire, and old Ewing had to cut the harses out of the harness to save them, and the wagon burnt right to the ground, so it did. Right to the damn ground."

I was just going to say it served the fellow right when Willy broke in.

"And the straw, Jimmy, did the straw burn to the ground, too? Heeyah, heeyah!"

"Well, of course it did."

"And old Ewing, Walt," said Dave, "he had two wooden legs. He burnt to the ground, too! Heeyah, heeyah!"

A beer bottle bounced off the wall by Dave's head. Freddy rescued the situation by getting Jimmy to tell some more horse stories, but Willy and Dave had heard them all before, and soon Jimmy's face looked longer and sadder than ever. When I made an attempt to show interest Jimmy embarked on the story of his life.

He came from a small town outside Galway in Ireland. He had a childhood sweetheart and, after he'd finished his apprenticeship, they were able to be married. The very day of the wedding, however, his bride "took a fever." Jimmy saddled up the mare, rode all the way into Galway to get the doctor and brought him back. He waited in the kitchen while the doctor went into the bedroom. A short while later, the doctor came out, laid his hand on Jimmy's shoulder and said, "She's gone, Jimmy. Flossie's gone.

Jimmy never even went into the bedroom. He gathered

up a few belongings, got back on the mare, rode into Galway, got off, sold her and bought himself a steamer passage to Canada.

The room was very quiet when Freddy finally spoke.

"Sing it, Jimmy . . . sing it to us."

Jimmy cleared his throat, tilted his head up and began to sing in a distant and tremulous tenor:

> "If you ever go across the sea to Ireland
> It may be at the closing of the day
> You will sit and watch the moon rise over Claddach
> And watch the sun go down on Gal—"

But he didn't finish. Tears choked him on the last phrase and he sat there, silently shaking his head in apology. It was all too awkward and I looked away. I thought of the years of loneliness and hopeless labour this man had put into the stony fields of a strange land and it filled me with sadness.

When I looked back . . . they were all asleep.

I got up, went out onto the verandah and thought about going home. The moon had gone down and the night was inky black and quite cold. I could just make out the shadowy shape of trees around the house and, far off down the lane, the distant lights of my own house. Groping down the lane in the dark without a light was out of the question. The screen door creaked behind me, and I turned to see Spike, one of the hounds, squeezing his way out to join me.

"Hello, Spike," I said, rumpling the loose skin on the back of his head. "You sober, too?" I found myself suddenly sitting on the verandah and realized I wasn't quite sober either. Obviously, I was there for the night, what was left of it. I picked up a couple of chunks of wood from the verandah and took them back into the kitchen with me, made a quiet fire in the wood-stove without disturbing the sleepers and curled up on one of the old chesterfields.

When I woke up, I was alone, except for Spike the hound, who was draped across me like a throw rug. A light morning fog crept in over the window-sill. It was cold, my head ached and, even with a stuffed nose, I could still smell stale beer, kerosene, wood-smoke and . . . smoke, lots of smoke. Down the hallway a thickening grey cloud hung along the ceiling.

"Freddy!"

An answering groan came from the verandah. I dashed out to find Freddy curled up on a old church pew.

"Freddy, wake up! There's a fire! It's upstairs, I think!"

"Mm?" said Freddy. "Ah Jeez, not again!"

Freddy grabbed an old hoe handle and started beating on a steel rain barrel beside the verandah.

"Everybody up! We got a fire!" he yelled.

Things started to happen fairly quickly after that. Freddy's fire alarm had the same effect on the household as a swift kick to an anthill. Seven people I hadn't even met came out of side rooms. Jimmy staggered out, clutching a case of beer he'd rescued from under the kitchen table. A bucket brigade quickly formed; Dave manned the pump, Willy and Freddy raced back and forth, carrying pails of water up the stairs. They didn't search for the source of the blaze. When they reached the top of the stairs, they would kick open a bedroom door, heave the pail contents in on the floor and run back downstairs for more. Jimmy stood by the pump, snapping the caps off beer bottles and handing them to the fire-fighters.

"It's a damn shame they can't see us," he said wistfully.

"Who?"

"Why the neighbours, Walt. Look at the job them boys are doing. It isn't fair."

"What isn't fair?"

"Why, they could put the fire out and save the whole house and people would still say we were drunk." He shook his head sadly and bent to fetch out another bottle of beer.

I turned to see a pick-up truck coming down the lane at full speed. It was my neighbour to the south, Don the dairy farmer. Word was spreading quickly. Within the space of half an hour, the whole of Larkspur had heard about Freddy's fire, except the fire department. The place began to take on a carnival atmosphere. Cars lined the lane both sides right out to the road; children bounced up and down on chesterfields we'd dragged out onto the lawn and the ladies organized a lunch table for the volunteers. Eventually the fire truck arrived, skidded to a halt in the turning circle in front of the house, lights flashing and radio crackling. Moments later a fireman emerged from the front door of the house.

"Someone lit a fire in the wood-stove," he said in a stern voice. A great sigh went up from the crowd. I stepped forward and raised my hand.

"I did. It was cold and . . ."

I heard my words echoing among the seventy-five people present.

"He lit a fire in the wood-stove . . . he lit a fire in the wood-stove . . . he lit a fire in the wood-stove!"

Freddy came over to me, shaking his head wearily.

"Walt, there's no s-s-tove-pipe above the ceiling. We took it out after the last fire, when we put in the gas furnace. J-j-jeez, Walt. Everybody knows that."

I felt my face achieve the rich crimson of a Persephone Township sunset.

"Send me the bill for the damages," I said. There was nothing else to say. I left.

The morning did have one positive result. Apparently I now own a dog. Spike the hound followed me home over the fields from Freddy's without so much as a backward glance. He's been asleep in front of the fire ever since. I think Freddy's fire was the last straw for him. He's come here looking for some peace and quiet. I've decided he can stay as long as he likes. He's of an age now when he's no longer a danger to wildlife, and besides . . . he admires me.

He's probably the only one left who does.

Yours sincerely,
Walt

―――*June 10*

Dear Ed,

This isn't working out. Not at all the way I planned it. The book says that if you live in Zone 4a, you should have your spring planting done by June the tenth. Here it is and I haven't even finished ploughing yet. I finally got Feedbin and the new horse, Mortgage, harnessed together and ploughed a few wiggly furrows. But Feedbin turns only to the left and Mortgage must be Australian, because she turns only to the right. Then it clouded over and dropped about a foot of rain in the space of half an hour, with the result that my field now looks like Vimy Ridge.

I never realized what an opportunity there is in farming to make a complete idiot of yourself in public. Sitting here under the maple tree at my line fence, I have a perfect one-hundred-and-eighty degree view of failure on all sides. On the way down the Seventh Line you drive by field after field of beautifully manicured spring oats and barley. Then you get to my place. Cars stop and whole families get out to take pictures of the mess.

The people really are wonderful around here. I can hear them now down at the General Store in Larkspur, laughing and telling each other what a mess I'm making of the old Fisher place, trying to plough with horses.

There is absolutely no way to please them. If I had a half-million dollars' worth of farm machinery like my neighbour Don, they'd say I had more money than brains. If I hired one of them to work the fields for me they'd say I was lazy. If I had a four-year degree in agriculture like the McKees' oldest boy, they'd complain about all book learnin' and no common sense.

The only way I could possibly please them would be to arrange somehow to have myself born here fifty years ago and then do everything exactly the way I did it last year. Which is fine for them; they're the only people I know who can lose money thirty years in a row and then move into a big house in town for their retirement.

In the middle of all this I got a letter from the new chairman at MacFeeters, Bartlett and Hendrie . . . my old partner Alf Harrison.

> Dear Walt:
> The investment community has accepted the
> news of your departure and the company still
> survives. This letter is not intended to persuade
> you to come back. I know when your mind is

made up. But if you can't be reasonable, I will try to be for you.

You can play Farmer Brown for a year and we'll keep your name on the letterhead. If at the end of that time you decide to come back, no questions will be asked, no explanations required. In the meantime, I haven't told anybody about your determination to farm for a living. There's no sense ruining your reputation over this thing. I've just told them you're being treated for a drinking problem.

My best wishes to you in this colourful and exciting new venture. I remain,

Yours sincerely,

Alf

Clearly, I am disappointing people on all sides. But that's too bad. I may only get one acre ploughed, and it may not sprout till Hallowe'en, but at least it will be my acre and my crop.

Or so I thought until this morning. I was just preparing to harness the horses for yet another attempt at cultivation when the air around me was filled with the sound of engine noises. I looked up to see my neighbour Don approaching from the south on his big articulated Minneapolis Moline diesel tractor, pulling an eight-furrow plough. He swung in my gate and, without stopping, headed straight into the Vimy Ridge field and dropped the ploughs.

I yelled at him to stop. I shouted at him to get that tractor out of my field. He wouldn't listen. I chased him around the field twice, telling him what I thought of charity and modern machinery. He paid no attention at all and ploughed the whole field in less than an hour. Willy and Dave turned up with disks and cultivators, Freddy brought harrows and a seeder, and Jimmy and The Squire came just to pick stones. At one point there were five tractors in my field, whirling around at top speed, as if I wasn't there. The crop was in before dark.

I suppose I could have been more civil about it. They were only trying to help. But it left me feeling like a complete failure and I found it difficult to stand there and watch them make a mockery of my efforts to hang on to the old ways.

After they all left, Spike and I went down to the pond to sit on the dock in the dark. We just sat there in the cool night air, watching the little trout jump at mayflies and listening as a halting version of "Stardust" drifted over the fields from Don's verandah, where he sat playing his old trumpet. Up at Freddy's, it sounded like another coon hunt was being organized. It was one of those early June nights when you can actually hear the crackle and pop of things growing around you. We just sat there, not saying anything to each other, until finally, Spike said "Woof" in a conversational way. There was a rustle in the grass and we looked up to see the Squire standing over us.

"G'day, Walt."

Spike moved over a few feet to give him room to sit on the dock. We talked about this and that for a few minutes before we got around to the events of the afternoon.

"You see, Walt, there's just one deadline in farming that you don't mess around with and that's the spring planting. Now, me and the boys were content to let you . . . experiment with them horses so long as you didn't go past June the tenth. But come today and no sign of a crop, well, we did what we had to do."

"Why the hell do they feel they have to look out for me? Do I appear to be some sort of invalid?"

"They wouldn't want to see you stuck, Walt."

"That's extremely noble of them. But where I come from, a man is allowed to fall flat on his face if that is what he wants to do."

The Squire nodded and got to his feet. "I figure they'll leave you enough room for that, Walt." And he disappeared into the darkness.

"Woof," said Spike, looking at me with a straight face.

"Woof yourself," I said, and we went off to bed.

Yours sincerely,

Walt

———*July 1*

Dear Ed,

I have finally realized a long-held ambition and become a dairy farmer. This week, Don and I drove down to Wychwood, where a friend of his runs a storybook dairy farm, complete with herds of cuddly brown Jersey cows. Don picked out four flabby old girls who were used to being milked by hand during power failures and we loaded them onto the truck. I thought we should have at least one younger animal, to diversify the portfolio, as it were, and pointed to a young heifer that had just freshened. Don and his friend didn't exactly object, but I'm beginning to catch on to these characters now. They just stood there stroking their chins, and said, "You could do that," which, translated, means "Only a real idiot would do what you're about to do."

We got the registration papers for all of them, showing the sire and the dam, the sire of the sire and the dam of the dam, and they all had the most precious names—impossible titles such as Acme Heritage Shady Grove Apple Blossom and Jester Generation Emperor Fred. The first thing we did when we got them home was give them some real names: Lollipop, Cupcakes, Creampuff and Yoghurt. The little heifer we named Milkshake.

Don stayed to help with the first milking, showed me the basic rules of sanitation, measured out the required portions of sixteen percent dairy ration and demonstrated the art of stripping a cow of milk in about seven minutes. The old girls stood very quietly for all of this; then we got to Milkshake. She's a shy, delicate creature with a deep dish in her forehead and eyes that stand out like those of a frog underfoot. She evidently views the milking process as a form of indecent assault. Don showed me the correct approach.

He's an ex-welterweight boxer, with broad shoulders and a solid build. He fixed Milkshake with a determined glare, took a firm grip on the pail and the stool, strode to her side, bent over from the waist and then stuck his head into her flank just below the hip-bone. A brief struggle ensued, but the heifer was effectively pinned to the wall by Don's stance. He got the stool underneath him and, within a few minutes, he was milking away quite successfully. He milked out the back quarters, straightened up and handed the pail and the stool to me.

I strove to imitate his technique carefully. Matching Don's determined glare, I took a firm grip on the pail and the stool, strode to her side, bent over from the waist, stuck my head into her flank . . .

When I woke up, I was flat on my back some distance away in the straw. The doctor says I'll have two black eyes for a couple of weeks but there's no permanent damage to the nose. Milkshake is back home in Wychwood.

Yours sincerely,

Walt

———July 25

Dear Ed,

I was trying out the team again in a fairly simple exercise with a stone boat this morning. Since it has no tongue to break and no moving parts of any kind, I thought it would offer good training at low risk to life and property. But within ten minutes we had worked up to a level of excitement worthy of the Calgary Stampede. So I put both horses on report and went up to Freddy's to pick out an older, more experienced animal, before it went to Owen Sound for glue production.

Freddy and I leaned against the corral fence and I watched the herd mill by as Freddy listed the track record, pedigree and hoof size of any individual he thought might appeal to me. They were a pretty nondescript lot, but Freddy's patter buffed them up a bit.

"Well now, Walt, you see the big chestnut mare there? The one with one ear, yeah. You see the way she holds her head? What a stride! Don't pay any attention to that bit of mange over the withers, Walt. That'd clear up with the sun on it in no time. And you see that two-year-old? He'd make a dandy hunter . . . with a little work. You could have him registered, if you want."

In Freddy's eyes, any horse who can stagger onto a truck unassisted can be registered. A big colt lumbered by.

"That fella's mother was a thoroughbred . . . and his father was half quarter-horse."

Great, I thought, That would make him seven-sixteenths dog food.

"Sure, he's ugly," said Freddy, with his auctioneer's gift for perceiving silent scepticism. "Most yearlings are. But strong, you know. His mother won a couple of races at Woodbine. I've half a mind to take that young fella and race him myself. There's a lot of money in him, if you bring him along right."

Despite the brilliant future ahead for this colt, his price was the same as the rest: a hundred bucks.

"You're lookin' for somethin' heavier, are you? To draw, like? Well, come on inside and I'll show you old King."

Freddy opened the barn door and we stepped into the gloom of the stable. It was cold and damp and the air was heavy with the smell of horse, harness and hoof paint. Half-way down a row of hefty Holstein cows, a huge black work-horse towered fully three feet above the rest of the animals. Only the shoulders and hindquarters were available for viewing. The head was out of sight somewhere at the bottom of the oat box. It looked like a great big, black grand piano on edge.

As Freddy listed the options on this animal I began to wonder if he came with a head. I reached out to touch him on the flank and an enormous head rose up from the oat box and turned to look at me. For a moment, I felt as if I was looking into the eyes of some ancient priest of Shangri-La. In those luminous brown pools I caught a glimpse of yesterday, before the milk wagon, before the prairie schooner . . . even before King Arthur's court. This was a very old horse.

"Hullo, King," I said.

The head returned to the oat box.

"I guess this fella would be old enough to vote, Walt," said Freddy, edging up beside the horse to undo his halter. "But strong. As long as these fellas keep their teeth, they never quit. You fit him up with a set of dentures and he'll last you another twenty years. Hyep!"

Freddy leaned over the oat box and spoke very distinctly into King's left ear as if he were speaking into an apartment intercom.

"Back up, King. Back up."

I understand that the pilot of an airliner has to wait seven seconds after applying the throttle before the engines respond. It was the same with King. The head rose up from the oat box, a blast from the nostrils filled the stall with a fine spray, one enormous hoof rose and came down almost tentatively on the cement walkway. Joints cracked, bulk shifted and King was underway.

There is something very impressive about a really big horse. I remember when I was a kid going down to the Royal Winter Fair in Toronto and watching the big Belgians and Clydesdales line up for their events. I remember most of all their huge soft noses, big kind eyes and hooves the size of dinner plates that came down on the concrete with a clank you could feel through the soles of your boots twenty feet away. I can't say I ever dreamed of owning one; they seemed so impossibly big and far away. But I did dream of having one as a friend some day, to go and visit.

Once he was out in the sunshine, I could see that King was a far cry from those sleek bob-tailed Belgians and Percherons with their nickel-plated harness. But the eyes and the nose and the dinner plates . . . they were all there, all right.

"A hundred bucks, Walt," said Freddy.

Same as the rest. And so I led old King down the Seventh Concession, his great chipped hooves scraping along and his nose barely three inches off the ground, blowing up little hurricanes of dust every few steps. I opened the gate to the pasture, unsnapped the lead rope and gave King a slap on the rump as he plodded by me into his new home. The look he gave his new pasture-mates, Feedbin and Mortgage, was one of unspeakable weariness, as if he had seen so many pastures and so many pasture-mates that all sense of novelty was hopelessly lost for him.

I've never seen Don laugh so hard. I didn't expect Don to see what I see in King. But then, I didn't expect him to tell me that I could have saved a hundred bucks by throwing a horsehair rug over a rail fence and emptying the wood-stove ash bucket over it. The reaction elsewhere in the neighbourhood has been much the same. King's age has been estimated at somewhere between eighteen and fifty-five and his pedigree judged to involve Percheron, Clydesdale, Belgian, musk-ox or woolly mammoth . . . take your pick. But I don't care. I've always wanted a quiet horse with some character, and I've certainly got that.

I can see them all down in the pasture now; my herd—Feedbin, Mortgage and old King. King has a couple of birds perched on his back, just like a dead elm stump. He hasn't moved in over an hour. He just stands there, staring sadly at the ground, as if some great tragedy were unfolding in the ant kingdom below.

This place gets to look more and more like a farm every day.

Yours sincerely,
Walt

Dear Ed,

The step down from the barn floor to the ground is quite a jump for a man my age. Don and I made the hop in the dark last night and I went over on my ankle.

"Are you all right, Walt?" asked Don, holding me up by one arm.

I put my weight on the foot and found I could walk on it, but it was pretty sore.

"Walt, that's a dangerous spot. Why don't you clean your stable out?"

"Stable?" I asked. "What stable."

Don pointed to the narrow gap under the barn sill where a gap in the foundation made a crawl-space about five feet wide.

"That's not a stable," I said. "That's where old Fisher kept his chickens. He had to crawl in there on his hands and knees every day to get the eggs."

"Used to be a stable, Walt. I remember when old Fisher kept Clydesdale horses in there."

"He did? Where? When?"

"It's years ago now. But things piled up after a bit and the horses wouldn't go in. So, for a while he used it for steers. Things piled up a bit more and then he used it for veal calves. After that it was pigs. For the last five years or so he just kept chickens."

I looked again at the gap in the foundation.

"Do you actually mean to say . . ."

"Yep. Hard to believe, but down there . . . six feet or so . . . there's a concrete floor."

I remembered the story of King Eurystheus handing

Heracles a manure fork and telling him to clean out the Augean stables. Don, being more helpful than the average Greek king, offered to bring over his tractor and loader in the morning and help with the excavations himself. He suggested I ask Freddy for the loan of a tractor and manure-spreader.

At nine o'clock the next morning, I limped up to Freddy's place and found him, or at least his boots, sticking out from underneath his '62 Pontiac, a beer balanced on his chest, poking plug wires up through the manifold. Every so often, Freddy glares at the Pontiac like a peregrine falcon and declares that "this day, that car will run." It never has.

"That spreader . . ." he said, looking at the ground and grabbing his cheek-bones with his thumb and index finger to stimulate his memory. "Seems to me Willy and Dave borrowed that spreader last year. They're out the back, scuffling turnips."

Off we went in Freddy's newer-model Pontiac to see the boys. Now, Willy and Dave have a reputation for getting an enormous amount of work done in record time but whenever I chance upon them, their vehicles are all parked nose to nose in the field, protecting a case of twenty-four. It was in this position that we found them, sadly contemplating a bent rod, which was evidently an important element of turnip-scuffling machinery.

"G'day, fellas," said Freddy. "D'you boys mind the spreader you borrowed off me last year? Where did it get to?"

"Spreader?" said Willy. "Hey, Dave! D'you mind the spreader we borrowed off Uncle Freddy. Where'd it get to?"

"Gee, Willy, didn't that Italian fella up the Town Line borrow it last spring?"

"Yeah, but he lent it to Sparky McEwan, didn't he?"

"Well, most of Sparky's stuff's up at his old man's now."

"But his old man sold out in the spring. Jeez, Uncle Freddy, you did the auction sale, don't you remember?"

"That was my spreader?" said Freddy, looking genuinely shocked. "I only got a hundred bucks for it."

In the meantime Dave had climbed into the driver's seat of Freddy's Pontiac and was examining the dashboard with curiosity.

"Say, this old stove's in pretty good shape, Uncle Freddy. Did you ever think you might sell her?"

Freddy's interest in the spreader vanished. He leaned in the window and started his sales pitch.

"She runs real good, Dave. Now just last summer I put a new set of rods in her."

Dave fired up the motor and put his foot to the floor. There was a roar, and blue smoke spewed out the back as the engine revved up to full throttle. Dave cranked the car into reverse, and for a few moments it sat churning in the same spot, the inside filling up with dust until Dave disappeared from view like the fairy castle in one of those jars you shake up to create a snowstorm. Eventually, the car slid away and began a breakneck lap of the field, still in reverse, setting up a rooster tail of dust and turnip leaves in its wake. At our end of the field, we could still hear Dave's shrill, axe-murderer laugh over the distant roar of the car. As he completed the lap and entered the final turn, Dave tried a forward gear and the car did a lazy swerve towards us, travelled the last hundred yards or so sideways and finally came to rest in a thick clump of choke-cherries in the fence-row. Dust whirled out the windows and Dave gradually reappeared.

"She runs real good, Uncle Freddy," he said, running his

finger through the dust on the dashboard. "But you should get her cleaned up a bit! Heeyah, heeyah!"

Freddy wasn't amused. "C'mon, let's go find that spreader."

Freddy had sold the spreader to a man named McGrath. Sure enough, that's where we found it, sagging under a load of barn timbers, a forgotten shipment to a forgotten destination. Freddy studied the timbers for a minute and then decided we would unload them ourselves. Half an hour later, that job was completed and we hooked the spreader to the trailer-hitch on the back of the Pontiac. Just before we left, Freddy thought it would be a good idea to put a load of rails on the spreader for the stretch of fence out behind his house.

By lunch-time we were back at Freddy's. Willy and Dave showed up with their crew and we sat down to a banquet served up by Freddy's long-suffering sister, Maggie. We consumed a quantity of meat, potatoes and turnips, traded hog prices and land values with disbelieving whistles, and observed a moment's silence for the market report. Towards the end of the hour, Dave stood by the open window, picking his teeth with a toothpick.

"Uncle Freddy," he observed. "That spreader of your's got a flat tire."

That set the tone for the afternoon. We got the tire off the spreader by heating the lug bolts with a blowtorch, took it into town and got it plugged at Ron's. A mere two hours later the tire was back on the spreader, the load of rails thrown off behind the house and the spreader hooked up to Freddy's little red Case tractor. For a fleeting moment, it looked as if I might get away after all, but then a shout came from the turnip field.

"We're up to our axles in mud out here," called Willy. "Bring some of them rails and give us a hand."

Freddy turned to me apologetically, to see if I would mind. Of course I didn't. It turned out to be quite a show. By the end of the afternoon, a crawler had been brought to the scene, escorted by two township road-graders. Another case of twenty-four appeared and this time no fewer than seven different species of vehicle were parked nose-to-nose around it. At 5:23 p.m. the tractor emerged from the mud like an exhausted water-buffalo, to the cheers of men, the roar of machines and the maniacal laughter of Willy and Dave. They all escorted me back to the house, apologizing once again for having kept me so late.

"Never mind," I said. "These things happen." Besides, I pointed out that I could still get a load on back at the farm before supper. Freddy jumped up on the little Case tractor and pushed the starter button.

"RRR . . . RRR . . . rrr . . . rr . . . r . . ."

Freddy turned to me with a sigh. "Y'know, this little tractor never starts unless the sun's on it. I really should give it a charge overnight. Why don't you leave this until tomorrow?"

Why not, indeed. I bade farewell and trudged off down the lane, back to the farm. Maggie waved goodbye from the '62 Pontiac where she was watering geraniums. She always uses Freddy's car as a planter as soon as there's any danger of frost. The last picture of the day remains in my mind; Freddy's feet sticking out from under the car; Maggie absently watering flowers; Willy and Dave sitting under the hollyhocks by the driving shed, smoking roll-yer-owns and reading the racing news.

Back at the farm I discovered that Don had been there and gone ahead without me. A mountainous manure pile greeted me in the barnyard, which I picked my way around to discover my new stable.

There was no sign of King Eurystheus. He'd gone home for the day to milk his cows.

Yours sincerely,

Walt

——— *September 20*

Dear Ed,

Don and I were leaning on the pig fence the other day, watching the pigs wander around their pen.

"Say, Walt," said Don. "Those fellas weigh a couple of hundred pounds each. You'll be wanting to send them out next week."

"Mmm? Send who out? Where?"

"These pigs, Walt. They're ready for the freezer."

It gave me a chill, coming on so suddenly like that. I'd never really considered what life would be like without the pigs and I hadn't realized how attached I'd become to them. I tried to explain.

"Don, it's just that . . . well, these aren't just pigs, Don. These are my junior vice-presidents: Abernathy, Greenaway, Pomerantz, Pilkington . . . I recruited them. I brought them into the firm. I gave them objectives to meet—two hundred pounds in the first five months. And they all met the target. Well, maybe it was more like six months. They had a few sick days."

"There you go, Walt. They've outlived their usefulness. What would you do at the firm?"

That was a good question. The answer was . . . probably nothing. That's what they used to say about me at MacFeeters, Bartlett and Hendrie. They used to say old Wingfield couldn't fire anybody. I hired people every day but I always let Alf

Harrison take care of my mistakes. I just never had the stomach for it. Alf used to get upset sometimes and he often complained that his arm was getting tired waving goodbye. I was an ideas person. I thought up new things to do, got new people to join us, whipped everybody into a frenzy when we had a sales campaign, and poor old Alf came along behind me, sweeping up the debris.

Don listened to me for awhile, but before he left he warned me.

"You gotta fire these guys, Walt. They'll eat you out of house and home."

Then it struck me. Maybe I could go into pig-breeding in a really big way. Starting with this stock I could go on to produce the best herd of pigs this township has ever seen. Anybody looking at these animals could tell at a glance that they were superior stock; long, lean and chunky through the shoulders and hams, with a lovely pink sheen. Any farm would buy the progeny of fine pigs like these.

"You couldn't do that, Walt," said Don, flatly.

"Now, why not?"

"They've been fixed."

Yours sincerely,
Walt

—— *November 30*

Dear Ed,

Persuading these two horses that God meant them to work for a living is turning out to be no easier than getting a bond salesman to put in a decent day's work. Where is Alf when I really need him? But at least bond salesmen don't bite and kick. It amazes me how two sleepy old nags can turn into fire-breathing dragons the minute I hitch them to an antique piece of equipment that I have rescued from someone's lawn. To date, they have demolished two single-furrow ploughs, a stone boat, sheared off three mailboxes and kicked a perfectly charming little democrat wagon to kindling.

The day before yesterday they got away from me while I was cultivating the top field and broke for the barn. The cultivator wedged so tightly in the barn door that it took Freddy an hour to cut it free with an acetylene blowtorch. While the horses and I studied one another over the wreckage, Freddy stepped in between us to make a suggestion.

"Walt, why don't you get someone down here to b-b-break this team in properly. Someone who knows what he's doin'. People are startin' to take the S-s-sixth Line into Larkspur just so's they won't meet you and these horses on the road. It's true, Walt. I'll tell you what. I'll send Jimmy down in the morning to give you a hand, but, Walt, don't let him talk you into takin' him into town. He'll go on a toot for sure. He's real frail and he can't take the booze like he used to."

I agreed to this proposal and the next morning Jimmy appeared after chores and watched while I tethered Feedbin and Mortgage to the fence for the harnessing. The girls always stand quietly for this part. It's later on, in ticklish situations, that they start to act up. But the harness has been broken in so many different places now that it all has to be wired together with fence pliers. Jimmy watched this silently until I had finished and then he sighed.

"All right, Walter," he said. "It'll have to do for today. But, if it's all the same to you, we won't drive them through the fashionable part of town."

He noticed Mortgage striking her right front hoof against the fence, gradually splintering the cedar rails until there was a hole big enough for a man to crawl through. This moved Jimmy to poetry:

"If he bites and kicks, you mind him well,

But a harse that strikes is straight from hell."

For practice, Jimmy recommended that we hook the team up to the front bob of the heavy sleighs. This would let them turn or back up without damaging any equipment. He also suggested we work them in the ploughed field I had been cultivating, where the combination of uneven ground and wet snow would make them concentrate on their footing. I took a deep breath of relief. It sure was nice to be working with an expert for once.

Jimmy climbed onto the bale of straw we had tied on the sleigh bob and prepared to start. Now, when I start these horses I just loosen the tension of the lines and give a little chirrup, just like Marshal Dillon giving the schoolmarm a lift into town. Not Jimmy. He whacked the horses over the backside with the lines and yelled "GIDDAP!!"

The horses leapt forward and Jimmy somersaulted backward over the straw bale into the slush. I ran to intercept the runaway team and managed to get my hands on the lines. They were tight as piano wire. I turned to see Jimmy, still holding the lines, rising up out of the icy slush hole like a Polaris submarine, gaunt and terrible in his rage.

"Whoa, you rotten, scum-suckin', yellow-bellied son of a Scot . . ."

"WHOOAA!"

Incredibly, the horses stopped and stood trembling, waiting for Jimmy's next command. I don't think they'd ever heard anyone swear in complete sentences before. Jimmy climbed back up on the straw bale, icy water dripping off his chin, his eyes bright and his jaw set. Again he whacked the horses over the backside and yelled "Giddap!" even louder than before. Away they went, off up the lane towards the top field, with me cantering along behind. They plunged into the top field and for a moment all I could see was clods of half-frozen dirt flying through the air. They travelled in a wide arc around the field. It was a scene from the wall of a Roman temple: Pluto descending into the underworld. And then . . . his line snapped.

The horses swerved to the left, Jimmy hauling on his remaining line in a desperate attempt to head them into the fence before they gained the gate and a free downhill run to the barn. It was going to be close. I stood there in the gateway, shouting and waving my arms as the horses bore down on me. All the horse stories I'd ever read assured me that a horse would never trample a man in battle. But there we were, eyeball to eyeball at the gate, and my nerve left me. I jumped aside.

As always, it was a compromise. The horses cleared the gate but the sleigh didn't. One of the iron runners caught the gatepost and stopped dead. Jimmy followed the horses in a graceful trajectory that ended in a clump of thistles. The horses disappeared off down the lane, the loose ends of the harness still flapping in the breeze.

I am concluding this entry from the bar of the Commercial Hotel in Larkspur, where Jimmy and I have been holed up for the last day and a half. I'm wondering how to break the news to Freddy. Still, frail as we are, we're safer in here with the booze than we are out there with the horses.

Yours sincerely,

Walt

—— *February 4*

Dear Ed,

I trudged out to the mailbox this morning, through four-foot drifts of snow and an icy wind, for news of the outside world. My reward for the effort was one of those fat window envelopes from the credit-card company, just bristling with bad news. The amount-due box read $2,500.

I waded back to the house, wheezing and gasping and wondering where all that money had gone. In the summer kitchen, I paused to look again at the bill, and several individual items caught my attention. There was six hundred dollars for feed from the Co-op, including a bag of Hoof'n'Hock Horse Treat. The stuff costs more than granola. Three hundred dollars for hardware for the barn door that blew off its hinges and hit the Hydro line, before it came through the kitchen window. Two hundred and eighty dollars for alcohol for the space-heater in the bathroom. For the first time in years, I felt the cold, sinking feeling of insolvency. I hadn't felt like this since the last time I had bank money in my margin account and the market was on its way down. It seemed worse, in fact, to be starting through all this again at my age.

I looked up to see the township snow-plough coming down the lane, with Freddy at the controls; Jimmy, Don and The Squire riding shotgun. I thanked them all for ploughing me out, knowing that it would all blow back in within the hour.

"We'll take another pass at it on the way out, Walt," said Freddy.

"We brought you a case of beer," said Jimmy.

I let them all in and they settled around the wood-stove.

Still thinking about the credit-card bill, I shuffled around in my sock feet, making toast and coffee, listening to the conversation but not hearing very much. Don's voice brought me back out of my daze.

"Pretty quiet today, Walt. You gettin' cabin fever?"

I explained to him that I was just fretting about bills. They all commiserated, and soon I was telling them the full extent of my troubles. The firm hasn't given me a settlement because the term of our agreement ends on June first, when I'm supposed to decide whether I want to come back or not. But buying the land took most of my savings and the rest has disappeared with all the improvements and purchases I've made this past year. In the meantime, bills keep coming in. Feed, hardware, fuel; bills, bills, bills. It just never seems to stop.

"What income do you have, Walt?" asked Don.

"Income!" I exclaimed. "This is February. What makes money in Persephone Township in February?"

"Fox bounty," said The Squire.

"Well, how much is the fox bounty?"

"Thirty bucks."

I explained that the scope of my problems was a lot larger than thirty bucks, but Freddy persisted.

"You have to kind of m-m-manage the fox bounty," he said. "Now just last week, there's a fella got a fox and he took the right ear to Demeter Township and he got thirty dollars. Then he took the left ear to Pluto Township and he got another thirty dollars. Then he sold the tail to Persephone Township for thirty dollars. That's ninety dollars for a fox."

I wasn't convinced that this would help. I had no intention of shooting at a fox and besides, I hadn't seen one since I came up here. But they kept making suggestions until they were back on familiar topics.

"If you sent those pigs out when I told you," said Don, "you'd be back even by now."

"That orchard," said The Squire, "would have about forty cords of good burnin' wood in it. There's a lot of work but you could get twenty dollars a cord for it."

"Old King would run about seventeen hundred pound," said Jimmy, "Up to Owen Sound they'll give you ten cents a pound."

"For Pete's sake, Jimmy!" I protested. "I can't do that. I couldn't do any of the things you're suggesting."

The Squire shook his head sadly. "If you won't help yourself, Walt, there's nothing we can do."

Then I told them what was in the back of my mind. I told them about the letter from Alf Harrison this week, my old partner at the firm, asking me to come back, even if only for a couple of days a week. The market's been very slow, they're losing clients and they want me to go around and warm up business for them. I could take the train down and they'd pay my hotel bill for whatever nights I stay over. I thought maybe one of the neighbours might help with the chores when I was away.

"Don't do it, Walt," said Freddy. "Gosh, you're working hard enough as it is. It'd ruin your health."

"Freddy's right," Don said, in his solemn way. "You can't put a price on your health." He paused for a moment while we all absorbed the wisdom of this observation. Then he asked, "How much are they offering?"

"The usual," I explained. "A thousand dollars a day plus expenses."

I might as well have said a million. Their eyes widened and they all looked at one another with open mouths. After a moment, The Squire made a suggestion.

"Walt, maybe you could try it for a week or two. We could keep a close eye on you . . . see if you lose any condition."

It isn't exactly what I had in mind but maybe I should try it out for awhile. I'm not ready to give up the farm altogether; it would be too much of a disappointment to my neighbours. They say that watching me this past year has been the most fun they've had since the tax department tried to do an audit on Freddy.

Yours sincerely,
Walt

Chapter Two

Wingfield's

— PROGRESS —

ANOTHER NOTE FROM THE EDITOR

That's pretty much how it went the first year. Soon after his chat with the neighbours, Walt agreed to start back at the firm part-time. He bought a computer terminal and set up a trading link with the stock exchange in the summer kitchen. Two days a week now he takes the train to the city where he attends management meetings, gives motivational lectures to the staff and makes pronouncements to the media about the economy.

Things started to improve right away for MacFeeters, Bartlett and Hendrie with Walt back in the chair, doing what he knew best, but back on the farm, Walt was still going through his own private little recession. It would have finished you or me, but Walt didn't quit. He was determined to keep up with this divided life until the farm could pay its way . . . which will not be in his lifetime. But, finances aside, it was a smart move.

The change seemed to give him his old energy back. By the time the snow started to melt, he was writing out a corporate plan for the farm, setting objectives for all the animals again—"the staff" as he calls them. Then, one morning in late March, he pushed another one of his letters through the mail-slot. Just to look at him, you could tell he had regained his confidence and was all set to drive off another cliff.

He saw me through the window and stopped long enough to tell me that his pigs, Pomerantz, Pilkington, Greenaway, Abernathy and the boys, each weighed four hundred pounds and he had decided to appoint them to the board of directors.

And so, the correspondence began again . . .

———— March 17

Dear Ed,

The compensation for working two days a week in the city is the relief that comes with escaping back to the country on the train when business is finished for another week.

With each passing mile, the cares of the office leave me and my shoulders get a little further from my ears. But I don't get the firm completely out of mind until the train crosses Highway 13 and the hills of Persephone appear on the horizon ahead. The countryside grows more familiar and I start to notice some of the changes that have taken place in the few days since I've been away.

Oscar McKeown must have broken down and paid his taxes this week, because the township snow-blower is finally punching its way up Sharp's Hill to his place, through a ten-foot snow-drift.

The light was fading quickly as the train slowed for the Larkspur station. Standing on the platform was a gaunt old man in a ragged duffle coat, lime-green pants and a ski toque that said "Parker's Cleaners." As I stepped off the train he started towards me. It was Jimmy.

"G'day, Walt," he said. "I hitched up the team and the sleigh to give you a lift home . . ."

I couldn't believe it. Harnessing those two horses is tricky enough with two people. It would take a lot of nerve for a man in his eighties to try it by himself. But still, it gave me a warm feeling to think what my colleagues back at the firm would say. While they were fighting their way home on the expressway, here was I, skimming along over snowy country lanes in a two-horse open sleigh, sleigh-bells ringing, spirits singing . . .

"So, did you have any trouble?" I asked.

"Some," said Jimmy. "The bay mare wouldn't come out of the barn. She backed out of the stall all right but she wouldn't come any further."

"How did you get her out?"

Jimmy chuckled and I presumed he had come out the victor in this dispute.

"I put a good halter on her . . . and I put the harness on the chestnut . . . then I hooked the tugs into the ring on the halter and the chestnut pulled her out like she was on wheels."

It was my turn to laugh.

"You know all these tricks, Jimmy. Now, what would you do if it was a really big horse and it wouldn't leave the barn? What sort of technique would you use then?"

"What you do, Walt," he said, "first you take the halter off, and you make sure you got a good footing. Then you kinda let your shoulders go loose . . . and then you punch him right between the eyes."

"Good heavens, would you really do that?"

It was chilly and we had a long drive ahead, but Jimmy had time for a horse story.

"Oh yeah. Now, there was a fella . . . years ago . . . Orval Ransier. He had a place north of the Pine River. He was a big man and he had a big harse. And that harse quit on him in the stable. He couldn't whip him out and he couldn't drag him out."

I knew this part. "He just quit, right?"

"That's right. So he took the halter off . . . got hisself a good footing . . . and he leaned right into her. Now, you won't believe this, Walt, but that horse ducked. And his fist went right through the wall of the barn . . . and he followed it. When Orval sat up in the snow, that harse was standing right beside him. And the two of them got on just fine after that."

We both laughed and I picked up my suitcase. It was dark and time we headed for home. I looked over Jimmy's head to the parking lot but saw no sign of the sleigh.

"So, where are the horses?" I asked.

"The bay mare's at McKelvey's."

"Where's the chestnut?"

"After an accident . . . she generally goes once around the concession and then she goes home."

"An accident? Jimmy . . . are you all right?"

"I'm fine. Hard to tell about the car though . . . until they get her out of the ditch."

"You ran someone off the road?"

"Lawyer fella named Darcy Dixon. He tried to pass me over Short's Hill. You know how competitive them harses are."

"So . . . how is he?"

"Mad as hell, as far as I could tell."

Then I noticed the police cruiser waiting behind the station, and Jimmy explained that the young constable had offered to give us a lift back down to the farm. We climbed into the cruiser and drove off down the Seventh Line. At

Short's Hill we passed the abandoned sleigh and, a few yards further on, the Larkspur tow-truck was winching a big, black Cadillac up the side of the ditch onto the road-bed. Dixon was nowhere to be seen.

I must confess I felt awkward about being delivered home by the police. I suppose it's silly really, but I didn't like the idea of a cruiser driving down my lane for all the neighbours to see. I suggested to Jimmy that we drop him off first and I could walk down to the farm from there.

"No, Walter," he said. "Just drop me at the road here. I know this young fella's got business to attend to . . . criminals to catch . . ."

"Oh, I'm sure he doesn't mind. You don't have any criminals to catch tonight, do you, Officer?"

The officer gave a faint smile but made no reply. He swung into Freddy's lane and coasted down the lane to the house, which to my surprise was cloaked in darkness. The hounds jumped out in the headlights of the cruiser. We thanked the officer, got out and groped our way inside the house.

"Where do you suppose Freddy is?" I asked, fumbling for the light. "It's not like him to be out at this hour."

"Oh, I expect he's around somewhere . . ." Jimmy answered.

He stamped the floor with his heel three times. The trap-door in the middle of the floor rose about eight inches and Freddy's face appeared.

"Is that you Jimmy? J-j-jeez! . . . You scared the d-d-day-lights out of us!"

And up they came: Freddy and Maggie, with several assorted cats and dogs. When Freddy saw me, he sighed.

"Walt," he said. "We're glad to see you anytime. But if you want to bring the whole police force with you . . . j-j-just call ahead, will you?"

Just another quiet evening in the country.

Yours sincerely,
Walt

———— *April 1*

Dear Ed,

Winter lets go of this land with the reluctance of an old dog giving up a bone.

This morning, I stood on the hill across the road, looking back up the Seventh Concession towards Larkspur, and felt the light drizzle seep into every pore. Pockets of fog lay in the swamp and back along the stream to the barns, where a motley group of steers stood apart from each other, chewing and, every so often, coughing clouds of steam. The horses hung their heads out the barn windows, watching the icicles drip from the eaves into icy pools. The hens sat in a silent row on the pig-feeder, feathers fluffed. Everyone wore the same dazed expression that I remember so well from subway platforms and bus shelters, the unmistakeable sign that the novelty of winter has completely worn off.

Shrugging off the feeling of despondency, I started up, gave a shout to Spike and fell flat on my face in the wet snow. I sat up spluttering and saw that I'd tripped over an orange-tipped stake, the kind surveyors use on road projects . . . or building sites. But what was a surveyor's stake doing in the middle of an empty pasture?

I looked to my left and saw another one. To my right a

third. I shuffled around through the snow and uncovered about twenty-five of them over the next ten minutes, all the while wondering what on earth was being planned. If this was a building, it was no ordinary sugar shack.

"G'day, Walt. D'you lose a nickel?"

I looked up and saw The Squire, leaning up against his fence and watching me with an amused expression.

"Do you know who is putting these stakes in the ground?" I asked.

"Sure. Lawyer fella from the city bought this fifty acres off Calvin Currie just last fall. Everybody knows that, Walt. The stakes are probably from the deed survey."

"He's done more than survey it. He's got a building site marked off right here across the front of the property."

"Yeah, I know. It's gonna look real nice. They sent me a brochure that tells you all about it. Come on over and I'll show it to you."

We went back to The Squire's house and he pulled the brochure out of a drawer. It looked like a menu cover from one of those fern bars on Yorkville Avenue, all done in delicate pastel greens and pinks.

"Persephone Glen Homes," said The Squire, reading from the brochure copy. "A quiet enclave of distinguished residences in a country setting."

"Oh, no," I said. "Condominiums." My heart sank as he read on.

" . . . significantly only forty-two homes."

"Forty-two!?" I shouted, frightening one of the cats out from under the wood-stove. "Only forty-two homes! Good heavens, man! And you knew about this?"

"Oh yeah."

"I don't believe it. The man sneaks in, buys up land and puts up forty-two condominiums right beside you . . . and you don't object?"

"What would I object to, Walt?"

"It's good agricultural land."

"Good ag . . . ah, go on, Walt," he scoffed. "A rabbit couldn't live off that field unless he had a job in town."

"Well, all right then, maybe it isn't the best land, but . . . it's a natural area."

The Squire snorted again. "There ain't a fence, or a barn or a drain on the whole fifty acres and you call that natural? It's just waste land now, Walt. Wouldn't it be better for someone to make use of it?"

There was nothing I could say to rouse him to any sort of objection. I decided to strike out for the township offices and gather some information first hand. I dispensed with the horses and borrowed Don's truck for the trip. This was important.

The local government offices for Persephone Township are located in the hamlet of Hollyhock on the banks of the Boyne River. What draws most of the visitors to Hollyhock is a factory that produces ornamental cement statuary—rabbits, dwarves, deer, that sort of thing. Most people wouldn't notice the renovated schoolhouse at the corner that serves as our township offices.

In the office, I was welcomed by the receptionist and asked to take a chair. The township clerk would see me in a moment. She asked me if I would like to read something in the meantime and gave me a pamphlet on tile drainage. After a few minutes she came back and led me to the clerk's office. He was an immense man with a red splotchy face, a gentle expression of hospitality and a handshake that felt like grabbing the end of a two-by-six board.

"Won't you sit down, Mr. Wingfield?" he said in a deep, soothing baritone voice.

"Thank you. I'd like some information about a development that's being put up on the property across from me."

"Oooohhh yeah," he said in a singsong way that sounded oddly familiar. "What is the lot and concession number, Mr. Wingfield?"

"Part of the East Half Lot Twenty-six, Concession Seven," I said.

He flipped slowly through a large binder.

"Yeah. We give a permit to a Mr. Darcy Dixon of Toronto on or above the tenth day of February of this year."

"Well," I said firmly, "I object to it and I want to know why I wasn't informed."

The clerk raised his eyebrows and studied me more carefully. Then he said something I didn't understand.

"You reside on the Adjasson property, do you?"

"The what?"

"Do you reside on the Adjasson property?"

"Adj . . . I believe it was the old Fisher place. Could you spell that for me?"

"A-D-J-A-C-E-N-T."

"Oh . . . oh, yes. Adjasson. Right across the road, in fact. On the West Half of Lot Twenty-six."

The clerk closed the book and said with grave finality, "Then you was circulated."

"No, I don't believe I was. That's why I'm here."

A wrinkle appeared over his left eyebrow. "If you wasn't circulated then you gotta give us notification."

"That's what I'm doing right now."

A wrinkle and a dent appeared over his right eyebrow. "Then you hafta file an appeal."

"I'd like to do that."

A long line appeared over the dents and wrinkles. "Then you gotta fill out an appeal form."

"Could I have one please?"

He shook his head, gave a large asthmatic sigh through his nostrils, and I prepared for the worst. "Yeah," he said and produced a form from the top drawer of his desk. He licked a pencil, squinted at the page and began asking questions.

"All right, Mr. Wingfield. You live on the West Half of Lot Twenty-six. Does the subject lands lie within six hundred feet of the repellent? . . . Uh-huh. They do." He ticked off a box and continued reading.

"Are yous a full-time resident of the township?"

"Yes," I said, too quickly. He looked at me sceptically, smiled a conspiratorial smile and checked another box. Then he turned the page over and asked:

"Have you had rabies on the property in the past ten years?"

"What?"

"Oh"—he paused and scratched his head sheepishly— "that's another application."

He got me to sign my name at the bottom of the form and then we embarked on the question of when my appeal would be heard.

"The Planning Committee hears the appeals," he said. "They meet on the second Tuesday of the month." I looked at my watch.

"That was just yesterday. He'll have half the houses up by the next meeting."

"Yep," said the clerk, "it's the buildin' season. He'll wanna get into the ground next week."

"But what about my appeal?"

"Well, generally it's the Committee that turns the appeals down. But you could come to township council meetin' next Tuesday week and they'd do it for you then."

This didn't sound very encouraging but I pressed on. "I want to make my views known and get this decision reconsidered. This permit is just opening the door to anyone who wants to sell his farm for condominiums."

"I can see how you feel."

"Isn't there something that can be done before it's too late?"

The clerk leaned back in his creaky chair and took off his glasses.

"Well, you know, Mr. Wingfield," he said, "what you might do is go on over and have a chat with Mr. Dixon and see if you can't work something out between the two of yous. You just never know, and he seemed like a nice enough fella to me. I'm sure he'd listen to reason."

Condominium developers can hear a hundred-dollar bill drop on a thick carpet but they cannot hear reason.

"I'm afraid the time has passed for that," I said. "I would like to make a presentation to council."

"You want to have your day in court, do you? I understand. You come on over here on the fifteenth. Council starts at eight o'clock sharp."

I rose, shook hands solemnly with him and left. On the way home in Don's truck I began mentally constructing the case I will present in two weeks.

Yours sincerely,
Walt

——— *April 8*

Dear Ed,

When I left the clerk's office it was raining hard and it kept raining for the rest of the week, bringing the stream at the farm to its banks. Opening Day for the trout season is only a few weeks away and I sniff the air, knowing that the fish are already on their way upstream.

But if I were a trout in this township, I would want more than the law on my side. I was puttering at the workbench one day this week when Freddy turned up at the basement door, holding a plastic bag.

"Got a present for you," he said, stepping inside quickly. "Mind if I come in?"

I looked in the bag. It contained a big, fat, rainbow trout about two feet long.

"For Pete's sake, Freddy," I exclaimed. "If they catch you with one of these things they'll take your farm away!"

"Don't w-w-worry about it, Walt. There's no problem. We have native fishing rights up here."

"Uh-huh. So, how did you catch it . . . with a spear?"

Freddy looked shocked. "Good gollies, no. The fish are kinda preoccupied this time of the year. The McKee boy just kicked him out of the stream with his rubber boots."

When Freddy left, I closed all the curtains and stashed the body in the freezer compartment of the fridge. It seemed like the first place the authorities would look but I didn't really have much choice. I laid him out with a couple of bags of corn niblets over him but the tail still stuck up at the side. I put an oven mitt over it. The fish would have to stay there for at least a month before it was legal even to look at it.

Then there was a knock at the door and panic seized me.

I slammed the freezer door shut, opened a window and fanned the air with a magazine to dispel the fish odour. I opened the door a few inches. It was The Squire.

"Can I see your fish?" he said, shouldering his way in.

"How did you know I had a fish?" I asked, scanning the road for cars. The Squire went straight to the fridge and opened the door.

"Golly, that one's bigger than mine. Bigger than Don's too. Say, what's the oven mitt doing in there?"

It gradually dawned on me that Opening Day in Persephone Township is the day they all open their freezers and start to eat the fish they've been catching over the past two months.

With all the excitement of seeing a fresh fish so early in the year I couldn't resist the urge to practise a few casts with the fly-rod in the stream down by the road—without a fly, of course. Just feeling the spring of a good graphite rod and the tug of water on the line is all you need to make you think of daffodils and Baltimore orioles. It really is true that a man cannot fly-cast and worry at the same time.

My roll-cast and side-cast were both in surprisingly good shape after a six-month absence from the stream. I took a good footing and leaned into a double haul to see if I could generate something over my usual thirty feet.

"Hey there!" called a stern voice up on the road above me. It was the young constable from Larkspur, standing beside his car. I waded out of the water to the bank and waved back.

"I know the season isn't open, officer," I said. "I'm just practising my casting with this fly-rod I got for Christmas."

"You don't practise fishing. Either you're fishing or you're not fishing."

I explained patiently that I certainly was not fishing because I was not using a fly. I pulled up the line and showed him the end completely devoid of fly to make the point crystal clear.

"So you lost it."

While I was sitting in the back of the cruiser, the officer plugged into his national databank for poachers and I amused myself by looking out the window. A group of angelic twelve-year-old boys from up the road climbed down the bank in their rubber boots and headed upstream, little plastic bags sticking out of the pockets of their ski jackets. I was about to say something to the officer, but I let it go.

After all, these are just the recurring signs of spring.

Yours sincerely,

Walt

———— *April 14*

Dear Ed,

Doctors carry beepers to tell them when they're wanted in maternity. What is a farmer supposed to carry at this time of the year? My cows are calving, my sheep are lambing and I suppose my goats have got to be kidding. In the middle of all this, one of the steers conked out and was dragged away by Oscar Berry's Dead Stock Removal Service. Our sanitary measures are beyond reproach, we use the latest medicated feed, the penicillin syringe is never dry . . . but the casualty levels still remain unacceptably high.

As Freddy says, the Lord giveth and Oscar Berry taketh away.

I put an extension phone in the barn because I spend so much time down here. It hangs right beside the window in the feed-room and there's a sign on the window saying "COWS—In emergency, break glass, use phone."

The latest head-count is twelve lambs, three calves, a litter of nine pigs from Porkchop, the brood sow, and an unknown number of little bunny-rabbits from my New Zealand Red rabbits, Xerox and Gestetner.

But the big surprise was Feedbin, who has been dragging herself around as if she'd eaten a thirty-six-inch pizza and a case of Diet Coke all by herself. She's always had a great hay-belly but this time she was really bloated up and I got concerned enough to call in the horse experts, Freddy and Jimmy.

"Worms" was the verdict, so off I went to the Co-op for supplies. I gave her a great dose yesterday afternoon and this morning came down in the drizzling rain to find her in her box stall, looking very much relieved, with a little filly standing at her side. My mother used to say that nothing induced labour like a dose of castor oil. The horse experts reappeared and, forgetting their diagnosis of the day before, warned me of the dangerous effects of horse-wormer on a pregnant mare.

But all is well. The vet popped out to make sure they were both all right. He gave the foal a shot, checked to see the mare was milking properly, gave me two aspirins and told me to call him in the morning.

I suppose I'm embarrassed that Feedbin caught me by surprise like that, but then again, I won't have to go to pre-natal classes with her. Just imagine trying to get a horse to learn the Lamaze technique. You don't think about these things until you have to.

Freddy and I sat in the mow of the barn this afternoon, listening to the rain drum on the roof and waiting for the last sheep to bring forth her increase. While we were sitting there a large drop of water hit me on the head and we both looked up.

"Old Fisher," said Freddy, "used to shoot the odd pigeon in here. It's just a small leak, Walt."

"Yes, but it's dripping right where I do my best thinking."

"Do you want to plug her up right now while we've got a minute?"

I didn't think we should be climbing around on a tin roof in the rain. Besides, I didn't have a ladder that would reach that high.

"No, but you got a p-p-pulley rope on a track goin' right under that hole," observed Freddy, studying the barn ceiling. "You could winch me up there on the pulley and I'll put a plug of tar in her. Won't take a minute."

So, we set to work, fashioning a chair-lift out of nylon rope and a milk stool for Freddy to sit in. I started to haul on the rope. It was hard work, but Freddy rose a few feet in the air.

"Ah, Walt?" said Freddy. "Just in case we get into trouble, why don't we put a few b-b-bales of hay around here to give me something soft to land on?"

I let him back down and we prepared a comfortable landing area. I had my doubts about the safety of all this but Freddy reassured me.

"Safe as a church, Walt. Here we go."

I hauled on the rope and let it drop in coils at my feet as Freddy rose in the air. Higher and higher he went till he was dangling twenty feet up, at the second purlin timber, right where the roof was leaking.

"Pretty slick, Walt. I can reach her now."

By one of those funny coincidences that make farm life so interesting, two things happened at that moment. Jimmy appeared in the door of the hay mow and the phone started to ring downstairs in the feed-room.

"Jimmy," I said, "could you hold this rope for me? I'll get that phone."

Jimmy took the rope in both hands, bent his knees and braced himself.

"I got 'er, Walter. You get the phone."

I stepped away, remembering that while Freddy weighed about one-eighty, Jimmy was probably something under a hundred and ten. Jimmy lifted off the ground and sailed up, towards the ceiling. The coils of rope at my feet disappeared in an upward spiral and Freddy came down, crashed through the floor and into the stable below. For a moment, everything stood still. Then the empty chair-lift came back up through the hole in the floor. That meant Jimmy was on his way down. I half caught him and we rolled into the straw landing-pad together. Jimmy let go of the rope. I should have realized instantly what would happen next but I didn't. The chair dropped back down and bounced off my shoulder.

By this time, the phone had stopped ringing. Jimmy and I picked each other up, and Freddy appeared at the top of the feed-room stairs.

"Don't w-w-worry about the phone, Walt," he said. "If it was important, they'll call back."

While I continue to fret about the health of my animals it appears that farmers are far more likely to wipe themselves out before any appreciable dent is made in livestock populations.

By the way, if you need a small bunny-rabbit, or two or three . . . just give me a call.

Yours sincerely,

Walt

———— *April 15*

Dear Ed,

I felt a little badly last month when my two geese, Colonel Belknap and General Longstreet, got the chop. I had vague plans to keep them through the winter and try to raise some goslings this spring. But I couldn't tell a daddy goose from a mommy goose for all the pâté in France.

Imagine my surprise when Maggie bought both of them from me for a dollar a pound. That came to twenty-eight dollars—the largest single entry for the month of March. And do you know what they eat?

Grass.

The outlay per gosling was five dollars. Starter feed was two dollars. Summer pasture goes for about ten cents an acre in this economy. Labour costs involved in feeding, killing, plucking and cleaning, and running around trying to sell them are all dismissed as negligible because I haven't got anything better to do anyway. Total expenses: seven dollars and ten cents per goose. Compare this to an average return of fourteen dollars per goose and I think you can see the magic of multiplication working in my favour.

This is very exciting. The upside is nothing short of breath-taking. Today, I created a new subsidiary, Wingfield Pâté Limitée, and went off to Larkspur to purchase supplies.

The General Store in Larkspur is run by a man named McKelvey, who appears to be about the biggest employer in the township. He owns the store, the feed and hardware business out the back, a building supply across the road and five hundred acres along the Pine River, with several hog barns, feedlots and turkey sheds. It's a big operation.

Actually, I prefer to deal with his assistants because

they are more friendly. But this morning, when I rode into town, he was standing on the verandah of the store, having just loaded several bags of groceries into a woman's car.

"Goodbye, Mrs. Lynch," he said, pleasantly enough, until the car pulled away. Then he added " . . . and pay your bill sometime!"

He turned back to me and spoke as if I'd been following him around all morning. He has a whiny voice that turns up at the end of each phrase, unlike any other voice I have heard in the township.

"I'll be lucky to get paid for those groceries in six months," he complained, "but she still makes me carry them to the car. She wants me to drop everything the minute she comes into the store, chase around, get stuff off the shelves. Do I have time for that? No. I got a business to run. So what can I do for you?"

"I won't keep you a minute, Mr. McKelvey. I need some starter feed for goslings. Do you have any?"

"Where did you get the goslings?" he asked sharply.

"Ah . . . well, actually I haven't got them yet. I was going to drive down to the Waterloo sales barns and pick some up on Thursday."

"What do you pay for them?"

"Last year they were five dollars."

"Each?" The sound of his voice was beginning to grate on my nerves. "I can get 'em for you a lot cheaper than that!"

"You can?"

"I just got a hundred in this week."

"Well, I only need fifty."

"A dollar each if you take the whole bunch."

I stopped. A dollar each was a good price. "What about the starter pellets?"

"Ten bucks a bag and you'll need ten bags of it."

"Ten bucks? Last year it was five."

"Grain's gone up. I don't run a charity. Do you want the geese or not?"

"Where did they come from?"

"Hatchery away up north." He was being evasive. "They're good birds. They go real fast this time of the year. You want 'em or not?"

"All right . . . sure. Can you deliver them?"

"That's extra."

I told him not to bother, knowing I could get Don to help me. As it turned out, Don wasn't as impressed with the deal as I was. I found him in the mow of his barn, grinding corn, and when I told him what I had just done he turned off the machine and stared at me.

"You bought a hundred geese from Dry Cry?"

"Dry Cry? Why do you call him that, Don?"

"It's his voice, Walt. He sounds like he's cryin' but there's no tears. Did you look at these geese?"

"Ah . . . no I didn't. But they're all the same . . . aren't they? I mean, a goose is a goose . . . isn't it?"

Don was incredulous.

"You bought a hundred geese from Dry Cry and didn't even look at them? I'll tell you a story about that man, Walt. One time he went shares with his brother on five hundred turkeys. But he's so cheap he figured he could save a lot of money if he didn't put the medication and the supplements in the feed like you're supposed to. After a couple of months, half the turkeys were walkin' around on their elbows, all crippled up, so Dry Cry crated up the healthy ones and sold them all down at Waterloo. The next time his brother's in the turkey shed he looks at all these crippled turkeys and says, 'Those turkeys aren't doin' so good.' And Dry Cry says, 'Never mind, those are the ones that lived.'

"And that was his own brother, Walt. Let's go have a look at those geese."

As it turned out, they passed inspection. Dry Cry had them all packed up in those flat cardboard poultry cases with the air-holes in them. But Don unpacked each box and checked them over carefully.

"They look healthy enough," he said, sitting back on his heels. "A little dark . . . What kind are they?"

"They're French," said Dry Cry.

"French?" I said. "That's nice. Did you hear that, Don? French geese."

"Uh-huh," said Don in his solemn way. "They look a little dark to me."

So, we took them all home and Wingfield Pâté Limitée is in business with French geese. I've got them in the feed-room now. They should be ready to go out on the grass in a month. Spike has agreed to be development vice-president of the new company. He's aggressive, self-starting . . . and the only member of the staff who doesn't eat starter pellets.

Yours sincerely,

Walt

—— *April 18*

Dear Ed,

On Tuesday night I drove over to council to make my presentation, as planned. The meeting began at eight o'clock, just like the clerk said, but he neglected to tell me that petitions are not heard until the rest of the agenda is completed. I sat and listened as they waded through twenty-two items.

One of the vigilant correspondents was there from the *Free Press and Economist*. But we heard nothing from him the whole evening except for the sound of his head hitting the desk.

The reeve sat at the middle of the council table, wearing his chain of office with the township crest on it. On his right, in plain clothes, was the deputy-reeve, and on his left, the other two councillors. At a separate table sat my friend, the clerk, who prompted the reeve through the agenda. It all looked like a meeting of the Soviet presidium. None of these people was under sixty-five, and the one on the end looked like a contemporary of Wilfrid Laurier.

"Your worship," said the clerk, "the first item of business we have here is a letter from Demeter Township saying that they don't want to contribute to the Larkspur library agreement anymore."

"What are they whinin' about now?" asked the reeve.

"Seems they've checked over the records and they found that no one from Demeter used the library in the last two years. They say it ain't worth it and they want out."

The councillors looked at each other meaningfully, and the deputy-reeve said, "They ain't had no fire up there this year either, but they ain't askin' to get out of the fire agreement."

"Is it the wish of council," said the clerk, "that I write 'em back while they can still read and tell 'em to go to hell?"

The motion was carried unanimously. In this fashion, council disposed of an application for a trailer-park permit, paid nine sheep-damage claims and approved a permit for a dog-obedience school. They endorsed a circular resolution from a distant municipality calling for nuclear disarmament and then settled down for the road superintendent's report. At about half-past ten it was time for petitions. The clerk introduced me, and they all got up to shake hands with me, which struck me as very hospitable. The reeve invited me to speak.

"Mr. Wingfield," he said, "we sure do appreciate you coming out and takin' an interest in council. As you can see, we run an open meeting and anyone with a complaint can come in here and speak his mind, if he's got one."

"Well," I said. "I appreciate the opportunity to be here. I have a problem with a land severance and building permit you approved across from my property . . ."

The clerk interrupted to explain where my farm is located.

"Denton," he said, addressing the reeve, "this is the old Fisher place at the corner of the Twenty-fifth and the Seventh. Down in the valley there . . ."

"Oh, gollies, yes," said the reeve, nodding, "I know the property, Harold. The Fishers is cousins of my wife's family, and Harriet spent the summer over there the year before we were married, when her dad was burned out. Do you mind that, Ernie?"

Ernie was the deputy-reeve, a red-faced man of an excitable nature. The reeve's apparently innocent observation brought him to the edge of his chair as if a challenge had been issued.

"I took hay off the back fields down there with my dad ten years before that," he announced, "when the Fishers still lived at the home farm on the Sixth."

Wilfrid Laurier leaned forward from the other side of the reeve and hissed, "My grandfather put the first plough in them fields and held the original deed. It was him sold it to the Fishers."

There was a silence and the reeve looked back at me, inviting me to continue. I was somewhat puzzled by this exchange, but I carried on.

"The property I am concerned about is, in fact, *across* the road . . . the East Half of Lot Twenty-six."

"That would be the back of Calvin Currie's place, Denton," said the clerk, helpfully.

"Oooohh, yesss," said the reeve. "God, that's a stony field. Just a pasture now, but there was a time when it put up sixty bushels to the acre. Used to be a barn on that place. Do you mind that barn, Ernie?"

"Do I?" roared Ernie. "My dad built that barn. It was the first bank barn in the north end of the township. Damn near broke him but he built her. That's a long time ago."

Mr. Laurier leaned forward again. "My great-grandfather," he said in a voice barely audible, "was the first white man to set foot on the Currie farm. He did the original survey the year Princess Victoria took to the throne."

This was starting to get away from me.

"Excuse me," I said, waving one hand, "I would like to appeal a decision you have made to sever fifty acres off that farm and grant a building permit to Darcy Dixon for the construction of forty-two condominiums."

"Harold, did you circulate Mr. Wingfield?" asked the reeve.

"Yes, your worship, the said application was forwarded on or above the thirteenth of February, but the said application failed to arrive. He never seen it."

"You got a mailbox, Mr. Wingfield? Or do you pick it up at the store?"

"I had a mailbox but it disappeared on or above the thirteenth of February," I said, matching the clerk's turn of phrase as diplomatically as I could, "courtesy of the township snow-plough."

"That happens," said the reeve. "I expect it'll turn up when the snow melts and then we'll put her back up for you."

"I appreciate that very much, but what about my appeal?"

"Well, sir, it's too bad you didn't get circulated and no one feels worse about that than I do. I can see it weren't in your power to get your objection heard before the appeal period expired, but the rules is the rules and I'd be takin' the law into my own hands if I told you any different."

"The appeal period has expired?" I said. "When was that?"

"Today at twelve o'clock. Now, I'll tell you what we can do for you, Mr. Wingfield. Harold, here, will get the road superintendent out to your place and they'll fish around in that big drift till they find your mailbox and get her set up again. Now, you'll do that for him, won't you, Harold?"

"Oh yes, Mr. Reeve. We'll do that," said the clerk.

I glared over at the clerk's desk, but he was calmly drawing a heavy line through my name on the agenda. I listened to the reeve's speech of thanks for my appearance, shook hands with everyone and left.

I drove back to Freddy's, my sense of grievance growing with every washboard I drove over. In Freddy's kitchen, Maggie had the gas furnace turned way up, which didn't help. Even the cats had moved into the summer kitchen to cool off.

"If they approve this," I asked Freddy, "what next? Where will they stop?"

"Lot of taxes will be comin' outa that place, Walt. You gotta think of that. It's gettin' late. You want a bit of lunch?"

"Lunch? It's past midnight."

Maggie produced crackers, cheese, cold cuts, pickles, apple pie, maple syrup and a pot of tea, and called us to the table.

I pulled out a chair and said, "Dammit, Freddy . . . the only way to get this thing under control is to run for council myself."

I had expected Freddy to be surprised, but I wasn't prepared for the look of woe that contorted his face.

"D-d-don't do it, Walt," he warned. "You'll learn to hate yourself. You know what it means, takin' a job like that? Hand out dog licences . . . keep the roads fixed up . . . and have every lunatic in the township callin' you to get their lane ploughed out."

"There's a principle at stake here," I argued. "I'm going to put my name up for the municipals next September."

"Walter . . . people run for council when they've run out of stupid things to do on their own place . . . and you got a long way to go there yet. You haven't even scratched the surface."

"Freddy," I said patiently, "it's easy to be cynical. But you and I know that if you want good government you have to get involved, and where better than here? After all, government at the township level is the very touchstone of democracy. It's what built this country and produced its great leaders, people like . . ."

Names escaped me for the moment. But Freddy knew what I meant. I predicted that in a year's time the people of this great township will probably come to think of me in much the same way as the people of Illinois saw Abraham Lincoln, or the way the people of Rome saw Cincinnatus—one hand on the plough, the other on the tiller of the ship of state.

Freddy was impressed. "By golly, we got ourselves a public

figure here, Maggie. Gosh, Walt, that's powerful stuff . . . speakin' of which, let's have a toast to the candidate. What about that special bottle we got at Christmas, Maggie?"

Maggie opened one of the high cupboard doors and looked at a row of liquor bottles.

"Which is the special one, Freddy?" she asked.

Freddy poured us both a glass and Maggie offered to toast the occasion with a mug of hot Horlick's Malt. As we raised our glasses Freddy paused and said, "I gotta warn you, Walt. Elections around here are a little different than what you may be used to back home. If you're determined to go ahead with this, maybe me and the boys should give you a hand."

"Will you be my campaign manager?" I asked.

"Now, that would be a good idea. Here's to you, Walt."

So, there you have it. I am a candidate for the municipals in October and I've already done some work on my speech to the all-candidates' meetings.

> "My friends . . . for we are all friends here . . . Our challenge will be to face, head on, the promise of our future . . . without losing sight of the traditions of our heritage . . .
>
> Keeping one eye on the rich potential of our township . . . but, on the other hand, resisting the urge to creep before we walk . . ."

Well, it sounded better when I gave it to the steers this morning. And don't laugh. Freddy says he can get them on the voters' list.

Yours sincerely,
Walt

—— *June* 12

Dear Ed,

This used to be my favourite view. Looking out the hay-mow door, over the manure pile, I still have a commanding vista of the Seventh Concession and the Pine River Valley. But last week, bulldozers and back-hoes moved on to Darcy Dixon's pasture and began ripping it apart. What used to be an attractive natural setting of limestone rock and cedar trees is now one vast, gaping wound. It would take me and the horses a month to make it look like that. A huge billboard at the fence-line, in the same hideous pastels of the brochure, announces "Persephone Glen Homes—Elegance in Harmony with Nature—from $250,000."

Dixon told me he was going to plant a wind-break, so his buyers wouldn't have to look at my place. The next day a truck arrived carrying seventy-five Siberian elms twenty feet tall. By the end of the afternoon he had created an instant forest.

The neighbours think it's just great. "Good for the tax base," they say or, "You can't stop progress." I seem to be the only person on the concession who doesn't think it's a good idea. I tried to appeal to their sense of history by pointing out that Calvin Currie's farm has been in his family's name for a hundred and fifty years. He has a Century Farm sign at his gate.

I asked: "What does a Century Farm sign mean to you people?"

The answer was: "A hundred years without a single decent offer for your land."

It doesn't do to dwell on these things. I have other things to worry about, like my geese, for example. They just started growing their adult feathers and I had a good look at them on Sunday. They're not French at all—there's nothing French about them. They're Canada geese . . . all one hundred of them.

I had a visit from a wildlife officer of the Ministry of Natural Resources yesterday. He tells me it's illegal to feed Canada geese, and he gave me a week to release them back to the wild. That's all very well for him to say. A hundred geese haven't imprinted on his overalls.

I was right about one thing. They eat grass all right. There isn't a blade of grass left around the barn, and the only thing that keeps them away from the house is gunfire. They careen around the place like marauding riff-raff, terrorizing everyone.

My old rule for times like this is to stay busy as much as possible. Having declared my candidacy in public I decided to gear up the campaign committee in the clinch-the-deal atmosphere of the Little Red Hen Restaurant in Larkspur. I phoned Freddy late Monday night to arrange a power breakfast for the key strategists.

The rule at the farm is, the animals eat before you do, which may be one reason that breakfast meetings have never caught on in the country. We all staggered into the Little Red Hen the next morning, and I realized what time Don must have got up to milk fifty cows and get there by eight o'clock.

"Is this gonna happen a lot in this campaign?" asked Don, looking at me through bleary, red eyes.

"Breakfast meetings are important," I said. "They communicate a feeling of commitment and show people we're up early and working hard. Now, have you got any suggestions about how I conduct myself during the campaign . . . where I should go, what I should say?"

"You gotta stay outa sight until the vote," said Don.

I laughed politely and continued. "I realize that it's going to be a tough battle and all that, but this is the challenge of a campaign . . . the cut-and-thrust of debate, meeting the people face to face, main-streeting, door-knocking . . . do you think maybe I should go to the senior citizens' home?"

They looked at each other.

"I never thought of that," said Don. "We could get you a room there for the month with my dad. Nobody would know you were there."

"Now hold on a minute," I protested. "I can't hide from the people. A peekaboo campaign is not my style. We're going to face this thing head on and deal with the issues as—"

"What Don is saying," interrupted Freddy, "is that people don't know you as well as we do. Three weeks isn't much time to convince them to go votin' for you. You'd be a lot b-b-better off if we put some signs up and you just lay low down at the farm . . . Hey, Donna? Could we have coffee over here?"

"I'm as good as the next man. I pay my taxes. Is there something wrong with me?"

"You ain't been hit by lightning," said The Squire.

"Lightning?"

"Now you take the fella who topped the polls the last three votes. He was hit by lightning on his barn roof about ten years ago. Never was the same after that. Couldn't farm and he couldn't do anything else. So we said, why not put him on council? Perfect for the job. That lightning was the making of him as a politician."

"I see," I said. "He avoids controversy, does he?"

"He avoids breathin' when he can."

Donna brought four cups of coffee to the table.

"There you go, Walt," said Freddy, passing me a cup. "If you don't want sugar, don't stir. Now, you sure you don't want to go into the nursing home? They got a new pool table, and shuffle-board . . ."

"No," I said flatly. "The next item on the agenda is fund-raising. Have any of you ever done any fund-raising before . . . for something like this?"

"Oh sure," said The Squire. "We got three hundred dollars once for the furnace in the church."

"Great. When was that?"

"Nineteen fifty-four."

I pointed out that with printing and advertising expenses the campaign costs could approach a thousand dollars. Just then, the lights and the radio went off and the fan over the deep-fryer whirred to a halt.

"That'll be Willy and Dave," said Freddy. "They're takin' a m-m-maple tree down outside Dry Cry's."

"Looks like it's down now," said Don. "We better get out there and give them a hand."

"Yep," agreed The Squire. "If they try doing home repairs on them wires we'll have another couple of candidates for office."

We went outside. It was a warm June morning and across the highway in front of the General Store a huge maple tree lay in a splash of green. Willy and Dave stood sadly contemplating the exposed end of a Hydro wire, snapping and guttering on the ground. On its way down, the tree had caught on the cement porch of the store and pinned a table of fresh produce to the wall. This appeared to be the only damage to the store, but Dry Cry was in a temper, threatening to sue for willful damage and interruption of business. When the

Hydro truck arrived, the servicemen isolated the pole, recon-
nected the wires and handed Willy and Dave a bill for five
hundred dollars.

"Five hundred dollars?" said Willy. "Hoooooeeeeeey!"

A sum like that can take your mind right off an election
campaign.

"Hate to see a bunch of people get up so early and still be
this far behind," said The Squire sadly. "How are you at fund-
raising, Walt?"

Dry Cry was only paying Willy and Dave fifty dollars to
take down the tree in the first place. That left us four hundred
and fifty to raise from other sources. We set off up the street
to find someone who would either buy the wood or pay us to
take down another tree. Mrs. Cole's eavestroughing was suffering from the attention of a willow tree, and the rectory had
a patch of shingles missing where a maple branch was scraping the garage roof, but our reputation had preceded us. There
were no takers. However, the minister did offer to buy three
cords of firewood, cut and stacked alongside his garage, for a
hundred dollars. That left three hundred and fifty dollars still
to raise and the morning was already half gone.

We spent the next two hours in front of Dry Cry's hacking
away at the maple tree and loading it into Don's pick-up. The
racket from two man-killing chain-saws brought all conversation to a halt and we were each left alone with our fund-
raising plans for the afternoon. Back at Freddy's for lunch,
Maggie received the news in something less than stoic silence.

"You take on a job for half what anyone else would charge
and you come home owing a month's wages. We'd be further
ahead if you sat in there all day, watching television."

A Pyrex bowl of turnips hit the table with some force.

She returned to the kitchen, and Freddy leaned over the table to me.

"Don't worry about Maggie, Walt. She's just a bit upset with the boys because they might have been hurt with that live wire. She worries about them . . ."

From the kitchen Maggie shouted over the running taps: "For five hundred dollars I'd put them both in a hot bath with a toaster oven."

We finished the meal in silence and slunk out to the summer kitchen to plan strategy for the afternoon. We delivered the wood to the minister, piled it along the garage and returned to the store for a Coke. Sitting on the verandah, we listened to Dry Cry's attempt to extract damages from Willy and Dave for the bent table.

"I'm willing to forget the interruption of business, but look what you done to my table!" he whined.

"Ah, go on, Dry Cry," said Don. "There ain't a scratch on it."

Don was right. It suddenly struck me how sturdy a table it was to have carried the weight of a tree with so little damage. I peeked under the linoleum and ran a fingernail over a patch of exposed wood.

"I could use a table like this in the barn," I said to Dry Cry. He screwed up his face and I prepared for another assault on my ears.

"It'd cost me fifty bucks to make a new one."

"If I gave you thirty-five, would you take it?"

"Forty," he said, sticking his nose in my face.

"Don't give in to him, Walt," said The Squire. "He's so narrow he could walk through the strings of a harp without strikin' a note."

"Done," I said, and handed him two twenties.

Dry Cry looked at me suspiciously for a moment and then reached out and took the bills.

In Freddy's yard, we unloaded the table from the truck and I borrowed Don's penknife to score the old linoleum and turn it back. The table top was one solid pine board an inch and a half thick and thirty inches across.

"Gentlemen," I announced, "I believe we just broke even. With a little sandpaper and a coat of urethane, this table is worth seven hundred dollars."

"Who would pay seven hundred dollars for this?" asked The Squire.

"Darcy Dixon, QC."

And he did. Our campaign kitty now has three hundred and ten dollars in it.

Yours sincerely,
Walt

———— *July 5*

Dear Ed,

Just after breakfast this morning I went on a door-knocking campaign down the Sixth Line of Persephone Township. Freddy wasn't enthusiastic about the idea because he says no one has ever done it before. I suppose if everybody knows who you are, there's no need for it. But they don't know me and the quickest way to get to know them is to knock on their door.

The Sixth Line is new territory for me. I don't know a soul along here except for the farmer on the corner, whose mailbox I snipped off with the horses a couple of months ago. He was very good about it. But I thought maybe I would skip him and try the house across the road, a white clapboard bungalow with nicely kept flower gardens and some of those lovely concrete rabbits you often see in this part of the country.

I walked up the porch steps and read the sign under the window: "These premises protected by shotgun three days of the week. You guess which three."

I knocked on the screen door. At the end of the hallway, a face popped out from the kitchen and frowned at me. It was a middle-aged woman, wearing a simple print dress and a fairly stern expression.

"Hello," I said. "My name is Walt Wingfield and I'm running for council in the upcoming election."

The woman removed her hands from the sink and rubbed them on a towel. "Oh yeah," she said.

"I hope I can count on your support," I said cheerfully.

She nodded and came down the hallway to stand on the other side of the screen door.

"Would you like my campaign brochure?" I asked.

She opened the screen door a crack and took the brochure. There was a pause while she scanned it thoughtfully. Finally she looked at me over her glasses and said:

"I got no use for the way the government runs the post office."

"Ah, well," I said, "that's a federal matter and I am running in the municipal election."

"I know that," she snapped. "And I'll tell you another thing. It's terrible what they're doing to the hospitals."

"Ah, there again," I explained, "the hospital issue is a provincial matter and we are in the middle of a local municipal election campaign. I am running for a seat on council for Persephone Township."

She looked at me over her glasses again and said, "I know that. You don't have to lecture me, young man! What we need is a man like Mr. Diefenbaker."

"Yes . . . a wonderful man. But he has been dead for twenty-five years!"

"I *know* that. Things haven't been the same since."

The magnitude of the task in front of me was becoming apparent. I could spend a lot of time on this verandah.

"To my way of thinking it's time for a change," she said.

"I couldn't agree with you more."

"Then you may just have my vote, Mr. Winghead."

This seemed like a good moment to make my escape. At the next place I was trapped by an evangelical beekeeper who tried to recruit me to membership in the National Beekeeping Association. Then, I helped a man chase a cow back into his field. At the last house, a gentle-looking man in slippers and a housecoat came to the door.

"Good morning. My name is W . . ."

"Oh, I know you," he said, "you're Mr. Wingfield. I recognize your picture from your brochure. I picked up a handful at the general store. They're terrific."

"Oh, thank you. I feel strongly about the issues and I've tried to crystallize in a few sentences what this election is all about."

"Well, they're just great. Have you got any more?"

"Yes, I do!" I handed him the rest of the brochures. "This is wonderful," I said. "Frankly, you're the first person I've met this morning that has shown any interest in discussing it."

"They're perfect. You see, if you spread them out flat like this . . . they fit right into the bottom of the birdcage. I could use a hundred of them."

With my brochures gone I turned for home. The only tangible result of my door-to-door campaign was a rip in my pant leg and a jar of honey. No one came right out and promised to vote for me but at least I'm putting my name in front of the people and my face under the birds. . . .

Yours sincerely,

Walt

————July 12

Dear Ed,

I am learning, with the great statesmen of the world, that the price of peace is eternal vigilance, especially when you're in the poultry business. Late last night, just as I was settling into the feathers for the night, I heard the piercing scream of a chicken from down at the barn.

You have to hear that sound yourself to understand why it brings you out of bed at a dead run and sends you flailing down the lane in pyjamas and slippers. As the barn loomed up before me, I could hear squawks, flutters and thuds coming from the hen pen. I flung open the door and switched on the lights. There was a scurrying along the wall, and a small dark shape vanished through a crack in the boards.

In the hen pen, all was confusion. Four hens lay on the floor, feathers fluffed out and breathing their last. The survivors huddled together on the roost, clucking nervously and scolding me: "Book, book, book . . . you're the sheriff, can't you do something about this?"

I did my best to quiet the ladies and bent down to pick up the casualties. Boots appeared in the doorway in front of me and I looked up with a start. It was Don, carrying a twelve-gauge shotgun.

"Heard the noise," he said. "How many did he get?"

"These four," I said, pointing to the bodies lying on the straw. "What do you mean, 'he'?"

Don turned one of the hens over with the toe of his boot and pointed under the wing with the gun barrel.

"See that?" he said in a low voice. "It's tough enough to keep a hen layin' every day without a hole in it like that. That's the work of a weasel. They come in when it's dark and climb up on the roosts. They move so quietly that the hens don't even know they're there. Then they pick one out and grab it under the wing, just here . . ."

Don poked me under the arm and I jumped about six inches off the ground. He sat down on a cement block and cradled the gun in his arms.

"He'll be back before long. When he does . . . we'll be here?"

"We will? I mean . . . how do you know he'll be back?"

"Once he's got the taste of blood, there's only one way to stop him."

This was all starting to sound like an episode of *Gunsmoke*.

"Say, Don, you won't fire that thing without giving me a little warning, will you?"

"Turn out the light, Walt . . . and make yourself comfortable. We may be here for awhile."

I turned out the light and sat down in the straw, beside Don, facing the chickens. The hens were roosting quietly now, their little chicken pulses already back to normal despite the recent visit of a serial murderer.

"Don?" I said tentatively.

"Yeah?"

"Is it all right to talk?"

"I suppose so," he said. "But I'm not very conversational."

"How come?"

"I had a visit from Darcy Dixon today."

"You did? What did he want?"

"He told me he doesn't want me spreadin' any more manure on the front fields. Says it isn't good for business."

"What?" I exclaimed, a surge of adrenalin rushing through me. "What did you say to him?"

"Nothing," said Don.

"He can't tell you how to farm, Don."

There was a pause, then Don said quietly, "Maybe you were right, Walt. That Dixon fella's gettin' to be a real pest." We lapsed into silence again.

Time does not pass quickly in the dark, especially when you're fighting sleep. But the important thing in a stakeout is to stay alert.

My eyelids started to droop and I pinched myself awake. I thought about Darcy Dixon and his condominiums. That gave me a few minutes of wakefulness but soon I was drifting again.

Then I remembered the weasel and jerked upright. I had to stay awake. I tried to imagine what a weasel would look like up close, but the only face I could bring to mind was Darcy Dixon's. I had a vision of a weasel dressed in a pinstriped suit. He was sneaking along the wall of the hen coop, carrying a set of blueprints under one arm. He climbed up beside one of the hens and began to explain to her the advantages of zero lot lines and low maintenance. He was showing her the details of the model suite: breakfast-room and patio, broadloom throughout, ensuite bathroom . . . I was sure she was happy where she was, but she was listening to him, her head cocked to one side. I couldn't believe it. He was going to make the sale.

"Don't buy it!" I shouted. "He's a weasel! Don't buy—"
KABOOOOOM!

I woke up.

Don turned on the light. He was talking to me and point-ing to a hole in the wall, but I couldn't hear anything. The air was full of blue smoke and acrid-smelling cordite.

It was a weasel all right. We identified it, using dental records. The hens sustained three more casualties, whether from enemy action or friendly fire it was difficult to say. This morning, they were all interred under the apple tree with full military honours in a service attended by all staff.

There was one other casualty. I'd forgotten that Freddy's truck was parked on the other side of the hen coop. The blast from Don's shotgun flattened both front tires and I notice the radiator is now empty. I said I thought my insurance would cover it but Don isn't so sure. He read somewhere in the fine print of my policy that the company will not assume liability for acts of war.

Yours sincerely,

Walt

———— *August 12*

Dear Ed,

The pace has been blistering and it has taken my mind off condo-miniums, politics and everything else. After four solid weeks bringing in hay we went straight into the harvest without a break.

It has been stinking hot and muggy. Men, machines and animals are reaching their limits. Well, maybe not the animals. Mortgage and Feedbin haven't put in a full day since the first of May. When you get this bone-tired, the only relief comes when a machine breaks down. We had a good one today.

Don and I were baling wheat straw in my front field

yesterday with his ancient McCormick baler. I realize this compromises my earlier pronouncements about machinery and the old ways, but there is no older way to bale straw than with Don's McCormick baler. The forks on the roller in front pick up the straw, and an arm and a plunger do the rest. The arm pushes the straw into the chamber that makes the bale. Then it pulls back, and the plunger comes from the front to ram the bale, six inches at a times, out the chute at the back.

It goes, "Runch, crunch. Runch, crunch. Runch, crunch."

Don likes to tell people that his baler has broken fewer than ten bales in as many years, and he was warming to this theme once again when we paused at about four o'clock to adjust the string tension.

He pulled the power take-off lever to start us up again and there was a great ripping "sproing" from inside the machine. We both jumped back out of the way and watched from a safe distance as pieces of metal flew through the air. The arm and the plunger were out of sequence, both trying to ram at the same time.

"Stay put, Walt. This could get ugly."

The two arms smashed away at each other, pounding the machine without mercy, until the main gear was whizzing freely in the air, and the baler lay in a crumpled wreck. When Don thought it was safe, he slipped in behind the tractor and shut it off.

"You okay, Don?"

"Jeez," he said, "did you see that? Did you ever see a machine commit suicide like that?"

I confessed I hadn't.

"Well, to hell with it," he said. "Let's get cleaned up and go to the dance."

Every August, the Women's Auxiliary gets together and holds a dance to break up the harvest. They hire a one-lung orchestra from Lavender and wax the floor of the Orange Lodge for the occasion. A general amnesty is declared on Catholics and the pictures of King Billy crossing the Boyne are retired into the loft to avoid offending anyone. Half the community sits on a single row of squeaky folding chairs along the wall and listens to the band play through its entire repertoire twice—that's four tunes altogether. Meanwhile the other half stands in the parking lot outside and talks about crops and politics. After an hour or so, people start dancing.

I strolled out to get some air after the first set of square dances and found the boys sitting on the bumpers of a couple of trucks, smoking and drinking from stubby Coke bottles. Jimmy beckoned enthusiastically.

"Come here, Walt," he called. "You look like you been rode hard and put away hot. Have a cool drink."

"Just what I need. Thanks, Jimmy."

I had a long pull out of the Coke bottle and it burned all the way down. I coughed and handed the bottle back.

"Jimmy, you shouldn't be drinking this stuff."

I looked over at Freddy, but he grinned and said, "He's just had a couple, Walt. He's all right."

Jimmy pranced around the truck, holding the bottle high in the air and singing:

"Oh whiskey, you're the devil,
You're leading me astray . . ."

I leaned back against the truck and watched Jimmy whistling and shuffling in the gravel. The crickets were singing at high pitch, and every so often a truck whizzed by in the darkness on the highway. A cool breeze lifted the leaves of the horse-chestnut tree beside us, bringing with it one of those strange premonitions of summer's end.

"Naw, there's no back-hoe work over there," Freddy was saying. "He's got a couple of fellas up from the city with a flat-bed truck and two machines. I go over to ask him why he don't use a little local help and he tells me I should clean up my front yard. Called it a junk-heap. I told him, I says, 'It'll be a junk-heap to you until the day you come lookin' for a carburettor off a '62 Chev.' It takes a long time to build up an auto-parts business like I got."

"I don't like it," agreed The Squire. "You know that field out behind the construction? First off he rented it back to Calvin Currie for twenty bucks an acre but now he's gone and offered Calvin thirty bucks an acre to leave it alone. Told him not to farm it at all. Damn waste of land."

I jumped in: "And he tells Don not to spread manure until the fall. Now do you see why I'm running for office? You can't protect your right to farm unless you are represented on council. That's the way a democratic system works. You've got to have a voice in order to change things."

There was an awkward silence and I was beginning to think I'd said something wrong.

"Running for council isn't the answer," said Don, finally. "Look, Walt, we probably shoulda told you. You haven't got much of a chance."

"Why do you say that?"

"Now, d-d-don't take offence, Walt," said Freddy. "It's not that people wouldn't agree with what you have to say. It's just that you're from the city. They won't even consider you."

"That's right," said The Squire. "A fella lost the last election up here because his wife's grandmother was born south of Highway 13."

"You got about as much chance as a toad on the freeway," said Don.

"But you're right about one thing," said Freddy. "We've had just about enough from this D-D-Dixon fella. It's time we loosened his bolts a little."

Then The Squire said: "Jimmy had the right idea last spring, runnin' him off the road like that. Didn't make a proper job of it, but it was the right idea."

Jimmy was singing again:

"Ten years ago, on a cold dark night,
There was someone killed 'neath the town-hall light . . ."

"Now look, fellas," I said hastily. "Let's not get carried away. If you want to stop Dixon you have to figure out how to keep people from buying his condominiums. He'll finish one unit, invite a bunch of high-powered real estate people up from the city and then do some selling to finance the construction of the rest. The only way to discourage him is to figure out a way to turn those people off."

"Well, how would you do that, Walt?" asked The Squire. "They're gonna be real nice houses."

"And you can't b-b-beat the neighbourhood," said Freddy. "If you had the money and didn't have to farm, where else in the world would you want to live?"

I laughed. "You may be surprised to hear this but there are some things about life in the country that people from the city have difficulty getting used to."

"Oh, you mean c-c-cluster flies. Don't like them myself."

"Snow's bad in the winter," observed Don.

"Can't get CBC up here," said The Squire.

"Well . . . that's partly it. But there are other things as well."

Someone announced the draw for the door-prize and the men moved towards the hall, leaving me alone with Jimmy and the first faint glimmerings of a plan. Jimmy was sitting on the truck tail-gate, singing at the moon in his tremulous tenor.

> "And they shot 'em in pairs,
> Comm' up the stairs . . ."

"C'mon, Jimmy," I said. "Let's go in. You've had enough."

Jimmy swung off the tail-gate and came around to the front of the truck. He surveyed me solemnly, took a deep breath and said, "I'll come in with you, Walter . . . *if* you can put my hand down on the hood of this truck."

This was ridiculous. I couldn't arm-wrestle an eighty-five-year-old man. But Jimmy grabbed me with his gnarled old hand and mashed my arm down flat on the hood of the truck.

"Do you dance, Walter?" he asked, twirling away again.

"Sure," I said, feeling my bicep. "Waltz, tango . . . listen, they're playing a foxtrot. Why don't we go in?"

Jimmy listened. "Sure and it's no foxtrot, Walt. That's the Little Burnt Potato."

He shuffled his feet and a cloud of dust rose around his boots. It took me a minute to realize that he was step-dancing to the music inside. He put his hand up on my shoulder and I found myself hopping up and down, trying to keep up with his footwork. His eyes shone with a combination of delight and Crown Royal and by the time the band reached the final chorus, we had heel-and-toed our way to the front door of the hall. Jimmy waved cheerily and tottered into the crowd, to join a square of people half his age.

I leaned against the cool cement-block wall to catch my breath, laughing to myself and listening to the crickets' furious singing.

Yours sincerely,
Walt

———— *August 27*

Dear Ed,

The morning of Dixon's great condominium opening happened in the middle of what Don refers to as "the dead of summer," on one of those endless hot and muggy days, when everything has stopped growing and the whole township has turned brown. After chores I stepped up into the hay mow to make reconnaissance with a pair of binoculars. All the leaves had dropped from the Siberian elm in the heat, giving me a clear view of Persephone Glen. Everything seemed ready. Bunting fluttered from the sign. Lawn-sprinklers shimmered over the square of fresh green sod around the model suite. I'd almost forgotten what green grass looked like. The parking lot was freshly gravelled but still empty.

According to Dixon himself, seventy-five of the most influential real estate people from the city would soon be here. Waiting was the hardest part. The minutes ticked slowly by.

In my front field, facing the condominium, stood an ancient threshing machine, of the kind you see in pictures of the prairies before the Depression. It had been sitting unused in Freddy's driving shed for about twenty years but Freddy promised me that it would run. Beside the thresher was Don's massive John Deere Model "D" tractor and a hay-wagon neatly piled with sheaves of wheat. Jimmy was standing guard with a pitchfork.

They appeared on the horizon right on time. BMW's, Mercedes, Audis . . . ladies in pink and turquoise dresses emerged from the cars, stretched in the morning sunlight and wandered towards the model suite. From my vantage point I could hear the shrill "Howarrryaa!" and "Hi guy!" . . . familiar mating calls of the male and female real estate salesperson.

By eleven o'clock, the parking lot was full of cars, the men were talking together in groups on the front lawn and some of the women were wandering along the side of the road, picking wildflowers. I spoke into the walkie-talkie.

"All right, gentlemen. This is it. Let's move that stock!"

It all started very quietly. Don and The Squire opened their barnyard gates. Holstein cows spilled out onto the road on the right, and sheep on the left. Now, there's nothing odd about a few sheep on the road . . . or a few cows. But two hundred sheep and seventy-five cows trying to pass one another on what is, after all, a very narrow road, can make the competition for wildflowers pretty intense. I could hear Don and The Squire cursing each other, just as if it had been an accident. Slightly ruffled, and perhaps taken aback by the colourful phraseology, the line of pink and turquoise dresses scampered back to the safety of the lawn and resumed their conversations. We had them now. They would be there, quite literally, until the cows came home.

Again I spoke into the walkie-talkie: "Very good, gentlemen. The pincer movement seems to be working well. I think we can move to Phase Two now."

The Squire disappeared back up his lane. Don sauntered easily through the front field to the thresher and swung up onto the John Deere. The tractor went "Rrr . . . rrr . . . whooosh, thoop-thoop-thoop." Don pulled the power take-off lever. The long belt between the two machines started to move and the thresher came to life. Jimmy climbed onto the wagon and forked the first sheaf onto the conveyor belt. The thresher bit into the sheaf with a great whine and a clatter and belched a golden shower of chaff out through the blower. For a moment, Jimmy and the thresher disappeared, but then reappeared as the golden cloud drifted slowly towards the model suite. Another sheaf went into the machine. As I watched through the binoculars, Dixon stepped through the patio doors and reached for his phone. Then my phone rang in the stable downstairs.

It was Darcy. He wanted to know what the hell was going on.

"We're threshing today, Darcy," I said innocently.

"Why can't you do it some other day?" he demanded.

"Oh, can't do that, Darcy," I said. "Gotta make hay while the sun shines."

"Can't you do it more quietly?"

"More quietly? Gee, I don't know. I kinda think if you could do it quietly they wouldn't call it threshing. Tell you what. I'll ask the boys to hurry things up a bit."

That seemed to satisfy him and he hung up. I went back up the stairs and picked up the walkie-talkie again.

"Freddy! Willy! Dave! Squire! Let's give the place some atmosphere!"

Freddy came roaring out of his lane on his big red Nuffield, hauling a manure-spreader brimming with a fresh load from the feedlot. Right behind him came three more tractors and spreaders with The Squire, Willy and Dave. Each of them had gone to some trouble to find a full load, representing a complete selection from the barnyard. They wheeled into my front field and criss-crossed in front of Persephone Glen, spewing chicken, cow, sheep and pig manure in all directions.

This aroma is not just offensive to the nose. It grabs lower down. What appears to the eye to be clear air, the lungs will simply not accept.

Dixon clutched the iron railing on his patio, a handkerchief over his face. His guests were falling back inside now, seeking the shelter of the air-conditioning.

My phone rang again. I picked it up on the ninth ring and, before I got the receiver to my ear, I could hear Dixon's voice.

"For God's sake, Wingfield! That smell is awful!"

"Smell?" I said. "What smell? Oh, that! Gee, I guess we get used to that up here, Darcy."

"One of my guests just threw up on the carpet!" he shouted.

"That's a shame. We'll certainly have to ask the boys to stop. I'm a little busy . . ."

"Tell them right now!"

"Okay, Darcy. No need to shout. Bye-bye."

Upstairs I gave the final order into the walkie-talkie: "We have them treed, gentlemen. Turn up the heat."

The boys abandoned the spreaders and converged on the thresher. Jimmy leapt on the John Deere and pulled the gas lever all the way back. The threshing machine went through an awful transformation. I knew it hadn't been oiled once in this generation, but, even so, the noise it made was incredible. It shrieked and banged and shook like a demented dinosaur.

Then Freddy, The Squire, Don, Jimmy and the boys, all started feeding it wheat sheaves at once. The chaff boiled out of the blower, filling the air with a dust cloud so thick that the very sky went dark. I could no longer see the model suite. In fact, I couldn't see anything.

My phone rang once again. This time, we could hardly hear each other.

"Hello! . . . Hello? . . . Darcy? Gee I can hardly hear you."

"What the hell are you doing over there? My air-conditioning has broken down. We're suffocating in here!"

"I got the boys to speed things up, Darcy," I shouted. "They say they'll be finished by nightfall. That's too bad about your air-conditioning. That's a brand-new system, isn't it? Do you think something might have got in it?"

At this point Dixon sounded as if he was chewing on the receiver and I wondered if I might have gone too far. I tried sympathy.

"It must be hot in there with all that triple-glazing and no air-conditioning. I'd get it fixed right away, if you can find someone up here who knows anything about those systems. Listen, Darcy, I'd love to talk but I gotta run. Bye now."

I hung up and scampered back upstairs for another look. Suddenly, the barn timbers creaked and the feed-room door swung shut downstairs. For the first time in weeks, the wind was picking up. Today of all days. The dust cloud lifted from the model suite. Worse than that, I could now see that the threshing machine had spooked the sheep and cattle and they had returned to their pastures. Even if the wind died again we were running out of sheaves. The threshing machine banged and shuddered and stopped. I looked up out of the hay-mow door and was horrified to see blue sky and fluffy white clouds.

The patio doors on the model suite opened and people stepped back out onto the lawn. I heard a cheerful laugh. The party was starting again.

"Damn!"

Well, there was one last chance. It was an operation I had code-named "Canada." I knelt down beside Spike, taking his head in my hands and speaking into his good ear:

"Go on, Spike. Get down there. And remember, we're counting on you."

Spike floundered down the feed-room stairs. I hauled on the rope to the stable door where the Canada geese had been penned for the last two days on short rations. They were ravenous. They exploded out of the pen and struck out across the field, with Spike woofing behind them. At the fence they took to the air, caught sight of Darcy's lawn, the last square of green grass left on the Seventh Line, and descended on it.

They'd never been shy, those geese. After they finished the lawn they started on the hors-d'oeuvres. One of them even bit through the phone wire. I've never seen a plague of locusts, but if you ever need one and you can't lay your hands on enough locusts, I recommend geese.

In a few minutes it was all over. Car doors banged, engines roared and the parking lot emptied, leaving Dixon standing alone on what used to be his lawn, shaking his fist at the geese.

We were all sitting in the hay mow, enjoying a beer after the battle, when the figure of Darcy Dixon appeared at the doorway.

"Golly, Darcy," said Freddy, "it's real nice of you to come over to help. But the truth is we've just finished for the day. Grab a beer, why don't you?"

The Squire said: "We had a pretty fair day, Darcy. Got a lotta work done. How did you do?"

"Hey, Darcy," said Willy, "did you hear about the Newfie who had ten kids and didn't want any more so he bought a condominium? Heeyah, heeyah!"

Dixon stood for a moment, glaring at us, and his gaze came to rest on me.

"Wingfield," he declared, his voice thick with rage, "I'll sue you, I'll sue the whole lot of you."

"For what, Darcy?" I asked. "For farming? It's all in the agricultural code of practice. I checked."

"We'll see about that. My lawyers will call your lawyers in the morning." He turned, took a step to go, but stopped and turned back to me. "Well, what about those geese?" he demanded.

"Those are wild geese, Darcy. I don't control the wildlife around here."

"Ain't it lovely, Freddy," said Jimmy in his sweetest voice, "the way the wildlife's comm' back. You never used to see geese around here."

Darcy turned on his heel, tripped on the door-sill and left. I followed him to the door and watched him stalk angrily down the gangway, his black leather shoes slipping on the dry grass, making a dignified retreat almost impossible. Chuckling, I turned back into the mow and found my neighbours all lined up in a row, waiting to shake my hand.

Yours sincerely,
Walt

—— *August 28*

Dear Ed,

The morning after the Battle of Persephone Glen, the heatwave broke. Just before dawn I rolled over in bed and heard the first pit-pat of rain on the roof. It's a wonderful moment when you are wakened by that sound, look at the clock and realize that whatever was planned for the day is now cancelled.

I got up, headed down to the barn with a copy of the *Free Press and Economist* over my head to keep me dry and did the chores. Then I rode into Larkspur and did a leisurely crossword over breakfast at the Little Red Hen Restaurant.

After breakfast, I went into the General Store to pick up a few things. Mrs. Lynch was at the counter and Dry Cry looked up as I walked in.

"A couple of pounds of three-inch ardox nails, please, Mr. McKelvey," I said cheerily.

"I'll be with you in a minute," said Dry Cry shortly. "Did you find the cornflakes there, Mrs. Lynch?"

I picked up a brochure on steel siding and listened to the conversation with one ear.

"Just went out like a light, so he did," Mrs. Lynch was saying.

"What was it, do you reckon?" said Dry Cry.

"Hard to know. Just worn out, I guess."

"When did they say the funeral was?"

"Friday."

"Funeral?" I interrupted. "Whose funeral?"

Mrs. Lynch turned to me, her hand at her mouth. "Oh my goodness, Mr. Wingfield. Didn't you hear? Jimmy Bremner died last night."

"Jimmy?" I said. "That can't be . . . I was talking to him yesterday . . ."

"Oh, yes, it was very sudden," she said. "Mr. McKelvey was talking to Freddy this morning. They say Jimmy wasn't feeling well after supper and went to bed. When Maggie went to wake him this morning, he was gone, poor thing."

"Not much of a surprise, if y'ask me," said Dry Cry. "Seems to me he's been kinda overdoin' it lately."

The words stung. I stepped outside onto the verandah. It had stopped raining. All I could think of was Jimmy—sitting on a hay-bale in the barn the afternoon before, laughing his head off about the geese. He'd seemed fine.

On the way home, I stopped Feedbin at Freddy's gate and looked down the lane. There were several cars in front of the house, so I turned in. Freddy was on his way to the barn with two milk pails, but he turned back and came towards us. He was brief.

"G'day, Walt. We're a little late with the chores, here."

"I just heard about Jimmy . . ."

"Yeah. Maggie tried to call you but there was no answer."

"What happened? Do you know?"

Freddy shrugged. He seemed almost impatient. "Doctor had a look at him and said he didn't know. Just worn out, I guess. I better slip along and get these chores done. Maggie's in the house."

He trudged off to the barn. I would have gone in, but I thought Maggie would be busy with people and, rather than disturb her, I just went back to the farm. During the day I tried to keep busy but nothing worked. I tried to fix some fence. I tried to rehang the barn door but ended up sitting in the hay mow, looking out over the barnyard.

That evening after supper, the phone rang. It was Freddy.

"Walt? We're giving Jimmy a bit of a wake here. Why don't you slip on up?"

I knew the whole community would be there. They always tell you exactly what they think and it wouldn't be any different this time. I got out my blue serge suit, dusted off my black shoes and walked up through the fields. Freddy was standing alone among the cars in the lane. I could hear the hum of voices coming from the front room. Freddy looked at my suit.

"Funeral ain't till tomorrow, Walt. You didn't need to get all dressed up."

"Oh," I said, feeling a flush of embarrassment. "I thought I should put on a tie."

"You look good, Walt." Freddy grinned. "How are you doin'?"

"Oh, Freddy," I said, the words coming in a rush. "I'm so sorry. I had no business letting him do so much with the horses. I just forgot that he was so old . . . and all that business yesterday—"

I didn't get any further. "What are you talking about? Walt, don't you ever think that way. Maggie and I have been sayin' all day that he's lucky he had you and those horses. The doctor said this morning he'd never seen Jimmy lookin' better. Which was kinda odd, considering he was dead and everything. But I knowed what he meant. Jimmy did look good. He'd quit the booze, he was eatin' his meals and takin' an interest in things. For once in his life, he was havin' a good time."

"He was?"

"That's right. Everyone in there's been sayin' it's a wonderful thing you did for him, Walt. He had the b-b-best year of his life, taggin' around with you and them horses. Now, come on inside. There's a bunch of people here want to meet you."

He was right. The kitchen was jammed with people and the noise was deafening. Someone stuck a beer in my hand and I found a spot near the egg-washer to sit down and look around. The table was covered with plates of cold cuts, pickles, breads and cheese. The sideboard carried industrial quantities of creamed Jell-O salad studded with pink and green marshmallows, jugs of pink lemonade and Freshie lined the counter and a big stainless-steel coffee urn chugged away by the sink. The day's rain had brought the flies inside, but the heat from the stoves kept them up on the ceiling. The hum of twenty-five conversations washed over me in gentle waves and I sipped on the bottle of beer.

"Are you Walt Wingfield?" someone asked.

I stayed late, met fifty people, talked about inflation, axe handles, the gold standard, whipple trees, treasury bills, the hole in the ozone layer and the rising price of beer. We talked about Jimmy, too. One old guy told me Jimmy talked to him about me all the time. In fifty years of knowing Jimmy he'd never seen him laugh much but in the last year or so the mere mention of my name was enough to set him off. He said he wanted to come out to the farm some time and meet the horses. That would be fine, I told him. I've been laughed at by the best.

I squeezed my way out onto Freddy's verandah, finally, thinking about Jimmy's wheezy laugh. I took a deep breath of the cool night air, watched the moon rise over Maggie's hollyhocks and drank a silent toast to Jimmy.

We'll miss him.

Yours sincerely,
Walt

A NOTE FROM THE EDITOR

I was at the funeral the next day. The crowd was so big they had to put a bunch of us infrequent flyers downstairs in the church basement. I hadn't been down there since I was in Sunday School, but nothing had changed. The kids were still putting up the same follow-the-dot pictures of Jesus Christ on the wall.

The next day, Walt withdrew his name as a candidate for Persephone Township council and, to everyone's surprise, he was replaced by Don. In October, Don got elected and the first thing he did was appoint himself to the land division committee that reviews all applications for development. When it snows, Walt, Freddy, Willy and Dave and The Squire all take turns calling him to get their lanes ploughed out.

Darcy Dixon's condominiums drew about as much interest that summer as the Orangemen's Parade. By the fall he still hadn't received a single offer and one day he just gave up. He sold the property—model suite and all—to Walt. Then he drove south and we never saw him again.

Walt had an auction sale for the model suite. Dry Cry got his pine table back, for seventy-five dollars. Maggie bought the triple-glazed windows for her new greenhouse. There were no bids on the air-conditioning unit, so Freddy hauled it back to his junk-heap, or I should say, his front yard. He said you just never know when air-conditioning might catch on in the country and if it did he wanted to be ready with spare parts.

Willy and Dave made a bid on the structure itself. They stripped the roofing, siding, eaves-troughs, verandah and plumbing out of it and started a whole new business. Now Willy takes the trees down and Dave follows right behind him, doing building repairs.

The geese flew south.

I was out there during the mail strike, just after Christmas, picking up one of Walt's letters, and I stopped for a moment beside the pasture to look at the scene. There was still no snow and the bare concrete walls stuck up out of the ground like an ancient fortress. They had begun to acquire the serenity and majesty of a Mayan ruin, and I began to understand what Walt meant when he said:

"When I came here, this was a sprawling civilization. But with my bare hands, I turned it into a wilderness."

Chapter Three

Wingfield's

— FOLLY —

ANOTHER NOTE FROM THE EDITOR

No one's been doing very well out of farming the past few years, but Walt had more reason than most to be grouchy. By sticking to the farm the way he did, he missed out on the stock market's longest sustained rocket-ride of the post-war era. While his colleagues on Bay Street lined their pockets, Walt completed his second profit-free season on the farm.

Walt stuck with his part-time consulting role with MacFeeters, Bartlett and Hendrie. He found he could just about break even if he worked two days a week at the broker-age firm and three days at the farm. He couldn't afford to farm on the weekend though.

Whatever his disappointments, he didn't quit. And he gave me his personal assurance that the Letter from Wingfield Farm would be mailed each and every week . . . as long as he could afford the price of a stamp.

He delivered that week's letter by hand so I began to wonder how tough things were out there. The letter went like this:

Dear Ed,

The neighbourhood is deserted this week because everyone has gone on holiday for the March break. Don took his family to the Bahamas, The Squire went to Florida, Willy and Dave went to Las Vegas and Freddy took a horse to the races in Buffalo. They all invited me to go with them, but the way the farm is right now, I couldn't afford a weekend at the Commercial Hotel in Larkspur. I think they knew that and figured I'd do chores for them while they were gone. It's just a matter of breaking open a few bales at Freddy's and The Squire's, but Don has seventy-five Holsteins and the milking takes me a few hours.

I was flattered when Don first entrusted me with the milking, but then I found that Don's barn is so highly mechanized, a six-year-old could milk the cows if he could reach the buttons. I push one button to start the stable-cleaner, another button to start the compressor, one more for the silo-unloader and yet another for the stereo system. Don says he has a pitchfork around somewhere, but I've never seen it.

Hearing these familiar pre-supper noises brings the cows coughing and blowing to their feet. I guide the electric feed truck down between the mangers and give each cow its ration according to instructions stuck to the beam above each stanchion. Then I lug out the milking machines and a pail of disinfected hot water and begin my rounds. I like simple, repetitive tasks. It gives me time to think, and these days I have a lot on my mind.

When I came to the farm, I figured it would take me a couple of years to get the hang of things. And I knew I'd make mistakes, because everyone does. But I thought that through hard work and determination, and a willingness to learn, I would eventually make a living at it. That was two years ago.

Since then, the word "profit" has been erased from my vocabulary. Running a farm is like standing out in the middle of a field in a cold wind, tearing up twenty-dollar bills. Until recently, I thought it was just my incompetence that stood between solvency and me. Now I'm beginning to realize it's more complicated than that. The scary part is, even when I do get things right, I still lose money. And it doesn't just happen to me. My neighbours complain about it, too. Now, I wouldn't say this to anyone else, but I'm beginning to think there's something wrong with the system. I mean, all my instincts are telling me that agriculture might not be profitable.

Don's farm is prosperous because he operates under the protection of the Milk Marketing Board, which provides him with a steady income and a guaranteed price, as long as he meets his annual quota. The rest of the Seventh Line looks like Tobacco Road because we all operate in the open market without quotas or protection of any kind. As Freddy, my neighbour to the north, says, we're the only businessmen who buy retail and sell wholesale. I'd like to be a dairy farmer like Don, but the only people who can afford to buy dairy farms these days are rock stars and Mafia dons. Even if I could get my stock out of MacFeeters, Bartlett and Hendrie, which I can't, it still wouldn't be enough to build a set-up like this.

Freddy has a different approach to farming. He prefers to diversify. He practises fifteen different trades, from auction-eering to real estate, sometimes all in the same day. He says you have to keep a few other pots on the stove to get by. But between his used car lot and his gravel pits and his racetrack, he doesn't have much land left to farm. Not to mention the slot machines in his barn. If you kept on farming like Freddy you'd end up not farming at all.

Which brings me to The Squire, across the road, who doesn't even pretend to farm. He retired a couple of years ago when he got the pension and rented his fields. Now he shuffles around the neighbourhood with a big smile on his face, watching the price of land go up. He's decided to move to Florida when his farm hits five hundred thousand.

Then there's me, trying to farm in an affordable, sustainable way, on a scale appropriate to the limitations of the land, forging a partnership with Nature. The trouble is, Nature is behind on her payments. If this country is depending on the Seventh Line for food, we're in big trouble.

By six o'clock this evening, I had the milk safely in the tank, the milkers washed and hung up, the cats fed and the all-night Barry Manilow tape playing the cows to sleep. I stepped outside to find the weather closing in again, hard pellets of snow driving horizontally across the fields. This was Thursday night, my regular night for dinner up at Freddy's. Freddy was away, but his sister, Maggie, would still be there. I collected Spike, the hound, from my place; we trudged up the lane in the dark and tapped at the door. Maggie opened the storm door and pulled her sweater close about her shoulders against the cold wind.

"Hello, Walt," she said. "How did you make out at Don's?"

"Oh, fine. I've got it down to a science now. Pretty cool out here. You'd never know this was the first day of spring."

"Well, you know, Walt. The weather you get on the first day of spring is what you get for the next forty days."

"Forty days?" I said. "Of this? I'll be down to my last sled dog by then." I patted Spike's head. "No offence, Spike. Say, are you going to let me in, Maggie?"

Maggie frowned. "I guess I didn't expect you this week, what with Freddy away."

"Well gosh, Maggie. I don't just come to see Freddy, you know. I enjoy talking to you, too."

"That's nice, Walt," she said.

"So . . . are you going to let me in?"

"No."

"Well, why not?"

"People would talk."

"Talk?" I was flabbergasted. "About what? Maggie, we're both over twenty-one and unattached."

"Well, exactly."

She closed the door and left me standing out in the wind.

I turned to Spike. "How was I supposed to know Persephone Township would have rules of purdah?" Spike looked mournful but offered no explanation.

"Well, c'mon," I said. "Looks like it's macaroni again. And it's your turn to do the dishes."

Yours sincerely,

Walt

—— *April 20*

Dear Ed,

Two of my horses, Feedbin and Mortgage, both had undistinguished careers on the racetrack before they came to the farm. Since then they have smashed every horse-drawn implement on the Seventh Line. Jimmy used to help me handle them but since he died I've been on my own again. The only exercise the horses got this winter was chewing. But now that the days are getting longer I know that soon I'll have to face the planting. So this morning I decided it was time for spring training and a workout with the stone boat. Feedbin came out of the barn all right, but once again, Mortgage took three steps out of her stall and balked.

I pulled on the halter but she jerked her head up, almost lifting me off the ground.

"Now, Mortgage," I said. "Let's not argue about this."

Jimmy taught me how to handle a balky horse. It's just a matter of harnessing Feedbin, hooking her up to Mortgage, and, whoosh, one horse pulls the other out. As Jimmy used to say, "there is no loyalty among harses."

But there are a couple of challenges with this method. First, Mortgage is getting familiar with this trick, and second, she's a lot heavier this year. I put the collar and hames on Feedbin, drew the tugs back and hooked them into the rings on Mortgage's halter. It was time to play "choo-choo train."

I clucked to the horses. Feedbin stepped forward and established tension. Then she leaned into her collar. Mortgage's eyes bugged out and she slipped forward a few inches. Then she sat down. Feedbin kept moving and Mortgage slid along the hallway, her hooves scraping along each wall, forming a kind of snow-plough, bringing up brooms, manure forks, shovels and several cat dishes with her.

"Keep moving, Feedbin," I said through gritted teeth. "We're committed now."

I looked back to see that Mortgage's hind leg had snagged onto a large electric cable. As it separated from the wall in short jerks, staples fired across the barn like bullets. This was getting out of control.

"Whoa, whoa, WHOA!" I shouted. There was a flash, and the lights went out.

There is nothing more terrifying than a scramble in the

dark in a narrow hallway with three thousand pounds of horse. I flattened myself against the wall. A horse rump squished me flatter. There was the sound of wood splintering, and then everything went quiet. When I took my arms away from my head I found Feedbin still standing beside me but facing in the opposite direction. Mortgage was now on the other side of her, out in the barnyard, with her halter hanging in shreds around her knees.

It's got to the point where I can't even get these idiots out of the barn without breaking something. Now I have to hire an electrician to repair the wiring and by the time I have that done another day will be lost.

I think it's time I bought a tractor.

Yours sincerely,
Walt

—— *May 10*

Dear Ed,

Experience has been a stern teacher in my past ventures with livestock. In the past couple of years every animal I have purchased in hope and raised for profit has filled a pauper's grave. Ducks, hens, steers . . . why doesn't someone just put wax in my ears or tie me to the mast? The only animals that make a profit around here are the sheep, which is odd because they were the ones Freddy warned me about.

It was a conversation between Maggie and Freddy during my first summer at the farm. They had invited me up to supper, and Maggie served thick, juicy lamb chops with a sprig of rosemary and a spoonful of mint sauce.

"This is your own lamb, Maggie? It's wonderful."

That's when the idea struck me that I should raise sheep. I asked them both what they thought.

"D-d-don't do it, Walt," said Freddy. "You don't know sheep like I do."

Maggie turned from the sideboard. "What do you know about sheep? That's the closest you ever get to one, right there on your plate."

"I know there's no money in 'em," replied Freddy. "I never met a sheep yet that didn't die in debt."

I was puzzled. "What makes them so unprofitable? Surely they don't eat much."

"Never get a chance to," said Freddy. "Somethin' generally kills them first. Dogs run 'em to death, wolves sneak in and kill 'em one at a time. They get stuck in fences, they roll into holes and can't get out, they eat wild cherry leaves and keel over. No, the only money you ever see from them is sheep damage or w-w-wolf bounty."

"Sheep damage?" I interrupted. "What's that?"

Maggie explained that every time you lose a sheep to wolves or dogs you can make a claim to the township for compensation or "sheep damage." Some townships like Persephone still pay a bounty for wolves.

"Now here we go," said Freddy. "What Walt could do is raise a bunch of wolves down at his place. Then the two of yous could take advantage of both programs at the same time."

"Oh, Freddy," laughed Maggie. "It isn't that hard. Why, in the old days they used to get the village idiot to look after the sheep. I'm sure Walt could manage."

At the end of that summer Maggie offered to set me up with a few ewes. I called them "yous" as in "How many of yous are comin' up to the euchre party tonight" . . . but Maggie corrected me, explaining they are called "yose" which rhymes with "toes."

Freddy drove them over one day and backed the truck up to the orchard gate. They sprang out of the truck one by one and gambolled over to the new shed I'd built for them. Freddy slammed the tail-gate shut.

"The warranty expires as of now," he announced.

It was an odd feeling after hearing all those horror stories about sheep to know that six defenceless little critters were wandering around under the apple trees with "Kill Me" signs pasted on their rear ends. Every morning I opened the shed door and peeked in, braced for disaster.

Finally Maggie made a suggestion. "Either stop worrying about your sheep or get a goat, Walt. Goats aren't afraid of dogs, and the sheep stay quiet when they have one around."

That's fine for her to say. She's learned to live with them. But the trouble is, goats can't be fenced, they eat flowers, they make trouble with the neighbours, they smell bad and they have a poor reputation in literature.

"What about a cardboard replica of a goat?" I asked. "Would that do?"

Freddy drove over the next day and delivered the goat. She was sitting on the front seat of the truck, looking out the passenger window, quite calm and apparently enjoying her afternoon drive.

"Walt," he said, putting his finger in her collar and helping her out of the truck like a gentleman helping a lady out of her carriage. "I'd like you to meet Mrs. Pankhurst. She's a real pet and you won't have no trouble with her."

I tied her to one of the apple trees with a length of rope.

"How much do I owe you, Freddy?"

"No charge for the goat, Walt. I'd drive a lot further than this to get rid of a few more."

That afternoon Mrs. Pankhurst chewed through her rope, climbed over the fence and strutted off towards the house. Spike went tearing after her, eager to prove himself in this first opportunity at real-life shepherding. Mrs. Pankhurst turned, glared at him and stamped her foot. Spike ignored the warning and dove in for a snap at her heels. She stamped again—this time on his head. Spike yelped and rolled back out of the way, thought for a moment and then came back to me with the apology that he didn't "do" goats.

Mrs. Pankhurst climbed up into the maple tree beside the house. She has been there ever since. She does come down at night when it's time to go into the shed, but most of the time she perches on a limb of the tree like a jaguar waiting for some poor, unsuspecting dog to happen along.

Maggie was right. I stopped worrying about my sheep. Mrs. Pankhurst watches over the flock by night and day, and I couldn't be more relaxed about them if they were all trained in kung fu and carried .45 revolvers. Thanks to her my lamb crop last spring was just enough to pay the hydro bill.

This week I followed up an ad in the *High County Shopper* for a pair of shears and asked The Squire if he'd give me a lift. Since his retirement, The Squire's lifestyle allows him to join me on these spur-of-the-moment junkets. We drove up into the swamp farms of Pluto Township and found the address referred to in the ad, a farm belonging to a Mr. Baldwin. He met us in the driveway carrying a pail of eggs from his hen-house. I asked him what size the shears were.

"They're full length," he said. "Eight or nine feet, I guess."

"Eight or nine feet?"

"Yeah," he went on, "the wife won't let me keep them in the house. She says they're too hard to clean."

The Squire blinked once and then chuckled. "They're *sheers*, Walt. You know . . . curtains."

I guess spelling is not the *High County Shopper*'s strong suit. However the trip was not entirely in vain. Mr. Baldwin was very anxious to get rid of a hundred and fifty turkey chicks he had out at the back of the property in a shed. He offered me the lot for twenty-five dollars. It seemed like a good price and I turned to The Squire to see what he thought.

"They're turkeys, Walt," was all he said. The Squire is not fond of poultry.

"I know they're turkeys. I mean, they look healthy enough, don't they?"

"But they're turkeys, Walt."

I realize my record with poultry is not perfect, but the price-earnings ratio on these birds was looking extremely attractive. One hundred and fifty birds at twenty-five pounds a bird, and a dollar a pound. That's almost four thousand dollars. I could go to the Bahamas with that kind of money. But I have learned caution in these matters.

"It's a good price, Mr. Baldwin. Why aren't you keeping them yourself?"

"I'd love to," replied Mr. Baldwin. "But you gotta keep one step ahead of the turkey police, eh?" He looked at The Squire and giggled. The Squire grinned and looked at me.

By now I'm getting used to the fact that I don't get a lot of the jokes they tell up here. On the way home in the truck, I asked The Squire to translate for me.

"Never mind about that, Walt. You just keep those birds alive till Thanksgiving."

"I know I'm going to lose a few. But at that price I can afford to."

"You know turkeys, Walt. Ten percent."

He may be right but I still don't know what he's being so gloomy about. Ten percent casualties isn't that bad. No one knows better than I do how difficult it is to raise poultry for the pot. I have a year-old Rouen drake who has got into the habit of launching himself off the pig feeder every time I come down to the barn. Usually he just flies a few feet and lands on the stream, but this morning a gust of wind caught him and sent him in a wide arc around the orchard and back towards the barn. I could see he was out of control, and I shouted at him to pull up, but it was too late. He hit the side of the barn with a sickening thud and a puff of duck feathers. I put him in the freezer and posted a warning to the rest of the flock about unauthorized solo flights. The Flight Safety Board is investigating the cause of the crash.

Yours sincerely,

Walt

———— *May 17*

Dear Ed,

The idea that something is seriously out of whack with the system up here is growing on me. I was walking down Bay Street the other day on my way to the brokerage firm, making a few calculations about the value of my labour on the farm, when I came to a startling conclusion. On an hourly basis I make less than a parking meter. If I am to stay on the farm I have to find a way to raise my efficiency level. I don't know if my decision to buy a tractor will improve the situation, but I don't see how it could make it any worse.

A tractor doesn't bite, kick or get out at night. As long as it starts in the morning, I'm ahead of the game. So I announced my decision to the neighbours. Freddy was first on the scene.

"Walt, why don't you shop at home? I mean, I got almost all the parts for a '58 International right here."

Freddy says "almost" when he's collected four good tires and a steering wheel. So I went down to ask Don. He was washing out his milk tank.

"It's about time, Walt. Welcome to the twentieth century. Let's go see Percy Franklin. He's got a Massey 35 with a three-point hitch, a loader and a snow-blower. That's what you need."

Percy wanted far too much money, so last evening after supper I went for a stroll to rethink the whole thing. I walked through my field on the other side of the road right out to Calvin Currie's place on the Town Line. Sitting by the road in front of Calvin's house was a very simple-looking tractor with a fresh coat of green paint and a "For Sale" sign on it. A booming voice called from the verandah.

"How are you now, Walt? You lookin' for a tractor?"

Calvin is a big man in his sixties with a lantern jaw and great bushy eyebrows. He milks a few cows and keeps a few pigs in a ramshackle collection of barns and sheds beside the Pine River.

"Yes, I'm thinking seriously about it. Can you tell me something about this machine?"

"This here's the first tractor I ever owned, the John Deere AR Model. Used to be hundreds of them around this country. Sort of the Model T of farm tractors. Gas-powered, two-cylinder, stick clutch, about thirty-five horsepower . . ."

"Is that it?" This was the shortest sales pitch I'd heard yet. "So what does it do?"

Calvin's brow furrowed in puzzlement. "Do? Why, it pulls things, Walt. That's all it's meant to do. Pull anything. Cultivator, wagon, spreader, stone boat."

Calvin climbed up on the tractor and pressed down on the starter plunger. It turned over once and went " . . . kaPOW!! . . . clank . . . thoop . . . thoop . . . thoop-thoop-thoop."

Calvin grinned. "The old two-banger John Deere always was good to start. And they're no trouble. I've had her forty years. Never had a wrench inside her."

"Forty years?"

"I mind the day my dad brought her home. It was hot, and I'd been rootin' up the summer fallow, ridin' the cultivator all day behind those damn horses. The sweat ran off 'em like a warm rain, and when they switched their tails it came right back in yer face. Between that and the flies you had to shut your eyes and let the horses steer. Well, when I seen this tractor I took the harness off the horses and threw it up in the loft. Never took it out again. I guess it's up there still. Some people say they miss the horses, but not me. I couldn't wait to be rid of them."

"How much do you want for it?" I asked.

"Well now, Walt, I'll have to get what I paid for her."

"What, from forty years ago? How much was that?"

"Five hundred bucks."

"Seems reasonable. Anything that runs is worth that."

I studied the engine as it thooped away happily, sending a cloud of blue smoke up into the cool evening air. The engine parts were made of cast iron. The part numbers were stamped on them in relief for easy reference. The mud-guards were made out of quarter-inch steel. The gear-shift moved through a maze of channels to find the home of each separate gear. All the gauges still worked. It was a very spartan machine without any options for the comfort of the operator. No cigarette lighter. No radio. Not even an arm-rest. Just the tractor seat and even that was removable for those who prefer to stand. Calvin took me for a spin around the lawn, and when we came back I wrote him a cheque on the spot. Calvin waved the cheque gently as if the ink had to dry before he put it in his pocket.

"Now she pulls a little to the left, and she throws a bit of oil, but she's got all the power she had in '48," he said.

"Thanks, Calvin. Do you have any tips for driving?"

"Just keep her between the fences, Walt."

He was right. The tractor did pull to the left. There was one complete turn of free play in the steering wheel, which made navigation difficult. It was a bit like sailing in heavy seas, trying to correct gently as we drifted towards the centre of the road and then spinning the wheel madly in the other direction as the bow finally answered to the helm, and we veered back towards the ditch. I made it home in one piece and parked the tractor in the hay mow of the barn. Then, in ceremonial fashion, I gathered up the harness and lugged it upstairs to the loft just as Calvin and his father had done forty years before.

I looked in on the turkeys before turning in and found that two of them had joined the feathered choirs. I pulled them out and set them on a barrel, ready for morning burial service under the apple tree. It's nothing to worry about. The profit margin is still very healthy. It just means a couple less martinis when I get to the Bahamas.

Yours sincerely,

Walt

Dear Ed,

The trouble with switching from horse power to mechanical power is that all the implements have a different hitch. I now find that none of my horse-drawn equipment will hook up to the tractor. The morning after I got the tractor home, I took a saw and shortened the tongue of the cultivator and made a temporary hook-up with a chain and some black wire. By ten o'clock I was out on the top field with the cultivator bouncing violently along behind but scratching up the soil with some success. Once I got one front wheel to follow a furrow, the tractor travelled in a straight line, and I didn't have to touch the steering wheel at all. The wind was still raw and cold, and black smoke blew back in my face as I laboured up the hill alongside Don's cornfield. Don himself appeared at the crest of the hill, going in the opposite direction, in his big yellow Minnie with about sixty feet of disk ploughs behind him. He did a double-take when he saw me. Then he lurched to a halt, jumped out of the cab, peered at the AR and made his way across the slabs of dirt and sod to the fence. He watched impassively as I pulled the hand clutch back and shut the gas down.

"I thought you were gettin' a tractor. Where the hell did you find this?"

"I bought it from Calvin Currie yesterday."

"You bought it?"

"Yeah. It's a John Deere. You have one too, Don."

"It ain't forty years old, and it ain't the only one I got. Why didn't you get three-point hitch like I told you? It would do more for you, like run a snow-blower or a wood-splitter. What you've got there is just a slow trip to the mailbox."

"The Squire says I should stay at home when it snows and

read my Bible, and wood splitting is something I enjoy doing by hand."

"Suit yourself. Nice paint job."

He returned to the Minnie. At lunchtime, I drove the tractor up to Freddy's. He was at the tool bench in his drive shed pounding the rust out of a starter motor of uncertain parentage. When he saw the AR his face lit up and he dropped the starter motor.

"Gollies, where did you find her? Let's have a look. Squidge over, willya?" He climbed up beside me, cranked the gas up and shoved out the clutch. Our heads snapped back as we leapt ahead.

"Watch it," I warned. "The clutch is a little jumpy. Calvin Currie had it on his front lawn. He painted it last winter and just put it up for sale yesterday. It runs fine . . . except the steering's a bit loose."

"Loose?" said Freddy, laughing and spinning the wheel. "You sure it's hooked up at all? . . . Oop, there she goes!" He stood on one of the foot-brakes, and the tractor spun around. "Gollies, Walt. You got brakes and everything. Yer all set."

"You think it sounds all right?"

"She needs to be tuned up. One of the cylinders ain't firin' right. Must be a dirty plug. Let's pull 'er over here." He wheeled over beside a hay-wagon and pulled the shutdown knob. At that moment Willy and Dave came tearing down the lane in an ancient pick-up truck.

I have never seen these two come to a normal stop in a vehicle. They always arrive like TV detectives at a shootout, in a four-wheel drift and half out of the vehicle before it comes to a stop. A hundred years ago, Willy and Dave would have been right at home on the prairie, shooting buffalo from a railway car.

Dave grabbed a handful of wrenches from the floor of the truck and advanced on the AR.

"Hey, Uncle Freddy! You need a hand?"

"Yeah," said Freddy, snapping the distributor cap off with his penknife. "Do you want to set the points for us?"

"Sure can. What's the gap on this thing? You got the book?"

"They're all the same. Seventeen one-thousandths. About the width of a dime."

"Hey Willy, can you spare me a dime? Hyeh, hyeh."

"Haven't got a dime. You'll have to eyeball it. Hyeh, hyeh."

An hour later they were still "tuning it up." The tractor was now up on blocks, the wheels were off and green engine parts lay scattered about on the hay-wagon.

"It seemed to be running fine this morning, Freddy. It just pulled to the left."

"We'll fix that for you, too." He glanced up at me. "What's the matter, Walt? Did you have something on today?"

"Well, I have a ewe ready to lamb, and I really should get back down there."

"Oh, gollies. You don't want to leave her alone too long. Here, Maggie'll run you down. She's not doing nothing."

Maggie was doing something, but she graciously agreed to drive me home. She even came to the shed with me to look at the sheep. When I opened the half-door there was the usual scramble in the main pen, and a row of sheep faces peered over the partition. Maggie opened one of the side pens and knelt down.

"Oh, look. You've got a new lamb. She didn't have any trouble at all." She placed both hands under the slippery newborn and lifted it up to me, speaking softly to the mother.

"Oh, you're a good momma." I took it reluctantly and it slid into my chest. Maggie looked up. "You have to get the stuff off it, Walt. Check in its mouth."

I hesitated. "How?"

"You stick your finger in its mouth and make sure it's clear. Like this." She stood up beside me and gave the lamb's mouth a quick swipe with her finger. She glanced at me and smiled, then put her face to the lamb's woolly coat and breathed it in.

"I love the smell of them. They smell like popcorn, don't they?"

I sniffed for myself. "They smell like poop," I said.

Maggie giggled. "Not that. It smells fresh and new . . . like popcorn."

I sniffed again. "You may be right, Maggie. I guess it's been too long since I went to the movies."

Maggie stepped back and her eyelids fluttered. "Why, Walter. Are you asking me to take you to the movies?"

"Sure, why not? We could take Lamb Chop here with us and see if anyone notices."

Freddy's voice interrupted us.

"Walt, yer AR's throwin' oil, and there ain't enough pressure in them cylinders to b-b-blow up a balloon. If I know Calvin, he ain't had a wrench inside her in forty years. I brought the little Case down so you can get back on the fields."

Maggie brushed the straw from the knees of her jeans. "I have to go into town to meet Sid," she said. Freddy rolled his eyes.

"Guess Maggie told you she's thinkin' about startin' a business, did she, Walt? As if she didn't have enough to do around the place."

"Like what?" asked Maggie testily.

"Like ministering to the needs of the suffering humanity around you. Ain't that good enough for you? You want to be a rocket scientist or something?"

Maggie turned to me. "I'm opening a store in Lavender with an old friend from school."

"Oh, really?" I said. "What sort of merchandise are you thinking of?"

"Fabrics, dress materials, patterns, that sort of thing."

Freddy huffed. "There's no need for it. You look at all the stuff Dry Cry has on that second floor of his. Jeez, you couldn't chase a cat through it with a broom."

"You may as well dress up in a feedsack," said Maggie. "Those of us who care what we look like have to drive to Barrie for something to wear."

"Makes a lot of sense, Freddy," I said. "Larkspur could use some more retail business."

"There, you see, Freddy?" She nudged him out of the way with the bottom half of the Dutch door.

Freddy shrugged. "What time will you be back?"

"Don't worry. I'll be back in time to minister to the incapacitated humanity around me."

Maggie left and Freddy took me out to introduce me to the Case tractor.

"Now when you stop this thing, p-p-park it on a hill. I'm still workin' on the starter motor. We'll rig up a proper hook-up for your cultivator in the next couple of days. You don't want to p-p-plant anything yet anyway with the weather like this."

I thanked him and then inquired who Sid was.

"You never met Sid? I guess you wouldn't have. He's been away for a bit. He's been workin' in the city since he got his finance degree. He's got Maggie all cranked up about makin' a million. He figgers the way she works, she can make more in a month than the farm makes in a year."

At 9:45 the next morning the wind shifted around to the southwest, and by ten o'clock the temperature had risen thirty degrees. We went from winter to summer in fifteen minutes. I missed spring. I was inside washing the cream-separator.

I went out to bump-start Freddy's Case tractor, which I had left parked at the top of the lane. I let off the brake, trundled down the hill and popped the clutch. The tires grabbed on the dirt, but the motor failed to start. I got up speed again and tried once more. Still nothing. In this fashion the Case rolled all the way down the lane without firing once. I sat there, wondering how to get the tractor back up the hill, when old King lifted his head and nickered from the shade of the apple tree. It sounded like someone shovelling at the bottom of a well.

Then it struck me. King could pull the tractor back up the hill.

King is a draught horse, but he has one serious drawback. He does not respond to conventional horse-motivating words like "giddyup." In fact, you can't drive him with the lines at all. When I brought him home from Freddy's the first summer and hooked him up, I clucked and chirped away, but there was no response. I went up to the engine room and looked him straight in the eye, searching for signs of mutiny. His expression was as amiable as Brian Mulroney's. The problem seemed to go beyond ordinary balkiness. To make sure, I took up the lines again, leaned forward and slapped him on the hindquarters. King turned his head slowly and gave me a look of such mournful reproach, I never thought of doing it again. Since then I have led him everywhere by the halter, which makes it impossible to handle an implement at the same time. However he isn't bad at a dead-slow pull with a chain, for hauling a log out of the bush or one of the other horses out of the barn.

I climbed up into the loft of the stable to retrieve the single set of work harness. Feedbin and Mortgage exchanged knowing glances. When King saw me return, lugging the harness, his eyes brightened, and he lumbered over to me. He even dropped his head to let me put the collar on him.

I took a heavy chain and hooked one end to King's harness and looped the other end around the front axle of the tractor. I needed a piece of wire to secure the chain so I rummaged around in the tractor toolbox among Freddy's empty beer bottles. The tractor suddenly jolted forward. I looked up to see King, head up and motoring. For one terrified moment, I thought I had another runaway.

"Whoa!" I shouted. King stopped, and his head sank to ground-level. He let out a long, flapping sigh through his nostrils.

I was speechless. What on earth had made him start by himself? I couldn't imagine. I went back to the toolbox and sorted through the beer bottles. King's head flew up and the tractor lurched forward again.

"Whoa!" King stopped. I climbed up in the seat, leaned back and reached down to the toolbox. I rattled the beer bottles. He started. This time I let him go.

He was going in the wrong direction, and I had no lines to steer with, but at the rate he was going I had plenty of time to think. What would Jimmy say now?

"Gee!" I shouted. King tilted like a battleship, and we began a wide right-hand turn.

"Gee!" I repeated.

The scenery continued to rotate. I steered the front wheels around after him. At the top of the hill by the house I tried "Haw" and got a perfect left-hand, donut turn. The tractor was now set for another run down the hill.

"Whoa!"

I unhooked King, led him to one side, then let off the brake and trundled down the hill again. Again the tractor failed to catch, and came to rest beside the apple tree. This time I just turned the key off and gathered the beer bottles out of the toolbox. King and I were going back to work.

News travelled quickly, and by the time I had my old cultivator readapted for horse power, the whole neighbourhood came down to watch King in action. Freddy finally cleared up the mystery.

"Walt, I called the sales barn in Kitchener, to see if they had a record of who sold King to me. They said he come from Sarnia and give me the name of a fella . . . Harvey. So I called Sarnia and got this fella's wife. She says he died last November in Florida. Jeez, November's a helluva time to die in Florida. Pretty good time to die here. Anyways she tells me Harvey and King ran the last milk-wagon in Sarnia. Harvey got sick and tired of the school kids takin' off with him. So he trained King not to move when someone said 'giddyap' or the like. But when he give the milk bottles a shake, away he'd go."

This discovery about King has been something like finding the cruise control switch on a car you've been driving for a year. It is a liberating feeling to have a horse that actually works for a living. The Case is still sitting under the apple tree, and who knows when the green machine will return from the repair shop. But for now I'm not worried. I'm sitting under the maple tree on the line fence, watching King cultivate the field all by himself. I just have to shout "Haw" at him when he gets to one end of the field, and back he comes; "Gee" when he gets to the other end, and back he goes. As long as he stays within earshot I have complete control. Don passes by on his corn-planter every so often on the other side of the fence, but he is pretending not to notice. I don't know what he's being so grumpy about. We're not in competition here. He could work up the State of Nebraska by the time King and I finish this field.

But I can see now that this year we will get it finished. More important, when my field is planted, my investment will have been my time and nothing else. Well, King's time too. In the end, Don and I will each get a crop, but the difference is, I haven't spent any money. That really should be the first rule of farming: Don't spend money.

Now if there were just some way of extending that to the other parts of the operation.

Yours sincerely,
Walt

──── *June 21*

Dear Ed,

I had a lunch date with Maggie yesterday. Well, maybe I shouldn't call it a date. She was in town, working on her store opening, and I was at the library, reading up on turkey diseases. We bumped into each other outside the Little Red Hen Restaurant.

Now, I certainly didn't intend to talk economics the whole time, but that's what we did. You see, ever since that first afternoon in the field when the inspiration hit me, I have been working on a plan that might restore some sanity to the economy around here. It all came bubbling out when I sat down to lunch with Maggie.

"Walt," she said, "it makes a lot of sense. And I think the others would be interested too."

"You think so? Well, I was thinking about inviting the neighbours down to the farm on Thursday evening for a talk about a new economics for farming."

"Walt, that's a wonderful idea. Why don't you make it an economics talk and barbecue? Then people will come."

She was right. On Thursday evening The Squire was the first to arrive.

"Hiya, Walt. I hear you've got something cooked up for us. Hope it isn't one of your turkeys."

When Willy and Dave, Don, Freddy and Maggie arrived, I made sure everyone had beer or lemonade and started passing hamburgers off the grill. Then I began my talk.

"You know, for years now the price of farm inputs—land, machinery, feed, insurance, taxes—have all been going up. In the meantime the price of farm produce has remained the same and in some cases actually dropped."

"That sure is the truth," said Freddy.

"Now, this gap means more than just thinner profits," I continued. "It also represents a growing disparity between the real value of your labour and the price you are able to command for it."

"What did he say?" asked The Squire.

Maggie said, "He says these days you have to work twice as hard for half as much."

"Yes, thanks, Maggie," I said. "Now, as long as we have no control over the price of what we buy or what we sell, this situation is going to continue and probably get worse."

Don nodded agreement. "Yeah, and we gotta pay taxes, and we're gonna die. There's nothing you can do about it, Walt."

"Maybe we don't have much power. But there is one crucial moment when we could exercise a choice. That's when we spend money. The way we do it now, it all goes to some big company in the city for feed or fertilizer. We have no control over where it goes or what we get back for it. But imagine if we could just take our spending vote somewhere else. If we could spend in a different system, a system that defined the value of a day's labour in terms of the food it puts on the table or the value of an acre of land by the crop it produces, then we could restore some sanity to the economy and some dignity to what we do."

"Where were you plannin' on doin' this, Walt?" asked Freddy. "This planet's already taken."

"We could do it right here on the Seventh Line if we could subsist on what we get from each other. And we could do that if we developed a formal system of barter among ourselves."

"We always done a bit of that," said The Squire.

"Sure we have," I said. "But if we make it a guiding rule of our lives to stop at that crucial moment when we're about to spend money and ask ourselves: 'Can I get this from Don?' or 'Can I get this from Freddy?' and if eventually this can account for all or nearly all of our transactions—then we've done it. We've created our own system. We've taken control."

Don shifted in his chair and leaned forward. "Who would keep track of all this, Walt? I got enough paperwork as it is."

"I've done the paperwork," I announced. "I want you to

have a look at it and tell me what you think." With a flourish worthy of the boardroom, I showed them an example of the new Seventh Line currency I had been working on the past few evenings. "It is square to avoid confusion with the Queen's currency, and it promises to pay the bearer, on demand, goods or services at the rate decided on by the community."

I handed them out. "I've printed a hundred and seventy-five units, and I propose that we each start out with twenty-five."

Don looked at one of the notes and raised one eyebrow. "What are the income tax people gonna say about this, Walt?" he asked.

"I think we can all appreciate that there is a certain need for confidentiality here."

"Hey, Dave," said Willy, "it looks like the stuff you get at Canadian Tire. Only there's no picture on it. Shouldn't you have your picture on it, Walt? Hyeh! Hyeh!"

"I think my signature should be enough, Willy. That's all the central banker does, usually."

"You gonna be the banker?" asked Dave.

"Yes, my job would be to maintain the stability of the system by promising to redeem any or all of the units at the agreed exchange rates."

"So what do we call these things?" asked Dave.

Willy piped up. "Well, Walt printed them. We'll call them Walts. Hyeh, hyeh!"

"So what's a Walt worth these days?" asked Maggie.

"I've done some work on that too. Here are my proposed rates of exchange. One unit of the new currency would buy three pounds of butter or one rooster or three dozen eggs or two quarts of fresh cream . . . or one hour's labour. You see, that's the beauty of the system. We get to decide what an hour of our labour is worth."

"Now hang on a second," interrupted Don. "Whose labour are you talkin' about?"

"Why . . . everybody's."

Don shook his head. "You mean, an hour of my time is supposed to be worth the same as an hour of Freddy's?"

"That's r-r-right," said Freddy, rising in his chair. "Now what's wrong with that?"

"Takes you an hour to get out of bed," said Willy.

Freddy snorted indignantly. "I can keep up with any of you, sluggin' bales, forkin' sh—"

"Maybe you could make Don's hour worth Freddy's without the beer breaks or the smoke breaks?" suggested Maggie.

"I don't stop workin', you know, just 'cause I'm drinkin'," said Freddy.

"How come we all start with twenty-five Walts?" asked The Squire. "I should have a few more than Freddy 'cause he owes me a steer."

"Like hell I do!" retorted Freddy.

"That was the deal we made for my '62 Pontiac."

"Yeah, and I'm still tryin' to get that car to run."

"It was running fine when it left my place."

"So was my steer."

"Well, if you hadn't left your gate open, and if you hadn't driven so darn fast, you wouldn't have hit the steer."

"I don't know what you're complainin' about. You got a lot of hamburger out of that steer."

"Yeah," said Don, "you still got a lot of hamburger in that radiator."

Freddy turned on Willy and Dave. "What about that spreader you boys left at McKeown's? I never saw a nickel for that."

Maggie intervened. "Now look," she said firmly. "If you're going to start digging back into every disagreement you ever had, this thing of Walt's will never have a chance. Besides, if I had a Walt for every free meal I've dished out to you dignified labourers, you'd all be starting from scratch. We have to let bygones be bygones."

It went just like a board meeting down at the firm. You know how it goes. Someone makes a presentation they've been working on for months, and after they've finished, the discussion goes back and forth like a free-range chicken. You never actually hear anyone say "Approved." You just have to listen to the tone of the discussion to know whether the idea is going to fly. I think I knew for sure that we were in business sometime after ten o'clock, when The Squire waved one of his Walts at me.

"Hey, Walt. Can I get a beer with one of these?"

Yours sincerely,

Walt

———— *July 1*

Dear Ed,

I just got a registered letter from Alf Harrison, my old partner at the firm.

> Dear Walt:
> It's time to speak frankly.
>   In the past year at MacFeeters B., we've gone through three panic sell-offs, two lawsuits and an

investigation by the Securities Commission.
Every time, the crisis seems to coincide with
some Armageddon up at your farm and the result
is I'm left to handle things on my own. I can't
even count on you for your regular two days a
week we agreed to. Last week, it was only a day
and a half because your cow had milk fever,
whatever that is.

Walt, you've got to decide one way or the
other. Either come back full-time or make a
clean break and leave room for someone else to
take your place. I'm giving you six weeks to
make up your mind.

Yours sincerely,

Alf

P.S. When you come down for the hearing before
the Securities Commission, will you leave that
dumb hat at home?

Six weeks doesn't give my currency scheme much time
to prove itself. Supply-side economics is supposed to trickle
down over a period of time. I'm going to need a waterfall.
Going cold turkey on my brokerage firm income will be a
major shock to the system.

Speaking of cold turkey . . . this afternoon the body count
rose to sixteen, and I called the vet in Larkspur.

"What are the symptoms, Mr. Wingfield?"

"They're dying," I said. "How's that for a symptom?"

"I see. How many birds do you have?"

"A hundred and fifty."

"A hundred and fifty?" He sounded startled. "I'll be out there right after supper. I'd get some help if I were you."

Before I could ask what sort of help I would need, he rang off.

I called The Squire over, and when he arrived I asked him if he knew what the vet meant.

"Once they start goin', Walt, you need a good man with a shovel. Ten percent . . . just like I said."

"You said I might lose ten percent. It's more than that now."

"No, I meant that's what you might end up with. Ten percent . . . in a plastic bag, paid for, in somebody else's trunk and goin' out that lane. Ten percent."

Freddy appeared in the door of the shed. "Bring out your dead!" he called. "Bring out your dead!" He looked around the floor at the sick turkeys and grinned at me. "Gollies, Walt, you sure got the touch here, don't you?"

The vet arrived and moved through the flock, stooping every so often to hand me a limping bird. He suggested we separate the sick ones and house them somewhere else. Before long, Willy and Dave joined us. We formed a turkey brigade between the turkey shed and the infirmary I arranged in the other barn. None of them seemed terribly concerned about any of this and they kept up a running banter as they worked.

"Hey Walt," asked Willy. "You still planning on that trip to the Bahamas?"

"Nah," said Freddy. "You don't want to go to the Bahamas, Walt. You'll just get sunburned and catch a cold when you get back. Come with me to the races in Buffalo."

I asked the vet if he had any ideas for treatment.

"We'll just have to pour the antibiotics into them and hope for the best. Avian diseases are tricky. By the time you know what the strain is, half the flock's gone. I'll send this one down to the agricultural college at Guelph for a report. Should know in a couple of days."

"Send it?" I asked. "How do you send it."

"Well," said Freddy. "That one's flat enough now, you could put a stamp on it and mail it."

"We use a courier," said the vet. "Have you got quota for these birds?"

"What?" I asked.

"Quota," he repeated. "If you have more than fifty turkeys, you're supposed to buy quota. That's the law."

Before I could answer him The Squire spoke up.

"This is kind of a co-op here, Doctor. Each of us has fifty birds, and Walt feeds 'em for us."

Freddy indicated a bird lying on its side with one wing stretched out. "Yeah, that looks like one of your birds there, Squire. Too bad, huh?"

"Well, it's none of my business," said the vet. "If this keeps up you won't need anything except maybe a back-hoe. I'll call you in a couple of days."

After he left I looked at the others.

"Quota?" I said. "Nobody ever said anything to me about quota."

"D-d-don't worry about that, Walt. Have a beer," said Freddy.

"Am I going to have some marketing board down my neck because I don't have quota? . . . Huh?"

I'm getting used to the fact that some of my questions don't get answered around here. It used to bother me, but now I know it's nothing personal. It just means that disaster is at hand, and they'll try to help if I co-operate. Past experience has persuaded them that I co-operate best when I don't know what's going on.

Yours sincerely,
Walt

———— July 10

Dear Ed,

It is now more than two weeks since the Walt was introduced and everything is going fine. I did a brisk trade in eggs, cream and roosters. I helped Freddy on the hay for a couple of days, The Squire hired me to replace some boards on his barn and Willy and Dave got me to make a few trades for them on the stock exchange. Everyone covered their purchases with the new Walts. I was delighted. Even Don came over and offered me five Walts for a pile of cedar posts I had sitting beside the barn.

"I sure don't mind using your currency if it cuts down on the time I have to listen to Dry Cry whine at me," he said. Dry Cry once sold Don a flat of eggs that were so old they started to hatch on the way home on the seat of the truck. Then he accused Don of stealing chickens.

While I was in town this week I actually did walk into Dry Cry's myself, for a bag of fence staples, my only purchase of the week. I was digging handfuls into a paper bag when I heard his voice right at my shoulder:

"Haven't seen much of the Seventh Line this week."

"I expect everyone's busy on the hay," I said, avoiding his gaze.

"I hear you got a scheme goin' down there for savin' money. Is that right?"

"You heard?"

"I hear a lot of things. Printin' your own money and everything."

"Well . . . it's just a little experiment. We don't mean any harm by it."

"Of course you don't mean no harm. Sounds like a real good way to save a dollar." He turned and waved at a customer. "Yeah, I'll be with you in a minute."

"Don't let me keep you, Mr. McKelvey."

"I'm not too busy to talk to a valued customer," he assured me, leaning against the shelving. "So, what are you, some sort of economist?"

"Oh, not really. But I am concerned about the way money leaves the rural community. It all goes straight into the hands of the banks and the oil companies, and the farmer never sees it again."

"Yeah. It's no way to get rich. The farmer's gettin' the same price for a pig he got twenty-five years ago."

"So our plan is to keep money here at home as much as we can. You may lose some grocery business today, but you'll make it back on the hardware eventually."

"Maybe I don't need to wait. If these things have any value, I might take them across the counter myself."

"Well, we could talk about that."

"Can I see one of them?"

I handed him one and he held it up to the light. "You're welcome to it," I said. "I'm pleased you don't think we're trying to take advantage of you."

"Of course not," he laughed. "If my customers can figure out a way to save their money these days, I'd have to be a pretty hard man to stand in their way, now wouldn't I?"

He was taking this all rather well. This was a side to Dry Cry I had never seen. He was a lot nicer than I had imagined, and I'd found this out almost by accident, just by taking the time to stop and chat with him. It all goes to show we shouldn't be so quick to judge a person. You just never know, do you?

Back at the farm I found Don standing beside his pick-up truck, waiting for me.

"You got any more posts?" he asked. "I could use another fifty."

"Well, not here, but of course there's a lot more down in the swamp."

"You can't get at them down there. You'd need a bulldozer."

There is a cedar swamp that sits on our property line, mainly on Don's side. It's hard to tell, though, because it's never been fenced. It's difficult to get at because the slope going down into it is about ten degrees too steep to negotiate safely with a tractor.

"You know, Don, I think I might get those posts out with the team."

"Just 'cause you got two horses doesn't mean you got a team, Walt."

I'm getting used to this sort of dig from Don. "Well, be that as it may, if I do get those posts out, what's it worth to you?"

"I'll pay you the same as I did for these others," he promised, "in Walts, of course. But you're wasting your time. You need a bulldozer."

Next morning, I was down in the cedar swamp bright and early with The Squire's chain-saw, buzzing down every straight cedar I could reach. By noon I had twenty trees down and trimmed. After lunch King and I got Feedbin and Mortgage out of the barn. I took the heaviest harness I own, trussed Feedbin and Mortgage together like a pair of kidnap victims and clattered off to the swamp, dragging a heavy chain behind us. As we made the descent they jostled and banged against each other, frothed at the mouth and stared wildly at the scenery, but I had gravity on my side. At the bottom of the hill, I looped the chain around the butt end of one of the cedar trees and turned the girls in the direction of home. Unreliable as these horses are, once they were headed towards the barn, I guessed it would take more than some old cedar tree to hold them up. I unsnapped the lines from the bridles and stood safely to one side.

Then I yelled, "Giddap!"

Heave-ho and out they go! They went sailing up the hill like an artillery unit in the Boer War. I scrambled up the hill after them and watched as they flailed home to the barn, the tree bouncing along behind.

Persuading them to return to the swamp was the tricky part. I took them in a wide circle around to the far side of the swamp. Then I turned them in the direction of home. You could just feel the power surge through them as they found magnetic north. They plunged down into the swamp and then came to an abrupt halt when they found themselves back among the fallen cedar trees. You should have seen their faces. They looked just like voters the morning after election day . . . right back where they started without any idea how they got there.

This time I hooked up three smaller trees. When I yelled "Giddap!" they galloped off up the hill towards home. On the fifth trip, they trotted. On the ninth, they walked. At the end of the afternoon, two cross-eyed horses and a half-dead stockbroker stood in the barnyard and watched as Don loaded twenty Walts' worth of cedar posts onto his stake truck.

He didn't say anything about it at the time, but on the way into church on Sunday morning I was telling Maggie about it when Don passed by and touched me on the sleeve.

"Walt," he said. "I wonder if I might borrow your team someday."

Maggie let him pass by and smiled at me. "Hear that, Walt? Your team!" She winked at me.

Back at home, I took stock of the situation. I was exhausted, my freezer was empty of produce, and one hundred and seventy-two Walts were back in my hands. That didn't bother me. After all, as the central banker, it's my job to establish public confidence in the new currency. For the system to work properly, the neighbours must satisfy themselves that the Walt has real value. The acid test will come next week, when I go out into the marketplace myself, as a buyer.

Yours sincerely,
Walt

—— July 17

Dear Ed,

The turkey situation is desperate. They are dropping like flies now, and the vet has pretty well thrown up his hands. I've given up morning burial service under the apple tree. I think I'm going to need a landfill site. I got the old freezer running in the garage and started throwing the bodies in there until I have time to deal with them properly. It's very depressing. If there's a vacation for me in this it will be at the psychiatric hospital in Penetang.

This morning I went off to see if my barter system would work both ways. My first visit was to The Squire. I asked him if he would part with some electric fence I needed for the sheep pasture.

"I would, Walt. But I haven't got any. Why don't you try Willy and Dave? Oh, and how about some more of that cream?"

I explained to him that I couldn't barter with him unless he had some of the currency.

"Oh, I still got some," he said and produced five Walts out of his kitchen drawer.

That's funny, I thought. I was sure that all but three of the Walts were back in my hands. I must have miscounted. I walked back out to the mailbox and found myself surrounded by Shorthorn cattle milling along the road in the ditches. Willy and Dave were standing on the road in a dust cloud, rolling cigarettes.

"Do you want some help getting your cattle in?" I shouted.

"In?" said Willy. "These cattle aren't out, Walt."

"Well, why are they on the road, and not in the pasture?"

"This is a pasture, ain't it, Dave?"

"Sure is, Willy. This here's the *long* pasture. Heeyah! Heeyah!"

"Hey, Walt, we're havin' a chicken barbecue in a couple of weeks, and we need about ten more of your roosters. Can you spare them?"

I repeated what I had said to The Squire. Without the currency we can't barter. To my surprise, he pulled a handful of Walts out of his back pocket and handed them to me. I must have flinched because Willy looked at me closely.

"You're still takin' these things, aren't you, Walt? I can still get a rooster for each of these?"

"Yes . . . yes, of course," I said. I was beginning to wonder what kind of shape I'd been in when I counted those Walts. I walked back up to the house. No sooner had I opened the door than the phone rang. It was a lady from up the other side of Larkspur asking for three dozen eggs. She wanted to buy eggs with Walts. How had someone from Demeter Township managed to get their hands on a Walt? The phone rang again. Another lady was asking the price of butter.

"Why don't you phone the general store?" I asked. She said she wanted to know the price in Walts.

The most important quality in a central banker is calm self-assurance. There can be no hint of panic. The phone rang again. I did the only thing possible. I yanked the phone out of the wall, took it to the back porch and pitched it as far as I could into the pasture. The market was closed for the day.

I left the house and walked straight up to Freddy's where Maggie answered the door. Freddy and Don were sitting at the kitchen table.

"Ah, I was just wondering . . . does anyone have any Walts left?" I asked, trying to appear calm.

"Yes, I have three," said Maggie.

Don looked in his wallet. "I think I've got five," he said. "Yep, five."

Freddy took off his hat and checked. "I got a couple."

I took a deep breath. "There's something terribly wrong here. I just printed one hundred and seventy-five of these things, and right here on this table there's almost two hundred."

Freddy held one of the Walts up to the light. "Say, this one's different, Walt. Yer signature's printed on. It ain't done with a pen."

"Looks like someone's got his own printing press goin' Walt," said Don. "Who else besides us did you give these things to?"

"Nobody," I said. "Except Dry Cry."

Don raised one eyebrow and looked at me steadily. "You gave Dry Cry one of the Walts?" he asked.

"Yeah, as a token of good faith."

Don looked at the others. "I think we just found the printing press," he said.

I slumped down at the kitchen table. Dry Cry! I should have known! By the end of the week, the Walt would be taking a beating against all other currencies and I would be fighting a losing battle against inflation. Heaven knows how many more of those things are out there.

"What am I going to do?" I wailed.

"You gotta do like Mexico, Walt," said Don.

"You mean devalue the currency and take my losses? I've lost two weeks' worth of labour and all the stuff in my freezer."

"Unless we get that printing press stopped you're gonna lose a lot more than that."

"Oh, my Lord!"

Freddy pushed his chair back from the table and stretched. "I think it's time we organized a little work party here," he said.

Maggie took an apron off the stove hook. "It gets dark at nine-thirty. You want me to put on a bit of a lunch?" she asked.

Don nodded and looked at the wall clock. "I gotta get milked and fed up. I should be done around seven."

"Beer store closes at eight," said Freddy. "I'll pick up Willy and Dave on the way back. They're good with locks. And The Squire, he wouldn't want to miss this. Walt, bring that Coleman lamp up with you when you come."

They were all talking so calmly I wasn't sure if they were planning a break-in or a church supper.

Larkspur is a pretty dark place at night. There is only one streetlight and Dry Cry supplies the light bulb for it—35 watts. At ten o'clock, Don and The Squire picked me up and we drove into town. We parked under the sign of the Little Red Hen Restaurant, the appointed meeting place. All I could see was a wall of fog rolling slowly up the street from the Pine River. As it passed the streetlight, everything went completely dark. I rolled down the window. We could hear voices across the street at Dry Cry's store.

There was a great ripping "sproing" from the darkness at the side of the store, a voice cursed softly and a flashlight rolled on the ground. We got out of the truck and stepped quickly across the street.

"Jeez, Willy!" hissed Freddy. "I told ya to take it easy!"

"Well, it's open, ain't it?" said Willy, in a voice that would carry through triple-glazed glass.

"Shhh!" said Freddy.

The three of them were standing at the side of Dry Cry's store, contemplating a door with a large section pried out of the edge of it. Freddy looked up at us.

"Hi, fellas. Willy and Dave just figured out the combination here. You want to hold the light, Walt?"

I took the flashlight and shone it through the doorway, down the stairs. Freddy went first. For some reason I went second. Don, Willy, Dave and The Squire followed. At the bottom of the old wooden steps we came to a dirt floor. The air was cool and damp.

We had come to a large room full of filing cabinets and office machinery.

"Looks like we're in Dry Cry's mortgage department," said Don. "Pump up that lamp, willya, Walt, and let's get some light down here."

"He lends money, too?" I asked.

Don nodded. "I guess most of us have had a second mortgage with Dry Cry at one time or another. He lends to any farmer that gets into trouble. That's how he got all those farms down the Pine River. Give me the flashlight, will you, Walt?"

Willy riffled through the top drawer of one of the filing cabinets and pulled out a file. "Hey, Dave! You want to mark ourselves paid up till Christmas?"

"You fellas stay out of those files," ordered Freddy. "We got work to do."

"Well, what d'you know . . . look here."

Don was standing beside an old, hand-operated printing press surrounded by piles of in-store display cards and other advertising matter. Freddy picked up a stack of price tags on stiff white paper.

"McKelvey's Discount Days," he read. "What do you know? Does it all by himself."

"Let's see if she'll crank for us," said Don.

He turned the handle and the platen came back to reveal a lead plate stamped with a reverse image of one of the Walts.

Don looked at the boys. "She cranks all right but she's a bit stiff. What do you think, Willy?"

Willy nodded. "I can't think but what she might need tunin' up, Don. Got any tools there, Dave?"

"Just the ten-pound sledge."

"That'll do fine," said Don. "Hand her over."

I was mentally adding up the list of offences we had already committed: break, enter, vandalism, conspiracy—when The

Squire lifted the lid of an old freezer. He looked in and glanced back over his shoulder.

"Hold it a second, fellas. How long do you figure a grocer could stay in business if he got a reputation for selling tainted meat?"

"Not long, I reckon," said Don.

"I mean, what would the public health people say if they found a bunch of oh, say . . . turkeys that just got sick and died, in a grocer's freezer with price tags on them?"

"They'd take a pretty dim view of that."

"And where do you suppose a fella could put his hands on about a hundred dead turkeys?"

Freddy scratched his head and grinned. "Let's see now. We could ask around."

Suddenly the phone rang. We all looked at each other. It rang again. Willy shrugged his shoulders and picked it up. Using his best Dry Cry imitation he said, "Hyelloooo! McKelvey's . . . What can I do for you? . . ." Then he said, "Oh, Jeez! Okay," and hung up. "That was Maggie. Dry Cry just pulled up in front of the store."

"We got to get out of here," said Freddy.

"What about the printing press?" I whispered.

Willy put both hands on the printing press handle and jerked it off the machine. "We'll just take this with us." He twirled it in the air and cackled. "She turns just fine now. Hyah, hyah."

The next morning after chores I did an inventory. Even with Dry Cry's printing press out of operation the damage is considerable. I'm cleaned out of produce, and the devalued Walt is now practically worthless. Even if I could recover my losses, I still haven't figured out a way to survive without a salary. I decided to phone Alf Harrison and ask him if he would give me an extension if I promise to come in to work three days a week instead of two for a while. My phone was out of order, so I went up to use Freddy's.

The day had dawned windy and hot. The cicadas were singing with a penetrating whine, and a blue haze darkened the sky.

Maggie answered the door. I felt better right away, just seeing her and hearing a sympathetic voice.

"Those new phones just don't take the punishment they used to," she said. "Come right on in."

On the phone I managed to raise Eileen, who told me that Alf was out for the morning. She asked me what it was about but I told her I'd better talk to Alf myself later in the day. I was just hanging up the phone when a car horn beeped outside.

"That'll be Sid," said Maggie, grabbing her purse off the table. "Stay as long as you like, Walt. I'll be back in an hour." She stepped out and brushed passed Don and Freddy in the doorway. Freddy shook his head.

"Jeez . . . he still thinks that car horn works as good as a doorbell. Mum used to hate that, do you remember, Don? Maggie always said he wouldn't come to the door because he was shy."

Don snorted. "How could you call a man shy when his car horn played 'Chantilly Lace'?"

"Yeah," said Freddy. "He had that '52 Monarch with the flathead eight motor in it, bored right out. They had the big generator sittin' right up on top of the motor, remember?"

"I saw one of those flatheads in a gravel truck once," said Don. "You could spin the wheels with a full load."

"Maggie and Sid went out together?" I asked. "I had no idea. What happened?"

"You know how these things go, Walt. They never last. She rusted right out from under him."

"She what? No, not the car. What happened to Maggie and Sid?"

"Oh," said Freddy. "Sid went to college in the city and got himself a job down there. That was the end of it. Haven't seen him again till this summer. Now he's back it looks like he's set to pick up where they left off."

I heard a loud, buzzing noise that sounded like the cicadas had started up again outside the house, but it was actually coming from my own eardrums. I suddenly felt I needed to sit down. So Maggie has a beau. It never crossed my mind. How stupid of me. Well, everyone deserves a chance to be happy, and Maggie deserves it more than most.

I turned to see a rather formidable, legal-sized document spread open on the table. It was the partnership agreement for Maggie's fabric shop. Now I don't normally read other people's contracts, but it was open at the revenue-sharing section, and a couple of phrases caught my eye. It was all done in percentages and cross-referenced back ten pages. I flipped back and forth several times, working out Maggie's share at different revenue levels. Each time I got the same paltry figure. And the liability clause left her obligated for everything but her firstborn child.

I have no idea how long I stood there. Freddy and Don had gone out to look at a flathead motor behind the barn, and when I looked up, Maggie was standing in the doorway.

"Hi, Walt," she smiled. "I see you found the contract. What do you think?"

"I think the Better Business Bureau should have a look at it," I said, with more heat than I intended.

Her face clouded in a puzzled frown. "What do you mean?" she asked.

"I mean some huckster is trying to cheat you out of your money."

"Hucks—? Now, Walt, Sid may not know as much about contracts as you, but he's not trying to cheat me out of anything."

"Uh-uh, Maggie. If he wrote this contract he's a crook. Have you worked out your return on investment after the net-net-nets in this thing? Did you notice that your percentage refers to residue, not to the gross? And this liability clause is like something out of the Old Testament. I've never seen anything like it. Where did this man take his business training, on the Spanish Main?"

"Walter, that's enough! I won't listen to this. I think you're awful. The one chance I get to really do something, and you want to spoil it all."

"I'm not trying to spoil anything, Maggie. I just want you to be careful. I'm thinking of your happiness."

"No you aren't. If you were, you'd just leave me alone. But you can't. You can't stand to see anyone have a chance to be happy, because you're a frustrated old . . . bachelor!"

She headed upstairs. I left. I stumbled down through the fields to the farm and spent the rest of the afternoon in the hay mow, looking out over the valley. I've been a fool. Of course Maggie would choose someone who's from Larkspur. It's only natural. She's lived here all her life. It's the same mistake I've made all along. I don't belong here. I've nothing to offer these people.

At suppertime I was reheating a tuna casserole of uncertain vintage when Freddy appeared at the screen door.

"Good news, Walt. Yer tractor's fixed."

I let him in. He was carrying a cast iron housing, which he set on the table.

"What have you got there?" I asked.

"I dunno. We put her back together, and this was left over. Don't think we oughta throw her out just yet. What's on your mind, Walt? You got a face as long as a wet week."

"Everything, Freddy," I sighed. "My currency scheme is a mess, and when people find out about Dry Cry's stunt, I'll be a laughingstock. My turkeys are a disaster. All I've got to show for my efforts this summer is a stack of play money I printed myself."

"And you had a bit of a s-s-scrape with Maggie. I wouldn't worry about it too much, Walt. You're in a bit of a moult. You'll get your feathers back."

"It's more than that, Freddy. I've got to get out of here before I do any more damage. Maggie's right. I'm a frustrated old bachelor, meddling where I don't belong. It's time I went back where I came from and forgot about this pathetically stupid pipe dream once and for all."

"Walter, I know you're upset. But give yourself a bit of time here. You don't want to do something you'll be sorry for later on."

"No, my mind's made up. I'm going to phone Alf Harrison in the morning and tell him I'm selling out, and I'll be back to work full-time in a couple of weeks. So I'll have to get things cleared up here right away. Freddy, I want you to book me an auction date as soon as possible."

"Jeez, Walt . . . Okay, if that's the way you want it. But folks will be real sorry to see you go."

Me too.

Yours sincerely,
Walt

———— July 27

Dear Ed,

The morning of the auction I got up and went down to the barn to do chores for the last time.

I started with the milking. As I was tying Cupcakes' tail to the post, I wondered if maybe I ought to put tags on some of these animals with instructions for the new owners. No reason they should have to find out the hard way. Porkchop, the brood sow, is on day five of a ten-day penicillin course. The penicillin bottle and syringe should be sold with her, I suppose.

When I came back from the barn Freddy and his team were in action, pulling machinery into rows. The hay-wagon was parked in the drive, and it carried the accumulata of the past three seasons: old harness, a chicken-feeder, cream cans, a pitchfork . . .

My meagre collection of equipment was lined up along the orchard fence. There was the single furrow plough that the horses and I cut our teeth on, the cultivator that Freddy has welded back together more times than I can count, the sleigh Old Jimmy used to pick me up at the railway station— one runner still carrying a smudge of black paint from Darcy Dixon's Cadillac—and the AR that did only two laps of the field for me.

People started to arrive about ten o'clock to check out

the merchandise. By noon there was quite a crowd. Freddy came over to me and asked me one more time if my decision was firm.

"Walt, are you sure you want to go ahead with this? I mean, everybody would understand if you changed yer mind."

"No, my mind's made up. Go ahead, Freddy, start the sale."

Freddy jumped up on the hay-wagon and began his sale warm-up spiel.

"Ladies and gentlemen, gather round and let me acquaint you with the t-t-terms and conditions of this sale. I have been commissioned to sell by public auction the effects of one Walter Wingfield of Persephone Township, the sale consisting of those articles listed in the bill of sale, which you will agree are too numerous to mention. If you are a successful bidder, please be so kind as to identify yourself to the clerk, speakin' of whom, I'd like to thank Henry here for standing in at short notice in this capacity t-t-today. The terms are cash, cheque or whatever arrangement you are able to make with my clerk. So without further delay, we will proceed to the first item and drive on. Henry, bring out Lot Number One."

At most farm auctions the hay-wagon and machinery are sold first and the livestock is held to the end. The theory is that a crowd won't thin out while there are animals waiting to be sold. In my case, Freddy had decided to reverse the order, explaining that he thought some of my animals were so old they might not make it through the afternoon.

Lot Number One was Old King. He blinked in the sunlight and stared at the crowd, sighed, and his head sank to ground level. I guess he knew all about auctions.

"Here y'are, boys," said Freddy. "When the energy crisis comes back yer all set with horse power and the

Arabs can't touch you. What am I bid for this old fella . . . who'll start me off at four hundred dollars? Whoolabid-muh-hundadollah-whoolabidmuh-hundadollah-and-abidmuh-hundadollah-NOBODY-bimuhhundadoLLAH? . . . Well, say fifty and let's get away. Fifty bid-an-whoolabidma-fifty-fifty . . . ?"

The crowd was silent. Old King examined a gum wrapper on the ground and remained motionless.

"Fifty-fifty . . . C'mon, boys. Now, granted, he's not fast. But don't think of it as buying a horse. Think of it as buying a landmark. When folks come calling, you can tell 'em, turn right at the horse." Freddy sighed and looked around at the crowd for a moment. "We're gonna hold him back for now. We got other buyers comin' up later on in the day. Walt, those fellas from the museum are comin' up . . . we might get lucky. Henry, bring out Lot Number Two."

Lot Number Two was Feedbin and Mortgage harnessed together. I had warned Freddy this was not a good idea. They're settling down now, but they're not used to a crowd. But one of his helpers claimed he could drive any team that could be harnessed. They came around the corner of the barn on their hind legs.

"Here's a good strong team, folks, broke to ride and to draw. Take notice now! Worked every day and lots of energy to burn. Took three years to break 'em, and it'll take ten to wear 'em out. Jeez, don't she buck! Keep them children back, Henry! We'll sell the harness separate. Who'll start us off at five hundred dollars for the team?"

A voice at the back spoke up. "I'll give you five dollars for the neck-yoke."

"Well, that's a start. I have five for the neck-yoke. Who'll give me ten? Ten is bid-an-a-habna-five-and-a-bidna-ten-whoola-bidma-ten . . . I beg your pardon. Six? Jeez, I never thought of that. I have six dollars here. Who'll give me twelve?"

At that moment Feedbin and Mortgage turned towards each other, flipped the neck-yoke over their heads and headed back towards the driver. He dropped the lines and fled. The horses galloped off towards the stream, passing on either side of a butternut tree as they went; the neck-yoke snapped like a matchstick. The crowd cheered.

"Golly! We'll sell them if they come back."

The Jersey cows came next: Lollipop, Cupcakes, Creampuff and Yoghurt.

"No, ladies and gentlemen, these are not antelope, but here's your chance to own the last four Jersey cows in the county. Who'll give me a hundred apiece for the Jersey cows? Wonderful animals. Used to see them all over, but hunters shot them, thinkin' they were deer. Okay, seventy-five, who'll give me seventy-five? They're good milkers, right, Walt? Sure, good milkers—or they'd make a dandy set of seatcovers."

Freddy prattled away to the impassive crowd, but nobody wanted Jersey cows either. Freddy leaned down and whispered, "Walt, I guess yer livestock's kinda exotic for these people. Why don't you let me take them up to Owen Sound for you, and we'll get on to the other stuff? Crowd's gettin' restless."

"Sure, Freddy," I said. "You know best."

Freddy straightened up. "Okay, folks, this hay-wagon is gonna go next. You see for yourself it's got good tires and a strong axle. She's been customized for horsepower, but it wouldn't take a lot to put her back the way she was, I suppose. Who'll start us off at two hundred dollars for the wagon?"

Freddy prattled away at the silent crowd and the price of the wagon dropped steadily until he reached ten dollars.

Suddenly, Freddy singled out a barrel-chested man in coveralls and a John Deere hat. "Hector, Walt paid you a hundred two years ago, and he's put a new rack on it. Helluva way to treat a neighbour, folks. Who'll say a dollar? Thank you, sir. I have one dollar from The Squire. Who'll give me two? I have two dollars from Don. Thanks, Don. Who'll give me five?" A little guy from Pluto Township waved his hand. "Five? Thank you. Jeez, we got a pulse goin' now. Who'll give me ten? Ten-anabid-ten-anan-abid-annabid-wannabid-whoolgimme-ten-anabid-wannabid-gottabid-muh-TEN. Hector? Are you gonna bid me ten dollars for this hay-wagon? Huh?" Hector blinked slowly. "Thank you. SOLD! Hector is the bidder. Ten dollars is the price. Come on, Hector, smile! Okay folks, you can see there's gonna be some bargains here today. What are we gonna sell next, Henry? The root pulper? Okay, this root pulper is gonna go next. Who'll say half a million dollars?" He grinned and fired his finger at the crowd. "Okay, okay, say two hundred dollars."

At that moment the crowd turned to watch as Willy and Dave came roaring down the lane in Freddy's Pontiac. Maggie was in the back seat. They slid to a halt sideways in the drive and got out of the car. Willy and Dave were carrying large brown paper bags.

Maggie advanced on the hay wagon and announced in a clear ringing voice. "I want to buy the farm."

Freddy shushed her with one hand. "Just a second, Maggie. We're sellin' a root pulper here."

Maggie ignored him and continued, "I'm prepared to offer five hundred thousand."

Freddy stopped and stared at Maggie for a moment. Then

he looked up at the crowd. "Hokay, we're gonna sell the farm now. I'll take the root pulper, Henry."

Maggie said to Freddy, "I'll buy the farm on the condition that you stop the sale, and nothing leaves the place."

I'd never seen Freddy caught off-guard in a public situation and it took him a minute to regain his composure. "We got a bid here, ah, conditional on . . . just a second, folks." He dropped down on all fours at the edge of the wagon and said, "Maggie, like conditional on, where the hell are you gonna find five hundred thousand dollars?"

"Frederick," she said firmly. "It isn't your job to question the source of the funds. Your job is to conduct the sale."

"But Maggie," he said.

"Freddy—conduct the sale!"

Freddy straightened up and took a deep breath. "Okay, folks, we got a bid here. Five hundred thousand for the farm and everything on it, 'cept you and your cars. Do I hear a better offer? Five-hunah-thousana-fiveanabidna-five-annabid-nabina-bidna. Probably NOT, eh? In that case . . . sold." He suddenly found himself talking to the backs of the retreating crowd who were now trotting to the parking lot to beat the traffic. "Folks," he called after them, "don't forget our next sale is on the Fourth Line of Demeter on the twenty-third of this month. Some real fine Depression glass and another chance at a root pulper—so don't miss it."

He shook his head, put one hand on the edge of the hay-wagon rack and jumped down to the small knot of Seventh Liners that remained. "Now, would somebody please tell me what the hell just happened here?"

The Squire rubbed his chin and said, "Looks like Maggie bought herself a farm."

Don nodded solemnly. "Five hundred thousand is a lot of money, Maggie. Did you raise it yourself?"

"I had help," said Maggie. "Willy and Dave turned it out for me last night after they took the turkeys up to Dry Cry's. It's there in these bags."

Freddy opened one of the bags. "But these are Walts!" he cried.

"Yep," said Willy, feeling his shoulder tenderly. "We took the printing press handle with us. Been at it all night. Hardest five hundred thousand I ever made. Hyah! Hyah!"

"This is no good," protested Freddy. "You fellas must be crazy. Walt, the sale's null and void. I'll set you up another . . ."

I held up my hand and looked at Maggie. "Just a minute, Freddy. Maggie, why have you done this?"

"I had to figure some way to stop the sale and give you a chance to change your mind," she said.

"Change my mind about what?"

"I took the contract to the lawyers. They figured something was wrong and called Sid. He said he'd explain everything, but no one's seen him since. You were right, Walt. I'm sorry. I shouldn't have shouted at you."

"No, I'm sorry, Maggie. I shouldn't have trampled on your feelings about Sid."

"What feelings? Don't be silly, Walt. That was all over years ago. This was just a business deal. Turns out, I gave him the deal, he gave me the business. So, you see, there's no reason for you to leave."

"It doesn't change anything, Maggie. I'm a failure as a farmer. I can't go on like this. I've made a mess of everything."

Maggie shook her head. "You haven't made a mess of anything. Let me tell you something, Walter. You may not have noticed, but when you came here, we were all standing around looking over the neighbour's fence, wondering who was going to get the highest price for his land. Then you walked in and started farming like it was 1905. Sure we laughed at you. None of us thought the way we live made much sense, and it seemed you were just trying to turn the clock back. But you showed us that it does make sense, the way we all live in each other's kitchens, keep gardens, trade stuff around and help each other out. It scares me when I think how close we came to forgetting that."

"Maggie's right, Walt," said The Squire. "This past while, the Seventh Line's been more fun than Disney World. I think I'm gonna retire right here. Might keep a few sheep, too."

"A man can't farm without neighbours, Walt, even if he's got a milk quota," said Don.

"Me and Dave are gonna keep farmin'," said Willy. "Hell, we'd just get arrested if we tried anything else."

Freddy grinned. "That settles it. I'm goin' to Buffalo."

"No, you are not," said Maggie, not unkindly. "Dynamite couldn't move you off the place, and you know it." She turned back to me. "So you see, Walt, if you leave now, it'll be a sad day for the Seventh Line and for me, too."

"You, too?" I asked. Her eyes held mine for a long moment.

"Well, go on, Walt Wingfield. Let me make a fool of myself. I suppose it's better than waiting for continental drift to bring us together."

"Say," said Freddy. "Do you two want to step inside and talk in private?"

"No, I don't," said Maggie. "You'll hear about it soon enough. This way you can all get the same story. Well, Walt, what about it?"

"I'm not much of a catch, Maggie," I stammered. "I don't know if I even have a farm."

"Well, you can take it all back . . . or you can settle for half."

"I'll settle for half, Maggie," I said. "If you will."

Yours sincerely,

Walt

A NOTE FROM THE EDITOR

The wedding took place in the church in Larkspur. Freddy gave the bride away. Alf Harrison came up from the city. He told us he'd come to give the groom away. Don and The Squire were ushers. Walt asked me to read a poem.

"Let me not to the marriage of true minds . . ."

I took a photograph at the reception when no one was looking and got the whole Seventh Line on the lawn in front of Walt's and Maggie's place. Willy and Dave, standing by the barbecues, smoking roll-yer-owns and pouring beer over the chicken. Don, with his back to the camera, whacking a baseball out into the orchard for the kids. Freddy and The Squire sitting under the locust tree with their jackets off, debating the merits of the clip-on tie. Spike, the hound, being sick on too much chicken. King, in a rare moment with his eyes open, making his way over to the salad table. In the middle of it all, Walt and Maggie admiring a gift from Ron who runs the gas station—a set of Texaco beer mugs illustrating the Dogs of Canada.

The Walts gradually went out of circulation. I guess everybody had to have one as a curiosity, and before long they were all framed and hanging on walls across the township. They even got one hanging up at the Revenue Canada office in Barrie. So we all figured economics would return to normal on the Seventh Line. But it's a funny thing. It seems the spirit of the Walt lives on. By the middle of the next winter they all actually had some money in the bank. Freddy surprised everyone and got himself a housekeeper. Maggie opened her fabric shop. The Squire invested his savings in it. Said it wouldn't change the way he dressed though.

And Walt and Maggie? In February they spent four weeks in the Bahamas.

Chapter Four

Wingfield

— UNBOUND —

ANOTHER NOTE FROM THE EDITOR

When people call me up here at the newspaper office, I always ask them how things are going. A lot of them say, "Well, I can't complain." But they always find a way. I'm not saying all the calls and letters we get here are complaints. Some of them are lawsuits.

Just listen to this humdinger:

> Dear Sir,
> As we stand at the threshold of a new century,
> what hope can there be for the fate of mankind?
> Anarchists strike at the very heart of civilization,
> our youth lack any sense of direction, and each
> day the newspapers carry fresh stories of
> appalling murder and violence in the streets.

That is dated Larkspur, September 21, 1905.

I'll have to use it in my weekly column, "One Hundred Years Ago Today." I firmly believe that those who forget history are condemned to repeat the mistakes of the past. Knowing our history gives us the opportunity to make entirely new mistakes.

I always assumed I was the only one who read this column, until I dropped it a couple of months ago. There was a great outcry . . . from one person, Walt Wingfield. And I can't afford to antagonize Walt, because he fills the other side of the page with the "Letter from Wingfield Farm." Everybody reads that.

So Maggie left a life of hard work and poverty on the farm she shared with her brother, Freddy, and settled down to a life of hard work and poverty with Walt. Walt eventually reached a career compromise. He now has a permanent part-time position at the brokerage to subsidize his part-time farming.

I asked him how he'd compare the two professions. Walt said, "In farming the insider information is legal, but it's much harder to come by."

For the first three seasons, Walt was obsessed with the prospect that he would eventually have to admit defeat and slink back to the city with his tail between his legs. He still has his fits and furies, usually after some spectacular meltdown in the barn or a public humiliation on the sideroad with his unpredictable horses. But I'm happy to say that his old anxiety about making a success of the farm is fading into memory. Now it's been replaced by a new and more powerful anxiety.

The first letter he sent to me after his honeymoon went like this . . .

Dear Ed,

I left the office early today and caught the train out of the city, back to Larkspur. Maggie had a dinner meeting of the Women's Institute to get ready for and she was expecting me home to do chores.

It used to bother me that the whole train has to be stopped in Larkspur just to let me off. Then it carries on up to Port Petunia before going back to the city. Tonight, as soon as I stepped off, the locomotive shifted gears and chugged back the way it came. It appears that if I stop riding the train, we won't have one.

The station is boarded up now and the parking lot is usually deserted, except for whoever comes to pick me up. This evening there was no sign of Maggie, which puzzled me because she is always punctual. The only vehicle in the lot was a ten-wheel Freightliner tractor trailer. A sign mounted above the grille said "Kick butt!" There was a blast from the air horns and Maggie leaned out the window.

"Come on, Walt! I'm late!" she shouted.

I jumped up on the running board, grabbed the passenger door handle and hauled myself into the cab. Maggie popped the clutch and we went lumbering out onto Wellington Street.

"The Institute supper starts at six. I've got to get the casserole over to the hall."

"It's a big casserole, is it?"

Maggie smiled at me. "The 4×4 heated up this morning on the way back from the station. I took it in to Ron's and he said the water pump was gone on it."

"So, where did this come from?" I asked.

"This is Ron's loaner. I like it. It's big, but it sure gets around in the snow."

"Will we be driving this to the dinner tonight?"

"No, the 4×4 should be fixed by now. And it's a supper, Walt, not a dinner. Dinner is in the middle of the day."

I'm learning a whole new vocabulary since I married Maggie. A thin cow is said to be "gant" and a day with no wind is "cam." You don't "do" dishes, you "redd them up."

"Right, I forgot," I said. "But you're not dressed." Maggie was wearing blue jeans and a white cotton blouse.

It turned out that the pipes had frozen upstairs in the empty apartment above the store she rents for her dress shop, but they didn't notice until the heat of the day thawed them out again and water started coming through the ceiling. I guess it made a real mess, because her assistant Bernice was still mopping up. Maggie pointed at two parcels on the floor of the truck.

"I have to deliver these two orders, get back and close up, but it's going to take me another hour. So, I want you to take the 4×4 down to the farm, do the chores, iron my blue dress, leave it on the door and take the casserole up to the hall. I'll meet you there. Oh, and feed Spike."

Spike the hound started life next door with Maggie and her brother, Freddy, as an outside dog. In my first year here he defected to my place and became an inside dog. When I carried Maggie over the threshold she carried Spike back outside. This remains a bone of some contention between them. Maggie wheeled into Ron's garage and rolled down the window.

She leaned out the window and yelled, "Is that water pump done, Ronnie?"

Ron was standing in the doorway wiping his hands on an

oily rag. "Done like a dinner, Maggie," he said. "But we got you goin'. Found you a low mileage replacement from the road superintendent's truck. He won't be needin' his until after the Good Roads Convention."

Maggie turned back to me. "Now, Walt, do you remember what you have to do?"

This was always a tricky moment. I recited the list carefully to her: take the 4×4 down to the farm, do the chores, iron the dress . . .

"The blue dress," she interrupted.

" . . . yes, the blue dress . . . leave it on the door and take the casserole up to the hall. You'll meet me there . . . oh, and feed Spike."

Maggie smiled again. "Good . . . nice to see you, dear." She leaned over and gave me a smooch. I climbed out of the Freightliner and Maggie roared off.

Ron grinned at me from the doorway. "The keys are in it, Walt. I haven't got a bill done for you. We'll catch up to you later."

Maggie calls it "the casserole," but it isn't like any casserole you or I were brought up on. It's more of a ham and egg pie, and it is delicious. We hardly ever get it at home because Maggie gets asked to make it for every big dinner out . . . I mean, supper. As the 4×4 bumped down the lane at the farm, I could almost smell it cooking.

But as soon as I opened the door, I could see something was wrong. There in the middle of the kitchen carpet was Maggie's good casserole dish . . . licked clean, and Spike was standing beside it.

"Spike! Did you eat Maggie's casserole?" Spike's ears drooped even lower and he hung his head. "I'll take that as a yes," I said sternly. "And I hope confession is good for your soul. You know what Maggie will say. You'll be an outside dog . . . with no chance of parole . . . for life. And I may be out there with you." Spike ears drooped and he flopped to the floor.

This was serious. What was I going to do about the dinner? I phoned Freddy. He's been getting by with a part-time housekeeper since Maggie and I were married last year. We're on the party line, which means I have to hold the receiver down and listen to my phone ring about nine-teen times. When it stops it means Freddy has finally picked up the line. On this occasion it stopped after nine rings.

"Hyello! How are you now, Walt?"

"Fine . . . well, not so fine. Spike just ate the casserole Maggie made for the Institute."

"Gollies!" he chuckled. "He's not even a member, is he?"

"This isn't funny, Freddy. You know how Maggie is about the Institute. Would she have any of her old recipe books up at your place? The dinner starts in an hour and a half!"

"It's a supper, Walt. Dinner's in the middle of the day. But come on up. I lived with that woman for thirty-seven years. I know all her recipes. We'll put it together for you."

In nine minutes flat I was standing in Freddy's kitchen. In the old days, when Maggie lived here, the kitchen was the only place on Freddy's farm where anything actually worked. But in the short six months since Maggie left, the jungle has reclaimed its own. It looks like the set for *Cats*. Dishes piled in the sink, newspapers stacked on every chair. The dinner table has become a workbench and boxes of beer bottles are stacked against the wall. I suggested as delicately as I could that maybe we should try putting the casserole together down at my place.

"Naw, naw," he said, waving away my objections. "Just clear away a spot here. I remember how this thing goes. First you gotta have toast, lots of toast. You brought the eggs and the ham?"

"Right here. Do you cook the noodles first?"

"No, you just put in lots of water. How long is this thing supposed to cook?"

"It says an hour at 350 degrees."

"We're a little tight for time, Walt. Let's try half an hour at 700."

"Stoves don't go that high, Freddy."

"Actually, this one does if you put it on self-clean."

In ten minutes we had it slammed together and in the oven, which has to be a record, even for Maggie. When it was cooked, I rushed it out to the 4×4—waved a thank you to Freddy and blasted through the snow to the hall. At thirteen minutes past six I jogged up the steps of the Orange Hall and met Maggie, coming out of the cloakroom with a casserole dish in her hands. Her eyes widened in The Look, which is a strong indicator that what is on her mind can't be said out loud in public.

"There you are! What a relief!" she said in a tone that indicated she was feeling no relief at all. "I thought you'd gone into the ditch somewhere. Where on earth have you been? And what is that?"

"You wanted me to pick up the casserole . . ."

"I got the casserole myself, Walt. But when I got there, my dress wasn't ironed, the chores weren't done, and Spike was looking at me as if he hadn't been fed. Hello, Vi." She handed off her casserole to Violet McKeown and turned back, and her voice dropped again.

"Did you remember anything I said?"

"I thought Spike ate the casserole. He was licking out the dish when I came into the kitchen . . . Hi, Victor!" I waved at the superintendent of the Sunday school.

"That was some toast I put down for him after breakfast," she whispered. "The casserole was in the oven. I have more than one casserole dish, Walt. Now, what is that? Hi, Bernice." She smiled at the lady who delivers our mail.

"Freddy and I made another casserole. So, now we have two . . . Frank. How are you?" I nodded to the man who lives in the white house beside the church in Larkspur.

Maggie raised the lid on the casserole dish and examined the contents. "It looks . . . it looks lovely, Walt." Her voice dropped again to a whisper. "Take that back out to the 4×4 . . . right now."

It was a beautiful supper. Maggie looked divine in her blue dress. Her casserole vanished in seconds. She was reinstalled as Treasurer. Outgoing President Elsie Burton was honoured for delivering her ten thousandth meal on wheels for seniors. She was too shy to say anything but "thank yez all very much," and she was thrilled with her prize, which was a three-day bus trip to Nashville.

Spike got his kibble a little later than usual that night. We tried him on Freddy's casserole, but he couldn't eat it. Still, Freddy and I have decided to hang on to the recipe. We think we may have invented a new roofing material.

Yours sincerely,

Walt

——— *April 15*

Dear Ed,

I've acquired horses in descending order of mobility. My first, Feedbin, is actually quite spirited, though erratic. My second, Mortgage, is not a self-starter and would rather stay in the barn. Once on the move, though, she can do as much damage as Feedbin. My third is an old draft horse named King who hardly ever moves at all. If I buy another horse, it will have to be a statue.

I have no idea how old these horses are. Going down to the stable now is like going to the Legion. Feedbin's all grey around the muzzle, Mortgage has the beginnings of white-eye, and King . . . well . . . I understand if King lives another year he'll get a letter from the Queen.

This morning I decided to get Mortgage and Feedbin out with the buggy. I may be pushing the season a bit, but it's been a long winter and I figured it would do us all good to get the adrenalin flowing.

25 Sideroad is a tricky drive at this time of the year. Where the road follows the river you have to watch for people like Don, my dairy-farming neighbour to the south, who drives along the wrong side of the road, leaning out his window, scanning the creek for fish. This morning I could see him meandering along towards us after we turned the corner from the Seventh Line. Thankfully, he saw us in time. He yanked his truck back over to his side of the road and passed us. Then he pulled a U-turn in the intersection and came up alongside.

"So, how are you findin' married life, Walt?" he asked in that solemn, slow drawl he has.

"No complaints, Don. I'm a lucky man."

"We'll get you out here in a couple of weeks with a fly rod, Walt. Then we'll see if you're a lucky man. How're the horses?"

"So far so good. But if this is a visit, I think I'll tie them up to the road sign here."

I gingerly descended from the buggy, keeping a tight rein on the horses, and led them over to a new post the road department had installed at the intersection. It sported a bright new green sign with an unfamiliar name on it.

"What's this, Don?" I asked. "Regional Road Number Four? Is this some kind of joke?"

Don seemed puzzled by it, too. "Well, how about that?" he said. "I guess it's part of the restructuring."

"Restructuring?"

"Yeah, they got numbers now for all the roads."

"They *had* numbers. That's the Seventh Line. This is 25 Sideroad."

Don shrugged. "Thing of the past, Walt. They're putting all the townships together . . . Larkspur, too. They're gonna make one big local government, called the Region of Hillview."

"Hillview? When did all this happen?"

"It's been in the paper every week for about six months, Walt."

"That's unbelievable, Don. The township has been here for 125 years. It's the oldest continuous form of government in the country. How can they just do away with it?"

"C'mon, Walt. No one is goin' to miss it. It wasn't much more than a dry place to play cards. That's why I got off the council."

Don ran for council after the big controversy over the Persephone Glen condominium development across the road from my farm. We managed to stop that particular monstrosity, but Don soon found that the township doesn't have any control over development anymore. Anyone with deep pockets and good lawyers can build anything he wants, anywhere. In the past few years, monster homes have sprouted like mushrooms on the top of every drumlin between here and Highway 13. "View properties," they call them.

"But the history," I protested. "And the motto on the township crest: '*Passim arborem horarem luserunt.*' The changing trees are the guides to the seasons."

"Is that what it means?" said Don. "I always thought it meant 'Pass the bower, lose for an hour.'"

"Don, don't you see what's happening? Without history we have no memory. We're losing all the old signposts."

"You've taken down a few signposts yourself with them horses, Walt," said Don.

I glanced around and saw that we were blocking the road for an ancient Dodge pickup that belongs to my neighbour across the road—the Squire. Up here, when vehicles block the road it doesn't mean there is an obstruction. It means the meeting is called to order. The Squire must be close to eighty now, and he's all crippled up with arthritis. It was painful to watch him ease himself out of the cab and hobble around to lean on the fender.

"G'day, fellas. What's the matter with these horses, Walt? I never seen them stand in one place so long without busting somethin'. Say, is that horse goin' white in the eye?"

"The vet says she may be going blind," I replied. "He doesn't think there's much you can do about it at her age."

The Squire pushed away from the truck and looked Mortgage in the eye.

"You've great faith in the veterinarian, Walter. When I kept livestock I had more faith in the tobacconist. You can treat a horse with drugs all you want, but tobacco is the stuff that cures him. We used to give a horse chewing tobacco for the worms."

"And they swallowed it? That stuff's poison."

"I know," said The Squire. "Killed the worms dead. Never seemed to hurt the horses much. Of course, it is habit forming, but in them days it didn't cost that much to support a horse's tobacco habit. Whenever old Peanut flared up with the white-eye, I just spit tobacco juice in his eye, three times a day for a week; cleared it up every time. And the surprising thing is, we stayed friends . . . Anyway, you should ask Jimmy to come down and have a look at her."

Don and I looked at each other. Old Jimmy, Freddy's hired man, was the expert on horses around here for many years, but he died two years ago. Maybe The Squire meant someone else.

"Jimmy?" I ventured.

"Yeah, Jimmy knows the horses." The Squire nodded his head once quickly to punctuate the observation in that way he has, to signal that no further discussion is required.

"But Jimmy's dead," I said.

"Jimmy died two years ago," said Don.

The Squire tilted his head and frowned at the sun as if he just realized he'd left his wallet on the kitchen table. "I know that," he said impatiently. "I know that. I just meant you shoulda asked him if he was here, that's all. If you guys'll clear a path I gotta move on."

He shuffled off back to his truck, climbed in and drove off without a wave.

"Now what was that all about?" I wondered.

Don shrugged. "He's been getting confused lately, Walt. Kinda livin' in the past, I guess. Not surprising, considering the age he is now."

"I've noticed he talks more and more about the past. And the stories he can tell . . ."

Don raised his right eyebrow, which is the one he uses to indicate scepticism. "Well, that stuff about the horses is true," he said. "But some of the stuff he talks about now . . . I don't know where it comes from. Well, I gotta go. Do you want me to hold on to these guys while you get squared away?"

"Good idea."

Don held the bridles while I climbed back in the buggy. He stepped back, I gave a little cluck, and we clattered off again. But it wasn't the same. The conversation had put a damper on the day. I know The Squire can't live forever, but he's like a barometer for so much I see around me.

You know, for the first few years up here the biggest question on my mind was whether I could make a go of the farm and keep my head above water. Now that Maggie and I have worked out a balance between my work and hers, the future of the farm looks pretty straightforward. It's all the other ones around me that I worry about. Everywhere I look I see signs that the old rural community of Persephone Township is disintegrating. Half the farms have been sold because the owners have died or retired or just given up. The new owners are city people like myself, but they have no interest in farming. The barns stand empty, the fences have collapsed. And now this restructuring business. Fair Persephone displaced by the thudding dullness of "Hillview." Imagine what the committee looked like that came up with that clanger!

It's not just The Squire who's losing his memory, it's the whole community. It's not fair. It seems that just at the moment when I finally arrive at the place in life where I've always wanted to be, it decides to fall apart around me.

It should have been a great day for an outing. Water gushed in the ditches, the sun lifted the moisture off the horses' backs, and the air carried that distinctive spring smell . . . all those little furry things the coyotes had been eating all winter were thawing out. I decided to head upwind.

The drive down the Centre Road towards Hollyhock is one that never fails to lift my spirits. As you crest the first hill, you get a panoramic view of the Boyne River Valley through a picture frame of white cedars. The drumlins spill down like eggs out of a basket, with the tiny village of Hollyhock nestled at the bottom. It never was a busy place, but now it's like a cemetery with street lights. Doctors and dentists from the city who appear only on weekends have renovated the old houses. During the week, nothing stirs. You could say that Hollyhock has fallen on good times.

There's a bend in the river here and a pretty waterfall that tumbles into a dramatic gorge. An abandoned stone grist mill stands above it, and the old millstone lies on its side in midstream at the bottom. If these stones could talk, what stories they could tell . . .

Then it came to me. This would be the perfect place to preserve a glimpse of the old rural community. It could be restored as a museum where people could bring their children and grandchildren. Then, at least, if the old ways have to die, they won't have vanished without a trace. The foundations still looked sound and there was plenty of stone lying about to use in a new structure. A voice from behind me interrupted my thoughts.

"Hi there. It's Walt Wingfield, isn't it?"

I turned to see Dr. Winegard, a dentist who used to be one of my clients in the city. He was bouncing a basketball with his teenage son on the asphalt driveway of his renovated stone farmhouse. He threw the ball to his son and trotted over.

"Traded stocks for livestock, have you, Walt? Heh, heh. This is great. I just love horses. Chip, come and see the horses."

He walked straight up to Mortgage, who was tossing her head irritably, and reached out a hand.

"Ah, I wouldn't do that—" I cautioned him.

Mortgage pulled her lips back and grabbed the cuff of his sports jacket with her teeth.

Dr. Winegard jumped back and checked to see that the brass buttons were still there.

"Whoa, nice horsie . . ." he laughed nervously. He backed around to the side of the buggy, keeping his eye on Mortgage.

"Good to see you, Dr. Winegard. How's the practice?"

"Oh, you know me, Walt. Drilling, filling and billing. Managed to save enough for a little hobby farm here. I call it 'Tooth Acres.' You get it? Listen, we should get together sometime. Where do you go for lunch up here?"

"To my kitchen usually. I guess there's the Red Hen Restaurant in Larkspur. But they don't do cappuccino. How are your investments?"

"I'm not doing much in the market right now," he said. "I've got all my spare cash tied up in cattle."

I looked around. There were no fences on his little acreage, and the barn had long since disappeared. "Cattle?" I asked. "Where do you keep cattle?"

"Oh, no, not here. Bill Haddock is keeping them for me."

Bill Haddock. I couldn't think of any Bill Haddocks in the neighbourhood. Maggie is a Haddock, and so, of course, is Freddy. Must be one the relatives, I thought. Then it struck me.

"Do you mean Willy?" I asked.

"Yes. Very enterprising young man. He and his brother got me a load of western steers. Eighteen-month turnover. I do the money . . . they do the management."

Willy and Dave are Freddy and Maggie's nephews. The scary part about marrying Maggie was they suddenly became *my* nephews. They're wonderful fellows if you need tax-free cigarettes or venison . . . they call it government beef. But I've never thought of them as management material.

However, I kept my thoughts to myself and said goodbye to the dentist. The horses pricked up their ears as we made a wide circle on the road to face north again. I could feel the magnetic pull of the oat bin drawing them back up the hill to the farm.

I'm going to look into this museum business, Ed. It may not be the answer to all our problems, but if I can do some small thing to preserve at least the memory of the old rural community, I feel I owe it to the next generation.

Yours sincerely,

Walt

—— *April 25*

Dear Ed,

I went into the sheep pen the other day and noticed one of the ewes lying down in the normal fashion but with her head pulled back and her nose in the air, staring straight up at the ceiling. I tried to get her up, but she couldn't walk. Something was definitely not right, so I called Freddy in for a "consultation." Freddy studied the ewe for a few minutes.

"Mike Fisher had one just like this last summer and he had to shoot it," he said.

"That's terrible. What did she have?"

"I don't know . . . but it was fatal. I suppose you could give her a shot of B$_{12}$ and drench her with glycol. That sometimes helps a sheep with the staggers."

This did not sound promising. I went to the kitchen to get a second opinion from Maggie. Maggie has a whole cupboard dedicated to veterinary medicine. It is crammed full of pills, potions and lotions, drenching tubes, bandages and disinfectants. There is also an extensive library on the ailments of domestic livestock. The kitchen table has doubled as an operating theatre for small animals on more than one occasion. Maggie reached for her sheep book and flipped through the pages.

"It's not the staggers," she said after a moment. "It sounds more like pregnancy toxemia to me. Give her four cc's of B$_{12}$ and drench her with a half cup of glycol. She should come around by morning. If she doesn't, we'll call the vet."

The ewe did not come around next morning. She was till staring at the ceiling and drooling heavily. The vet doesn't make house calls anymore. So I had to figure some way to get the sheep into town. Freddy offered his truck but shook his head when he arrived.

"Jeez, Walt, I'm not much good at a dead lift anymore. She's gotta weigh over two hundred pounds, and we can multiply that by three if she doesn't want to go."

I had already figured that one out. Using the ancient Egyptian principles of the lever and the inclined plane, Freddy and I dragged the ewe slowly and painfully up a plywood ramp I had constructed and then rolled her as gently as possible onto the bed of the pickup truck.

Freddy wiped his hands on his overalls. "She sure is slobberin' a lot. You don't mind bein' sneezed on by a sheep, do you?"

"Why, is that a good shirt you're wearing?" I laughed.

"Ah, nothin' that won't wash out. Gotta hand it to you, though. You're not squeamish."

By the time the ewe was loaded we were both up to our elbows in sheep slobber. We drove into town and, as we waited at the stoplights, an old man on the bench in front of the drugstore noticed the sheep and glanced up at the sky to see what she was staring at. When the light turned green we left a small crowd of people staring at the sky. At the clinic, the vet came out, took one look at the ewe and put on a pair of rubber gloves.

"What, you don't think she's got rabies, do you?" asked Freddy nervously.

"She is showing some of the symptoms," said the vet. "The virus is carried through the saliva. It's important not to have contact with the saliva. Have you been handling her?"

Freddy looked at me and shrugged. "Don't worry, Walt, I've had the shots lots of times. They just give you one . . . a day . . . in the stomach. You get used to it."

"Actually, you take a pill nowadays," said the vet. He took a blood sample from the ewe and told us to call him in the morning for the results. "In the meantime, I can give you some glycol and B$_{12}$. That might help her."

"We already did that. Thanks, Doc," said Freddy. "We seem to be able to get that stuff cheaper than you do."

Next morning, Freddy came straight over after breakfast. If he was trying to make me feel more optimistic, he failed.

"Was that your sheep I saw chasing the school bus this morning, Walt? You haven't had any problems with uncontrollable thirst, have you?"

"Oh, stop it, Freddy," scolded Maggie. "He didn't sleep a wink last night."

"Actually, her neck is straightened out and she's eating hay. If it was rabies, she wouldn't be doing that, would she?"

"Nope," agreed Freddy. "Rabies isn't the sort of thing you shake off after a coupla days."

We called the vet to report the news. He sounded quite pleased.

"Sounds like you've turned the corner with her, Mr. Wingfield. I think what you're dealing with is a form of sheep polio. Don't worry. It's not contagious and the others aren't likely to get it unless there's a thiamine deficiency in the flock."

"So, what's the treatment from here?"

"The B_{12} mixture you've been giving her has thiamine in it. So just keep it up and pour half a cup of glycol down her throat every six hours."

I thanked him and rang off.

"Well, ain't that a corker?" said Freddy. "We've been through the textbook on sheep ailments from toxemia to polio and the treatment remains the same. Anyway, congratulations, Doctor."

"Let's not count our chickens," I said. "The doctor says she will probably have some brain damage."

"Oh, yeah?" said Freddy. "And, like, how would you tell with a sheep? Their brains run on two penlight batteries. You know, the double-A size."

"Well, she'll probably get by with triple-A now."

Over the next few days, it became clear that the ewe was indeed a couple of brain cells short of a full cortex. She didn't recognize me when I came into the stable in the morning. When she came back in from the pasture she looked at the barn in astonishment, as if to say, "When did they build this?" Now, whenever I put hay in the trough, she looks at it closely as if she's never seen hay before.

I understand that a fish never gets bored in an aquarium because each time it swims around the tank it forgets that it's been there before. No matter how many laps it makes, its view of the world remains forever fresh, which would be as close to a blessed state as any creature can achieve in this life. So it is with this sheep.

Yours sincerely,
Walt

—— *April 30*

Dear Ed,

Still in the middle of lambing out here, and the results are nothing to boast about.

Maggie is the expert on sheep and she says we really have to buy a ram. She made this pronouncement when Freddy came down for supper last Monday. I have had the sheep for two years now, but I have managed to do so without investing in a ram of my own. Freddy just opens a gate in November and lets his old Corriedale ram into my pasture for a few weeks. Five months later, sometime in April, little lambies appear. I throw terms like "Corriedale," around loosely, but, of course, Freddy's sheep are by no means purebred. Anyway, Freddy was a little prickly about it. He was tilted back in the pressback armchair at our dining-room table when Maggie brought the subject up.

"So, what's the matter with my ram, Maggie?" he asked, gouging one of his molars with a toothpick.

"Well, look at the lambs he throws. They're no good for wool or meat. We could only sell them to vegetarian nudists."

Freddy shrugged. "I'll be the first to say it, they're not fancy sheep, but by gollies, they're tough. Actually, they're more of a hunting sheep. I might use a couple of them up in the county forest this fall to track wolves."

Maggie fluffed out the *Hillhurst County Shopper* and pointed to the auction notices. "There are some rams listed in tomorrow's sheep auction for the Pluto sales barn," she said.

"Yeah, I saw them," agreed Freddy. "There's always rams up there, Walt. People trade them around this time of the year to kinda freshen up the gene pool."

The Pluto sales barn is a great place to get rid of livestock, but I've never bought anything there. I'm always leery about bringing some animal health problem back to the farm.

"But sales barns are an incubator for disease," I said. "Don't you ever worry about that?"

"Sure I do," nodded Freddy. "But when I'm over at Pluto I use my elbows to open the washroom doors and I never order anything with gravy on it, if I can help it."

"You can take the 4×4, Walt," said Maggie.

"But will a ram fit in the back of the 4×4?"

Maggie looked at me serenely. "Rams can be dangerous," she said. "If it doesn't fit in the 4×4, don't bring it home."

Gassing up at Ron's in Larkspur the next morning I noticed a tractor-trailer parked across the road. It was carrying a load of last fall's calves. Not the usual scruffy Shorthorn crossbreeds from the local pasture farms in Persephone Township. These were smooth, fat Limousin calves from the west. A lot of them. I know just enough about cattle to know that I couldn't afford six of these, let alone a hundred. Around the corner of the trailer came Willy and Dave. Willy flashed a gold-toothed smile at me.

"Wanna buy some cattle, Uncle Walt? We can get you in at the special family rate! Aren't they pretty?"

Willy and Dave are two lanky fellows in their mid-twenties with charming manners and high-pitched laughs that sound like the shriek of a startled parrot. They have omnivorous taste in employment. They are self-described "cash-croppers," by which they mean that all of the land they work is rented and they're always short of cash because it's buried in the soil at the moment. But despite all that, they're usually at the wheel of some immense machine, like this huge truck.

"They certainly are pretty," I agreed. "They must be worth a pretty penny."

"Yeah," said Dave. "They'll sure raise the standards around home."

"Oh, of course," I said. "These must be the ones you got for Dr. Winegard, the dentist down in Hollyhock."

Willy glanced at Dave and bobbed his head. "Ah, yeah. Some of these would be his, too, I guess. Say, Walt, we were lookin' at the Chicago price for cattle on your computer. We were wondering how you get into the futures market if you want to make a trade. Do you ever do that?"

I've been introducing Willy and Dave to the fundamentals of the market via my computer. They're keen students and with a bit of coaching they have already done reasonably well with a few simple trades I made for them.

"Well, we can look at that together some day. You have to have the password."

"Password?" said Willy. "Oh, right . . . a password."

Dave elbowed him and climbed up into the cab.

"Come on, Willy," he shouted. "Let's keep these dogies movin'. Rollin' rollin' rollin' . . . RawHIDE!"

At the Pluto sales barn I scanned the pens and soon found the rams. They were a dreary-looking bunch, with matted wool and patches of bare skin showing. They'd had a hard winter. In the very last pen there was a good candidate: a very tall and noble-looking Oxford ram, all freshly clipped to show off his muscles. He looked like an aging golf pro in long underwear. A ram of this quality would probably bring a high price, but he was worth a try.

I sat in the bleachers, listening to the hum of the sale and waiting for the rams to come out. The first five sold for about fifty dollars each. Then they brought in my Oxford. The auctioneer started the bidding at twenty-five dollars, and I stuck up my hand, bracing for a fight up to two hundred dollars. The auctioneer took my bid, prattled to the crowd for about ten seconds and then pointed to me.

" . . . twenty-five and a bid now thirty and a bid now thirty and a bid now thirty and . . . sold for twenty-five dollars. What is your number, sir?"

I was amazed. Twenty-five dollars for a ram like that was a real bargain. This didn't make sense. I rose and trotted down the stairs to have another look at him before they ushered him out of the ring. He walked without a limp, his eyes were clear and he wasn't coughing. Past that you couldn't really tell. He certainly was big. Very big. But he didn't look dangerous. He had a slightly offended look, like a lawyer being asked to wait in line.

As it turned out, I almost needed a shoehorn to get him into the 4×4, but with the help of two attendants we got him loaded. Back at the farm Maggie helped me extract him and put him in the stable.

"Walt," she said. "He's the size of a small horse. Where did he come from?"

I told her the story.

"You got him for twenty-five dollars?" she said, and then put her hand to her mouth. "Oh, my goodness, this must be Floyd McLean's ram."

"Floyd McLean?"

"Floyd McLean farmed in Demeter Township. He had a problem with his nerves. They had him up in Penetang for a while, trying to calm him down. The experts had a theory that the colour pink was good for violent people and they had the whole room and everything in it painted pink. When Floyd came back he was all right, as long as he took his medication, but he always had a problem with the colour pink after that."

"What happened to him?"

"He had another attack in April. Easter was always a difficult time for him. They put him back in the pink room."

"And it didn't work?"

Maggie shook her head sadly. "I guess not. They say he put his head right through the wall. Anyway he never came out. And the night he died, this ram was born. Folks up in Demeter believe Floyd's soul passed into the ram, and now nobody will touch it. They even named it after him . . . Pink Floyd."

The phone rang and Maggie went inside to answer it. I couldn't believe what I was hearing. It appeared the reason I got this splendid animal for next to nothing is that people imagine he is possessed by the spirit of his owner.

I put my hand under his chin and guided him to the main pen. He came peacefully; I bumped open the pen gate and let go of him. He blinked a couple of times and started chewing his cud. He wasn't hard to manage at all. I went hunting for a couple of sheep gates to block the door, so he could see out without getting out until he was used to his new surroundings.

Of course, what we're dealing with here is an Evil Eye culture—people have all kinds of superstitious beliefs dating back hundreds of years. Some of them make sense. For instance, don't plant until the frogs sing three times—that actually works. But there are others. If you leave new shoes on the table, or dream about a birth, or plow down snow—these all mean certain death. Obviously these are loony notions, like this business with the ram. What perplexes me is that people up here make no attempt to distinguish between taboos against things that are genuinely dangerous and ones against things that are utterly harmless. I finished wiring the sheep gates together, blew my nose on a pink handkerchief and stuffed it in my back pocket. Then I bent over to pick the fence pliers off the floor of the pen.

At the hospital, I was treated for concussion and something with a Latin name that actually just means a pain in the butt. When I woke up, the Squire was sitting in a chair beside the bed.

"How are you now, Walt?" he asked. "I brought you some stuff."

I was expecting him to hand me a newspaper and some of those Western novels he reads. Instead, he opened a cardboard box and pulled a little electric fan out of it. He placed it on the bedside table and plugged it into the wall socket. It made a soft little whirr that was quite soothing.

"This is for when the sun comes around to the west, Walt. It can get stinkin' hot in here. And I got you a fly-swatter, too. It's bad for flies in the evening. And this here's in case you ever need a nurse."

He reached into the box and drew out a large brass school bell.

"There's a call button right here, attached to the bed," I pointed out.

The Squire shook his head. "That's not hooked up to nothing. And I got you some cigarettes . . ."

"But I don't smoke!"

"Neither do I. They're for when the school bell doesn't work. You light up one of these, you get nurses comin' from all directions."

"Well, thanks," I chuckled. But I was puzzled. "How do you know all this? Have you been in here a lot?"

The Squire shrugged. "I just come in for the usual . . . you know, plugs, points and condenser. At my age I'm kinda past the warranty."

There was a familiar rustle at the door. Maggie breezed into the room and fluttered a kiss on my forehead. She sat down on the other side of the bed and smiled.

"Hello, dear. I brought you some flowers."

The Squire pulled himself to his feet. "I'll push along now, Walt. And remember, rule number one for the shepherd . . . never turn your back on a ram." He grinned and shuffled out.

I turned back to Maggie. "So, how is Pink Floyd?"

"He's all right," she smiled. "I decided to start training him. I left your overalls with that pink handkerchief sticking out of the pocket hanging on the concrete gatepost. He's having a sleep now. Are you feeling better, dear?"

"I'm all right. Did you know the Squire is a regular patient here?"

"Just the past couple of years. He gets run down from time to time. None of us lasts forever, Walt."

"I know that . . . I guess that's why I want to press on with this museum idea. It would help to keep things from disappearing completely. At least we'd have some kind of permanent record of a way of life."

"You may have a permanent record of your encounter with Floyd. When we brought you in here I noticed you had one of your antacid tablets in your overalls pocket where Floyd hit you. It looks like a tattoo—you can actually read it."

"What does it say?"

"It says 'ᙎMUT.' It makes it look like I married a biker."

Yours sincerely,

Walt

—— *May 25*

Dear Ed,

Maggie's gone for a few days to move her aunt into a chronic care hospital in Barrie. I decided to spend the time seeing what the township council had to say about my museum proposal. I called the township clerk and got a spot on the agenda for the regular meeting on the fourth Thursday of the month. Since Maggie had the 4×4, I borrowed Freddy's truck for the drive.

The township government has been housed in the old Hollyhock schoolhouse for the last forty years. I got there at eight o'clock and let myself in the east door, over which, embossed in the brick, were the words "Boys Entrance." Some wag had painted in front of the inscription the word "Old."

I had been here once before, two years ago, to protest Darcy Dixon's condominium development. They were sitting in exactly the same position as I last saw them. The reeve, wearing his thirty-pound chain of office, sat at the centre of the table, with the deputy reeve on his right and the other councillors on his left. Harold, the clerk, sat at a separate table and prompted the reeve through the agenda. It crossed my mind that we had the makings of a museum right here.

Harold was just starting up the machinery of government as I came in.

"Your worship," he was saying. "We have two applications for permits on the Conservation Area picnic ground. The first is from the Persephone Animal Rights Action Committee."

The reeve scowled and shot a glance towards his deputy. "You got somethin' to say about this, Ernie?" It wasn't a question.

Ernie squared his shoulders and closed his eyes as if someone had just heaved a tomato at him. "I'm agin' it," he said flatly. "Last time I went for my wolf bounty cheque I had to cross their picket line. They spattered me with animal blood. Called me names."

"What's the other one for, Harold?" asked the reeve.

"It's for the Larkspur Rod and Gun Club barbecue, your Worship."

The reeve glanced to his left now, at a man who appeared to be the oldest elected representative in the British Commonwealth. "Wilfrid?" he prompted.

Wilfrid's eyes opened slowly, like a crocodile contemplating a flamingo leg.

"They're just as bad," he hissed. "I had to cross their picket line when I went to register my twelve-gauge. When I came out, my car windshield was soaped."

"Turn 'em both down, Harold," snapped the reeve. Harold paused with his ruler on the page and his pencil poised above it, ready to draw a line through the agenda item.

"Your Worship, might I point out that both applications happen to be for the same date? Might I suggest a motion to grant both permits for the same spot?"

There was another pause while the reeve studied the portrait of Queen Elizabeth and Prince Philip on the wall behind me. He glanced to his left and right and said, "Carried. What have we got next, Harold?"

"Your worship . . . we have a deputation." He nodded in my direction.

"I can see that, Harold. Mr. Wingfield . . . nice to have you back before council. I understand you have a proposal for a museum you want us to have a look at."

"Yes, I do."

I stood up and approached the bench. They looked slightly bemused as I plopped a three-page proposal in front of each of them and launched into my presentation. I talked about the rich history of Persephone and the distinctive way of life that makes it such an interesting place to live. Then I moved on to the rapid changes we have seen in the past few years, the loss of farmland to development, how the old family farms are being bought out, the owners retiring and their children looking to other kinds of employment or leaving the township altogether. The demographics of Persephone are changing rapidly and the community's memory of itself is slipping away. I stressed the need for some way to preserve what we know of that old rural community before it is lost forever, and explained how a museum would help.

"And in conclusion, gentlemen, I cannot stress too heavily the benefits of an institution that would preserve the rich history of Persephone Township, a world that I fear is slipping away."

"That sounds like a real fine idea, Mr. Wingfield," said the reeve.

Ernie reached behind him for a large axe leaning up against the wood panelling.

"And I got something here you'd want to have in that museum. Belonged to my dad but I know he'd want to donate it. This here's the axe that was used to clear the first farm in Persephone Township . . . over here on the Fourth Line in the Back Settlement . . . woulda been 1836."

"Really?" I said. "That's remarkable. It doesn't look that old."

"Somebody put a new head on it just after the war," said the reeve.

Wilfrid came to life again. "And my father replaced the handle on that axe in 1972," he quavered. "One of the last things he ever did."

"But it's the very same axe," said Ernie, daring the others to contradict him.

Wilfrid placed both hands on the table and raised himself slowly. He was wearing a Sam Browne belt and a scabbard dangled from his side. "Now, if you want some real history," he said, "my great-great-grandfather, who did the first survey of this township, cut his way up through the bush swinging this sword . . ." With a flourish, he drew a navy cutlass from the scabbard and gave me a shaky salute. The other councillors ducked.

"Careful, Wilfrid," warned the reeve.

Wilfrid leaned over the table, pointing the sword at me. " . . . the same sword he used to drive the Americans across the Niagara River at Queenston Heights in 1812. The dark spots on that sword are American blood."

"Maybe they are, Wilfrid," said Ernie. "Or maybe Laura Secord's cow peed on it."

"Yeah, well, one thing for sure," said the reeve. "That strongbox Harold uses to keep the minutes in was a gift from the first tax collector sent out by the Lieutenant Governor in 1841."

"Really," I said. "That's an odd gift."

"Gave his horse, too," added Ernie.

"And his watch," cackled Wilfrid. "And a signet ring. And a gold tooth . . ."

"Ah, I see," I said. "That's fascinating . . . and, of course, the museum wouldn't just be a place for artifacts; it would preserve the living history of the community, stories like the ones you told just now."

"Sounds like the kind of project we'd all like to get behind, Mr. Wingfield," said the reeve.

This sounded promising. "That's wonderful. What kind of support could I expect from council?"

"We can give you an agreement in principle to the under-taking . . . or an undertaking that we are principally in agree-ment . . . either one."

"But I meant, would there be any chance of funding?"

The reeve handed off to Harold, the clerk.

"Your worship," sighed Harold. "I am given to understand by the restructuring committee that our funding is to be held in abeyance pending the results of negotiations on the provin-cial funding formulas."

The reeve turned back to me to interpret. "What Harold is saying, Mr. Wingfield, is we don't have a budget right now."

"When will you get one?"

The reeve looked back at Harold.

"Your worship," he offered patiently. "Budgets would be struck by council once it is reconstituted, and that again is attending on the ratification of the new boundaries by the Legislature."

"It's up to the province, Mr. Wingfield," explained the reeve.

"But . . . if you have no budget," I protested, "no jurisdiction and no constituency, why are you meeting?"

All eyebrows went up as if I had asked the silliest question in the world.

"Council's the fourth Thursday of the month," said Ernie. "Always has been."

"Now, Mr. Wingfield," said the reeve. "Had you given any thought to where this museum might be located?"

I explained to them the possibilities offered by the abandoned mill property just down the road from the township office. "I understand the land belongs to the township. It's central and it appears to be structurally sound . . ."

Their silent stares brought me to a halt.

"The mill?" asked Ernie in astonishment.

"Did he say the Hollyhock Mill?" echoed Wilfrid.

"Any thought to anyplace else?" asked the reeve.

"Well, no, I thought—"

The reeve cut me off. "G'day, Mr. Wingfield. Thanks again for comin' to council. Harold, do you have the hall committee report there?"

Apparently, my audience with council was over. Obviously, I'd put my foot wrong somehow, but I was at a loss to explain where. I gathered up my papers and left. Back at Freddy's, Willy and Dave pushed past me in the doorway, carrying cases of beer, followed by Spike and several other dogs. Willy set his case down and raised his hands in benediction.

"Rejoice, children, for those of ye who thirst shall be refreshed," he said.

Spike came over and put his head on my knee. I was surprised to see him. He doesn't usually wander away from the house when I'm not at home.

"What's Spike doing here?" I asked.

Willy's head popped up from behind the fridge door, where he was loading in party supplies. "Ah . . . we were down at your place lookin' at the Chicago price again, Uncle Walt."

Dave nodded and plunked a bottle of Labatt's 50 down in front of me. "Guess his old nose still works good enough to sniff out a party."

For many years, Maggie's absence from the community for more than twenty-four hours always served as the green light for one of "Freddy's benders." Even though Maggie no longer shares the same premises with her brother, her going away still triggers a powerful reflex response. The phone rang and Freddy answered it.

"Hyello?" he chirped, then suddenly whirled and shushed us to be quiet. He covered the receiver with his hand and whispered, "It's Maggie!" The others froze. Freddy put the phone back up to his ear. "Uh-huh," he said. "Uh-huh . . . sure, we will . . . you bet . . . Walt? No, haven't seen Walt all day." He leaned over the counter and squinted out the window. "There's lights on at the barn. I expect he's closin' up." He winked at me and grinned. "Okay . . . Okay. We'll see you then." He carefully hung up the receiver and turned to us. "She's safe and sound in Barrie . . . till Monday. Gentlemen . . . you may smoke!"

A little later Freddy came over to me and presented me with a handful of insulated wires. "Walt," he said. "Could you hang onto these till Monday?"

"Sure," I said. "What are these?"

"These here would be the coil wires for every internal combustion engine on the farm. It's part of our designated drinking program. If you hide 'em somewhere and don't tell us till Monday, chances are the township will be a safer place. G'day, Squire, come on in."

The Squire hobbled in the doorway and raised his eyebrows. For a moment I wasn't sure if he approved of the scene.

"G'day, fellas," he said. "My doctor tells me I'm not to do any work. So I figgered this is the place not to do it."

They all settled into couches, dogs flopped around their feet, Dave tuned up his guitar, and Freddy blew the dust out of his accordion.

"So, Walt," said Freddy. "How did your meetin' go with the Fathers of Confederation down there in Hollyhock?"

I told them that the meeting had gone quite well and the council seemed quite supportive until I mentioned the possibility of using the mill property in Hollyhock.

"The Hollyhock Mill!" said Freddy. "Is that where you were thinkin' of puttin' it? Now, Walt, you never told me that!"

"All right," I said. "Could someone please explain to me what the problem is with the Hollyhock Mill?"

"It's haunted," said Freddy.

"Haunted?" I laughed. "What nonsense is this?"

"Now, Uncle Walt," said Willy. "You don't mean to say you've been up here this long and nobody's told you the story of the Laird McNabb and the curse on the Hollyhock Mill?"

"You gotta tell 'im, Willy," said Dave.

"Okay, but I gotta have this." Willy lifted Freddy's accordion out of his lap, put one foot up on a chair and played a sombre minor chord.

"Long ago, when the land was young and men paid cash for their cars, the Laird McNabb owned all the land from Hollyhock up to the Glen. And though he was wealthy he was a hard, hard man.

"He grew a bit of corn, and he milled a bit of flour, and he stilled a bit of gin, but the chief delight he took in life was givin' the back of his hand to the poor country folk of the township.

"One night a banshee appeared to him as he was goin' to bed and said: 'McNabb, ye've cheated the honest farmers of this township long enough and if you do not mend your ways I will smite ye like ye've never been smit before.'

"That would have been good enough for the likes of you and me. Being interviewed by a banshee in the middle of the night while standing in your underwear . . . that would make an angel out of some of the worst cases in the Commercial Hotel. But not the Laird McNabb.

"McNabb would have none of it. He scorned the banshee's words, so the banshee caused the corn harvest to fail and dried up the creek so the mill would not run, and still the Laird would not relent . . . so she sent cluster flies to torment him, and still the Laird would not relent . . . and finally she sent a grant application form for tile drainage with no instructions on how to fill it out, and that cracked him. The Laird dove into the millpond to drown himself and broke his neck . . . it bein' dried up like it was. And so the mill sits crumbling and abandoned and a curse lies on it, down to this very day."

Freddy snatched the accordion back from Willy. "That isn't anything like the curse," he snorted. "Jeez! Let the Squire tell it."

The Squire sat forward in his easy chair and waited for quiet.

"The Miller McNabb, Walt, was the man who brought out the first company of Scots settlers to the bush here. He'd been a landowner in Scotland and he lorded it over the other settlers and treated them like a bunch of serfs. He set up the mill there in Hollyhock and wouldn't let anyone in the settlement trade anywhere else. And he got rich. He had three daughters, the prettiest girls in the Settlement, but the mother died young and it was left to the Miller McNabb to raise the girls. As the years went by, he got so he wouldn't let them out of his sight. Not for a minute. Every young lad in the township was tom-cattin' around, so McNabb told the girls they had to stay in the big stone house up by the mill.

"In spite of his efforts, these girls got to know young fellas, and they all fell in love, and one day they cornered the old man and demanded the freedom to get married. Well, the Miller McNabb flew into a rage, and he boarded up the windows, and he bricked up the doorways, and he had an iron deadbolt forged across the front door that locked with a brass key he kept on a chain around his neck."

"Good Lord!" I said. "How did he get away with this?"

"They were Presbyterians, Walt," said Freddy. "That kinda behaviour didn't exactly stand out in those days."

Squire continued. "Well, the young fellas hatched a plot to free the girls. And one night in a big storm, they surprised the Miller McNabb in the mill and knocked him out and stole the key from around his neck. They freed the girls and got in a boat tied down at the wharf below the dam and off they went. Before long, the Miller McNabb woke up, and he felt the key gone, and he ran down to the door of the house and found it standing wide open, with the key still in the lock. He looked out and saw them all floatin' off down the river. And he snatched up the key and climbed out on the dam at the height of the storm and screamed a curse at them, and then he started pulling boards out of the millrace. The water was already high and, first thing you know, the stones started falling out of the dam and the foundations around the mill wheel gave out. Then the whole works came crashing down: the dam, the mill wheel—"

"Twenty-five cats and his whole collection of moose heads off the wall—" added Willy.

"—and McNabb himself. And, last of all, the great millstone came tumbling down, and it crushed the Miller McNabb as dead as a nit in the riverbed."

"Yep," giggled Willy. "And the place has been known ever since as 'Miller Flats.'"

The Squire sighed and carried on. "The river flowed over its banks for three days and three nights. And when the flood was over they searched the river for the girls and the young fellas and the Miller McNabb, but none of them were ever found.

"And six men stood in the river and lifted with all their strength and they tried to raise the stone. They all felt a tremor pass through it. Like a live thing, it was. And they let it fall back, and they all ran away. And that stone has never been moved from that day to this."

"I guess everybody figured if it could move itself, why bother?" said Willy.

"Laugh if you want, Willy," said Freddy. "But of those six men, not one lived more than a year after that night."

"Of course they didn't. With the boss gone and nobody to tell them what to do, they drank themselves to death in the Hillsdale Hotel."

I agreed that this was quite a story but I pointed out that the problem with the museum site wasn't the mill itself. It was the millstone. That's the thing people won't touch.

"I don't know, Walt," said the Squire. "Folks are pretty spooked about the whole place."

"But," I persisted, "if people could be shown there's nothing wrong with moving the millstone, all their objections to the site would just fade away, wouldn't they?"

The Squire shrugged. "Well, that makes sense, but—"

"And don't you see, the story makes it even better as a museum site." I turned to the others. "That's the real living history of the community."

Freddy shook his head. "Some history is better forgotten, Walt. That stone is cursed, I tell you, and anyone who touches it will come to a bad end."

Dave nodded. "Uncle Freddy has a point. You know, Sparky McEwan went fishin' there once and sat on that stone by accident. And he sure has had a run of bad luck."

"Why? What happened to him?" I asked.

"He didn't get his property tax rebate this year, and his kids have all moved back home."

"Look, I'll move the stone myself. Nobody else needs to be involved. Then, when people see I'm not cursed . . . end of problem."

Freddy was unconvinced. "You may not be the right guy for this, Walt."

"What do you mean?"

The Squire patted my hand. "What Freddy's sayin' is, the

way you do stuff around here, it's hard to tell if you're in the grip of a deadly curse or just having a normal day."

Yours sincerely,
Walt

⸺ June 10

Dear Ed,

I haven't found any historical record of the Miller McNabb, but that doesn't prove much. It seems most of the early history here is in dispute. For instance, most accounts say the opening of the road from the Town of York started the flow of goods and people that really established the community. But I found this entry in a local history book—Dr. D.J. Goulding's *With Axe and Flask: The History of Persephone Township from Pre-Cambrian Times to the Present*:

> Reaching Larkspur under any conditions was a difficult and hazardous journey and could take many days. But building a road made the situation even worse because as soon as it was finished 39 taverns sprang up over a distance of 38 miles. Some people never made it to Larkspur at all. It wasn't until Prohibition in 1916 that people discovered you could make the trip in an hour and a half.

I had a small success with poultry my first year here. My two geese, Colonel Belknap and General Longstreet, grew to fourteen pounds each and fetched a dollar a pound. Modest, but an encouraging start, you'll agree. But it's like those guys in the midway who let you win a couple of times to get you hooked. Then they take all your money. I was out at the mailbox last week in another one of those impromptu neighbourhood roadside meetings, this time with no less than four vehicles blocking the Seventh Line. I was driving back from the Co-op in Demeter Centre with a flyer advertising day-old meat chicks from a Mennonite supplier in Elmira. I was hesitating because of the terrible luck I have had with whatever birds I try—ducks, chickens, turkeys, guinea hens, you name it. The guys were all sympathetic.

"You've buried a lot of birds here, Walt," said the Squire.

"Yeah," said Don. "You may as well call it a poultry farm, Walt. That's pretty much what the ground's made of now."

"It's not your fault," said the Squire. "All you have to do is look at a chicken and you can tell they were not meant to live. Everything loves to kill a chicken."

Freddy looked at the flyer. "You know, if you're thinking of going into these meat chickens, what you should do is, when you pick 'em up from the hatchery, set a flat of them on the front seat beside you and fire one at every mailbox you see on the way home. You try it, Walt, it'll make you feel better in the long run."

I read an article last year, from an organic gardening magazine, about an experiment at an apple orchard in Washington State where they were raising free-range chickens to help break the cycle of bugs coming up out of the ground and into the fruit. It sounded like a terrific idea, so I mailed away for fifty Dominique chickens, which are a rare American breed that the poultry catalogue described as independent, good foragers and "a pretty good meat bird." Then I released thousands of beneficial bugs—ladybugs, lacewings and tricogramma wasps—natural predators of apple pests.

I was trying to work in harmony with the natural world, but it turns out that the natural world is a pretty violent place.

As Freddy says, Nature's a lot like Revenue Canada. She sets her own rules and she doesn't always tell you what they are.

The chickens ate all the beneficial bugs; dogs ate the chickens. By the end of the summer it was dogs: 37; chickens: 0. In the fall, hunters snuck in and ate all the apples, and the natural cycle was complete.

I did manage to put seven chickens in the freezer in December. At seven months they weighed four and a half pounds each. We had one for dinner just before Christmas. It was the toughest chicken I have ever eaten in my life. It tasted like it had run all the way from Washington State. Maggie pointed out that these were the fastest ones out of fifty chickens, so what did I expect?

That left me with five hens and one rooster—with a very bad twitch. The rooster started attacking me, so I decided to teach him a lesson. Every time he came at me I whacked him over the head with a leather glove. I did this thirty-five times before I realized that a rooster's head is designed the way it is for a purpose. It is meant to hold a certain amount of inherited information but it will not accept new information. There is no room in that head for a new thought. So all you can do is take the head off, I guess.

I finally moved the survivors into protective custody in the henhouse for the winter, but even there they weren't safe. A couple of months ago, I came out and found that a raccoon had broken through the chicken wire covering the window in the middle of the night and killed three of the hens. I asked Maggie if there was anything you can do about a raccoon.

"Yes," she said. "You get one of those humane traps—it's called a Havahart Trap—and you trap the 'coon in the humane trap. Then you beat it to death with a shovel."

So the score started to even up a bit. But then I found that raccoons are a lot like taxicabs at the airport. You take one out and another one moves in to take its place. It's a lot of work burying a raccoon. Some of them weigh twenty-five pounds, and it can really put a dent in your morning schedule. But I've found you can drop them out at the highway and the Ministry crews will pick them up. Just don't drop them in the same place every time.

I'm down to my last chicken now. There were two, but this morning I opened the door of the henhouse too quickly, and one of them fell over with a stroke. Couldn't take the pressure, I guess. The Squire helped me bury it this afternoon.

"I'm beginning to see why this breed got so rare, Walt. They seem to prefer extinction."

I patted the shovel on the loose dirt and straightened up to find the Squire studying the hill across the road.

"My oh my," he said. "Where did that come from?"

I wasn't sure what he was looking at. "Look at that," he said, waving a finger at the view that stretched away to the east. Over the past week, with the warm weather, the trees were just now bursting into their full summer plumage. "Here, put your shovel down and look there. Fourteen shades of green, full of birds and bugs. Smells better than a bakery. If a fella can't take pleasure in a sight like that, he should go down to the real estate office and slap a sign on her today."

"It's nice, isn't it?" I agreed.

"And look at the way the old forest has come back on Calvin Currie's hill pasture."

I hesitated. There were a few cedars in the gullies on the side of the hill, but, for the most part, the field was grown up in dogwood and thistles.

"Forest?" I said.

"Yeah, look. There's maple up there and beech . . . there's even a stand of pin oaks. Come on, Walt, let's take a walk up through it . . ."

He took a step forward and then stopped. He blinked and frowned and looked back at me. After a moment he said, "You don't see it, do you?"

"No," I said carefully, taking his arm. "But you do. You remember it from a long time ago. Come on, I'll help you home."

We walked slowly back out to the lane and down to the mailbox. At the road, we stood together in the cool evening air, listening to barn sounds down at Don's. A gravel truck chugged up the town line in the distance. Two groundhogs chased each other through the ditch and out onto the hayfield.

"Are you all right from here?" I asked gently.

He smiled and patted my shoulder. "You're very kind to an old man, Walt. You have a way about you. I don't know what's the matter with me. There's never been a stand of pin oaks on Calvin's hill."

I watched him hobble back down his lane until he climbed up the steps of his verandah and the old screen door banged behind him.

Yours sincerely,

Walt

———— *June 21*

Dear Ed,

I was on my way out this morning when I met Willy and Dave at the kitchen doorway. I could tell from the look on their faces that something was up.

"Say, Uncle Walt," said Willy. "Do you got a minute? Me and Dave's got a little problem and we were thinkin' maybe you could help. You know that Dr. Winegard that bought the cattle with us? We just got a call from him. Revenue Canada is askin' him and his friends a bunch of questions, and there's a coupla government guys comin' up today to look at these cattle."

"Ah," I said. "An audit. That's not unusual."

"But they're not just looking at Dr. Winegard's books. They're doin' a bunch of his dentist friends, too."

Dave threw up his hands. "Like what kind of shady characters are these dentists, anyway?"

"Look," I said. "There's nothing to worry about. They're not auditing you. Just be polite and show them you have nothing to hide. You might take them to lunch at the Red Hen."

Willy scratched his neck. "Now there's a good idea," he said. "We're gonna be kinda busy. Could you take them to lunch for us? Like, you know how to talk to these people."

I don't know why, but I said yes. They asked me to be sure to put the visitors in the corner booth by the kitchen. By the time it occurred to me to ask why, they were gone. I met the audit team in the Red Hen restaurant at twelve o'clock. A man and a woman, carrying clipboards and a map of the township. I rose and introduced myself.

"So," I asked. "Are you all done?"

"Done?" said the young man. "No, no. We saw one herd this morning. We have more this afternoon, don't we?"

"Yes," said his partner. "There's another herd on the Second Line . . . that must be the other side of Larkspur."

I waved at Donna, the waitress, and she came over to take our orders. While we were sitting there, chatting, a movement at the window caught my eye. A cow's head

appeared. The next moment it bobbed its head and disappeared. Another cow appeared. I did a double take and
realized the whole street behind was obscured by the backs
of moving cattle. I went quickly over to the window and
closed the blinds.

"Gosh, that sun's hot. I thought I'd close the blinds,"
I said, grinning like an idiot. I snuck a peek out through the
slats and caught a glimpse of Dave on horseback at the back
of the herd, hat waving high above his head. I heard a distant
"Yipee-i-o-kiyay!"

"What was that?" said the auditor.

"Oh," I said. "That was me. I said, 'The pudding's tapioca
today.' Will you try some? Say, Donna, could you turn up that
radio? That's my favourite song, don't you love it? What's it
called, Donna?"

Donna stopped chewing for a moment, shifted her quid to
the other side of her mouth and said, "'I Used to Kiss Her on
the Lips but I Left Her Behind for You.'"

At four o'clock, I was back on my verandah trying to
make sense of the whole situation with Don.

"I feel like they were using me as a decoy," I said. "They
must have been trying to make the auditors think they
have more cattle than they actually do. The question is, how
many more, and why?"

Don nodded. "Mm-hmm. Pinning those boys down is
like trying to put six cats in a basket. When they get here,
we'll just turn them upside down and shake."

A few minutes later the boys drove in, grinning like
schoolboys on the last day of class.

"Good news, Uncle Walt," said Willy. "The revenooers
figger they hit a dry hole. They're headin' south."

"Is that right?" I said. "I want to see both of you . . . in my office. Come on, Don."

They filed in meekly and sat down on the couch beside the computer. Don and I drew up two chairs and sat facing them.

"Now," I said. "How many cattle do you boys have?"

"Let's see," Willy said, stroking his chin and studying the ceiling. "On the home place there'd be . . ."

"Never mind that stuff," interrupted Don. "We want a number. Now."

Willy swallowed, looked at Dave and looked back at us. "A hundred and twenty-five."

"All right," said Don. "Who do they belong to?"

"I guess, like, originally . . . Dr. Winegard."

"You guess. Now what cattle were those auditors looking for?"

"I don't know. Maybe . . . the other ones? Ya see, Dr. Winegard got nine of his dentist friends to send us a hundred thousand dollars each to buy cattle. Well, we got no place to put that many cattle. What were we supposed to do?"

"Normally, you give the money back," said Don.

Willy and Dave looked at each other in surprise. "Jeez," said Willy. "We never thought of that. Anyway we bought a contract for feeder cattle on the Chicago futures market."

"But how did you do that?" I asked.

"On your computer, Uncle Walt."

"But you can't do that. You can't speculate in that market without a licence. The machine won't let you make a transaction unless you use my password—"

"Spike," said Dave. "It wasn't that hard, Uncle Walt. We got it on the third try."

I got a sinking feeling in the pit of my stomach. "Omigosh," I said. "You bought nine hundred thousand dollars worth of cattle futures under my name?"

"Jeez no," said Willy. "It was a lot more than that. We put the whole wad in your margin account. All you need is five percent down. You can tie up a lot of cattle that way. Hey, Dave. What did we figger nine hundred thousand got us?"

Dave tapped on the calculator on my desk. "Let's see, if five percent is nine hundred thousand, then a hundred percent would be . . . is it this button here?"

I snatched up the calculator and punched in the numbers. Eighteen million dollars. I put a hand over my eyes and waited for my head to clear.

"What's the price of cattle been doing since you bought this contract?" I asked finally.

"Gone down like a stone," said Dave brightly. "Nearly twenty cents."

"So, in three months' time, if the price doesn't recover, you will both be on the hook for two point four million dollars. What did you plan to do then?"

"We thought the responsible thing to do would be to make a run for the border. Unless you got some ideas, Uncle Walt. You do have some ideas, don't you?"

"Yes, I certainly do. I call the Securities Commission. Then I call the fraud squad."

The boys shrank back in horror. Don put his hand on my arm.

"You can't do that to them, Walt," he said solemnly.

"Why not, may I ask?"

"They aren't employees. They're your kin."

I looked out the open window as a bumblebee bumped against the screen, dropped to the sill, crawled up and dropped again. Don finally broke the silence.

"Can you get them out of it?"

"I don't know," I muttered. "Maybe. We'll have to dump the whole business right now."

"But who's goin' to touch it?" asked Dave.

"As it stands right now . . . nobody. We'll have to make it more attractive. What I can do is put together a butterfly spread." They all looked at me blankly. "You know, a hedge contract based on a matrix of contradictory speculative outcomes."

Willy nodded hopefully. "Oh, yeah. One of those . . ."

"Say you're deciding what to plant," I explained as patiently as I could. "The variables are temperature and rainfall. For hot and wet you plant rice . . . for hot and dry . . . cactus, I guess. For cold and wet . . . mushrooms. For cold and dry . . ."

"Martinis?" offered Willy.

"Whatever. If you plant all four crops: rice, cactus, mushrooms and juniper, one of them is certain to be a winner. So, we have to build an investment model that works the same way only for cattle futures. Now . . . let's see what's out there."

I leaned over the computer and tapped into the Chicago market. Over the next half hour we took large positions in cattle in three corners of the planet. For me it was like going back in time . . . to twenty years ago on the commodities desk at MacFeeters, Bartlett and Hendrie. The difference was, in those days I didn't know any better. And my nerves were a lot younger.

Willy looked over my shoulder at the screen. "What's that number there, Uncle Walt?"

"At this precise moment, that is our total liability."

Willy whistled softly. "Hokey jeez, I thought it was your social insurance number."

"All right," I said. "Now . . . we fold the whole thing together and put a 'For Sale' sign on it."

"You're not getting yourself into trouble on account of us, are you, Uncle Walt?" asked Willy. "Maggie would drown us in a sack like a couple of kittens."

Dave agreed. "She'd stake us out on an anthill—"

There was a beep and I looked back at the screen. An offer was coming up now. A very reasonable offer, it seemed to me.

"See there?" I said. "I can get you out of the contract for that figure."

Dave worked the calculator furiously. "I guess if we sell the cattle we got now, we could just pay the dentists back. But then we'll have worked all summer for nothin'."

"So what?" said Willy. "We worked last summer for nothin', too. Go ahead and sell it, Uncle Walt."

I put one finger up in the air. "There's one condition. Neither of you ever touch this machine again without me in this room. Is that clear?"

They both crossed their hearts and spit. I clicked the mouse on the "confirm sale" button and waited. The machine burbled for sixty seconds and a confirmation code finally appeared on the screen. I accepted it and the sale was complete.

"Done," I sighed.

"So . . . who bought it, Walt?" asked Don.

I looked at the bottom of the screen. "It says, 'The Christian Democratic Front for Peaceful Change of San Carlo de . . . ' Holy smoke, it's that new military junta in South America. We'd better do the paperwork on this right away. They have anthills, too."

Yours sincerely,
Walt

———— *July* 7

Dear Ed,

This morning, I decided to move the millstone. I've learned a bit about this kind of civil engineering over the past few years. Nothing beats a team of horses for moving something heavy and awkward up a slope that's too steep for conventional machinery. Last year, I won Don's grudging admiration when I managed to get Feedbin and Mortgage to haul a load of cedar posts out of the swamp. Since then I've refined the technique by putting King in the middle. He acts as a kind of chaperone to the ladies, keeping them from having too much fun. I even had a set of heavy harness made up to accommodate the three of them. I pulled a length of heavy logging chain out of the shed and we set off down the Centre Road in the direction of Hollyhock.

The village was its usual idyllic self. Some kids with their parents were at the playground by the bridge. There were several cars parked and some fishermen on the bridge itself. I waved to them as I steered the horses off the road and we made our way down the steep embankment. The fishermen waved back. When we got to the riverbank, I tied the horses to a cedar branch.

The millstone lay, as I'd seen it before, half-submerged on a gravel bed below the ruined millrace, creating a little V-shaped eddy in the water. I waded out through the steady current with the logging chain and studied this fabled piece of masonry. It was a fairly ordinary millstone: about four feet across and maybe ten inches thick. Standing this close, I could see it wasn't lying flat; it was wedged into the gravel and on the high side there was a cavity of about six inches underneath. It occurred to me that it would be possible to haul this thing out of the river without actually touching it. Not that it made any difference, of course. I bent down and put my hand in the cold water, gingerly reaching towards the millstone.

"FFFFDDDDDD!" said Feedbin from the riverbank. It gave me a start. I looked up and down the river and found no hazards in sight. A small crowd had gathered on the bridge. They appeared to be watching me. I dropped the hook end of the chain through the hole in the stone and reached into the water again to pull it through the other side. Something moved against my hand and I jerked it out again, almost losing my balance in the current. A crayfish shot out from under the stone.

I looked up at the line of faces on the bridge. "Crayfish," I called to them and smiled. I picked up the hook again and fastened it snugly back on the chain. Then I waded out of the stream to the horses, who were now staring at me.

"I didn't touch it," I promised. "No hands."

I untied them, backed them gently into the water and hooked up the chain. Now, using King as an anchor horse in tricky pulls like this has always made the kind of difference that an insurance company would really appreciate. Without him, as the poet says, things fall apart; the centre cannot hold. With him, we have two speeds: dead slow and stop.

I gathered up the lines and clucked softly. The horses stepped forward, the chain snapped up out of the water, the stone slid a few inches sideways and disappeared under the surface. The crowd at the bridge watched intently. The mill-stone slid a few more feet, bounced gently against a stone and emerged at the water's edge.

"Okay, you guys . . . but slowly now . . . Giddyup!"

We started up the bank. Suddenly I felt that old familiar tremor pass through the horses. Feedbin started cantering on the spot, Mortgage stood up on her hind legs, ears flat, eyes staring wildly. I fought to control them. King held his ground. Thank heavens for King. Then, suddenly, King lost his mind. He took a gigantic leap forward, then another and another. I tumbled back, tripped over the chain and found myself face to face with the millstone, careering up the hill. I had two choices: either hang onto the chain or find out first-hand what the Miller McNabb had discovered about meeting the mill-stone at high speed. I decided to hang on, and an awesome force hauled me up the slope. My grip loosened and I slid down the chain until my feet were touching the millstone. The horses gained the crest of the hill, scrambled sideways and stopped, snorting and trembling. The millstone and I bounced along the face of the bluff, then swung out into empty space.

"Whooaa . . . whooaaa . . ." I prayed. The horses stood together, trembling above me. "This is okay," I thought. If they would just stay put. "Whoa there, horsies. For once in your pea-brained lives, please just stay whooaaed."

I'd swung out into a gorge where the embankment had eroded. The drop beneath me wasn't all the way to the river; only about halfway, but still far enough. King was calming down. I could see figures racing off the bridge. Help was on its way. If the horses stayed still and the harness held, everything would be all right.

It was good harness. The fittings were brass; the tugs were made of triple-laminated horsehide. Mennonites had sewn it all together by hand. They were good fellows, those Mennonites. They use that tough, sinewy, white thread . . . I looked up and saw some of that stupid, flimsy, white thread going pip! . . . pip!

At the hospital they took X-rays and put me in a bed for observation. When I woke up, Maggie and Freddy were standing at my bedside.

"You made the papers this time, Walt," said Freddy.

"Thanks for coming, both of you," I croaked.

Maggie shook her head. "I just seem to go from hospital to hospital these days. How's your head, dear?"

"Oh, I'm fine. I just got a bit of a bump."

"A bump?" said Freddy. "Walt, when you came around you made a speech thanking the rescue party for coming out to the annual meeting."

Maggie leaned forward and looked me squarely in the eye. "Are you well enough to tell me just what you thought you were doing down there at the mill?"

"I just wanted to show people there's nothing wrong with it as a museum site. They've got this notion that the millstone's cursed. I suppose you know all about it."

"Of course I've heard of it!" she exclaimed. "It's the excuse you hear whenever someone suggests cleaning up the trash in that river. I guess there's a few cursed washing machines and bedsteads down there, too. Walt, do you think you might give this museum idea a bit of a rest?"

"You think I'm being obsessive? It's just that it's a good idea, and it seems a shame we can't do it as long as people have this cockeyed notion of a curse."

Freddy looked at the ceiling and cleared his throat. "You may have dug yourself in deeper there, Walt. The newspaper story says a couple of the eyewitnesses claim they saw the Miller McNabb riding King up that bank, in a black robe, with no head."

"What? Oh, wonderful! But, wait a minute. If the rider had no head, how could they tell it was . . . oh, never mind."

Yours sincerely,

Walt

———— *July 15*

Dear Ed,

Last night Maggie and I were finishing up the dishes when the house shuddered. We both went to the window and looked out. The wind was up, but the sky was clear and the moon shone down on the fields. It all looked peaceful enough to me.

"There's water in her eye," said Maggie ominously.

"There's what?"

"The moon. You can tell there's a blow coming in. Are the barn doors shut?"

I looked again at the moon. There was a ring of vapoury blue light around it. I checked the wall barometers we got for our wedding. They all said "fair and dry."

"Never mind those things, Walt. Look at the moon. Did you latch the barn doors shut?"

By now I know that voice. I stepped out onto the verandah. The wind was up, all right. It whipped the screen door out of my hands and banged it shut behind me. I closed up the tool shed and the henhouse, then dashed over to the barn and pushed the big sliding door shut. I always get a surge of energy, battening down for a storm. When I'm done I like to stand for a minute on the gangway and marvel at the power of the elements. It's exhilarating to see the clouds tumble across the night sky and the wind make the young oak trees bend double and flap furiously.

Actually, I'd never seen them do that before. The sky certainly was an odd colour, too. Then, I heard a loud bang and looked over to see that the door of the henhouse had blown open. There was only one hen left, but I didn't want to lose the door. The henhouse was straight upwind, and it took me a few moments to get there. When I did, the door was flapping hard against the wall. It took everything I had to bring it around into the wind and close it.

A pail flew by. I guess the tool shed was open again. I jogged over to check on it. More stuff was blowing by me, including some pretty big wooden boards. Something soft bounced off my shoulder. It was the hen, headed east, out of control. I looked back and saw that the henhouse had disappeared. Then Maggie was there beside me. She was speaking, but I could barely hear her voice over the roar of the wind.

"Come to the house, Walt. NOW!"

Then the rain hit. We ran over to the house. In the shelter of the verandah, we looked back towards the barn. A flash of lightning revealed it for a moment, just long enough for us to see a section of steel roof curling up to the peak like an orange peel.

"There's nothing we can do," said Maggie. "Come inside."

We lay in bed in our bedroom off the kitchen, listening to the storm hammer the house. When a gust of wind hit, the whole house would lean and creak and go "whub-a-whub-a-whub." Then the wind dropped and it lurched back again.

"You don't suppose there's the slightest chance of the house blowing over, do you?" I asked.

Maggie looked around at the room. "If it does," she said, "this window will be on the floor, the floor will be that wall there, and the wood stove will come through," she glanced at the ceiling, "about here." We went down to the basement and spent the rest of the night on the sofa bed.

Next morning we went out to look at the damage. All the steel had blown off the south half of the barn roof and the boards were all blown out of the gable end. The big sliding door had disappeared. The tool shed was gone, the henhouse was gone and the yard was littered with debris.

"What a mess," sighed Maggie. "I'd better get down to the shop and see what the damage is in town."

As she drove off, the Squire appeared, carrying my hen.

"Found this bird on my verandah," he said, handing her to me. "I think she's about due for a therapist. And, say, is that your barn door floating in my pond?"

"In your pond? Good heavens. So, what's the damage at your place?"

"No damage. Why, did you get a bit of wind last night?"

"A bit of wind?" I snorted. "More like a hurricane! Look at the place."

"That's funny," he said. "I didn't notice anything. I had coffee with Freddy and Don this morning. They didn't talk about any storm."

We went back to the kitchen, where I made a few calls and verified that no one else on the Seventh Line was aware of a windstorm last night. I looked at the Squire.

"This is weird. I know isolated windstorms happen, but

do you think there might be something to this curse thing, after all?"

The Squire sat down at the kitchen table and took a big breath.

"Did I ever tell you about John Hand?" he asked. I shook my head. "John Hand had a great team of bloods, and he was very proud of them. They must have been the nicest looking team of horses in the county. John would spend extra time with them, feedin' them up and brushin' them till their coats shone. He loved them horses. On Sundays, if the weather was bad, he'd stay home from church rather than leave the team in an open shed. Well, one night in the fall, John Hand's barn burned to the ground. He lost all his stock, maybe twelve heifer cows and the same number of calves, all the year's hay and grain and that beautiful team of bloods.

"Folks pitched in, and we got John through the winter, and in the spring we helped him build again. I wasn't much more than a kid then, but I helped, too; I just got into the habit of walkin' up there when I could and I'd put in an afternoon with him. One day we were workin' on a fence and John turns to me and says, 'I know why that barn burned.' I thought he meant someone had set the fire on purpose and I didn't know what to say. And then John says, 'I was worshipping horse flesh instead of the Lord.'"

"Wait a minute," I said. "He thought God burned his barn down?"

The Squire nodded. "That's what he thought."

"And is that what you think?"

The Squire sighed. "Well, I don't know. But John Hand was the only man I ever knew who would smoke in a barn.

Myself, I think God kept that barn standing as long as He could and it was John who burned it down."

"So, what you're saying is that I should look for an ordinary explanation for all of this?"

The Squire did not reply.

"I'm going back to the mill and figure out what really made the horses bolt. Enough of this nonsense."

"In that case, I'd better go with you. Maggie asked me to keep an eye on you."

The Squire drove me down the Centre Road to Hollyhock. We parked by the mill and walked over to the edge of the bank. The millstone lay below us, halfway down the slope, caught in a cleft made by two birch saplings. We helped each other down the embankment, noticing the skid marks the stone had made on its way up the slope. Near the bottom, I saw the first deep gouges in the clay that showed where the horses got excited. I pointed to them.

"It was right about here that King went nuts. But I don't see anything." Something moved on the ground and made me jump.

"What is it, Walt?" asked the Squire.

We both looked closer. There was a rustle in a clump of dead cedar twigs and a big fat toad climbed out and blinked at us. I guess he was sleeping.

"That explains it, then," said the Squire.

"It does?"

"It made you jump, didn't it? A horse can't stand that sort of thing. Makes him think the ground is moving."

"Really? Well, so much for the curse, eh? Do you suppose if I kissed him he would turn into the Miller McNabb?"

We followed Mr. Toad as he hopped down the bank towards

the river. I looked out into the river to the spot where the millstone had been and saw a glint of sunlight reflect off something under the water. Something shiny. I waded out and took a closer look. It was a clover-shaped piece of metal, half buried in the gravel. I reached in and pulled out an old brass key.

"Well, I'll be . . ." I marvelled.

"Walt! Can you come here a minute?"

"Look what I found," I said, holding up the key.

"Walter! Come here . . . NOW!"

I jogged over to him quickly to see what was the matter.

"Are you all right?" I asked.

It made hardly a sound. I'd never have heard it from down by the water. Just a faint crack of wood, like a twig snapping. By the time I looked up, the millstone was flipping through the air like a huge coin in slow motion. It smashed into the riverbed right where I'd been standing and broke into three pieces.

Neither of us said anything for a long moment. Finally the Squire said, "I reckon that'll be easier to move now."

I stared at him in amazement. "You knew that was going to happen, didn't you?"

The Squire shut his eyes and nodded. "Yeah, I did. I saw it. A couple of days ago. At the time I didn't know when it was happening. Not till I seen you standing there."

"So these things you've been seeing, some of them, they are real. They just haven't happened yet."

"Maybe they've happened a lot of times, Walt. Just not to us."

"You saved my life."

The Squire nodded again. He looked frail and frightened. "Can we go home now?" he asked.

We hear a lot these days about the Internet, as if it were some kind of new development. We've had it in Persephone

Township for many years. Only we call it "the party line." Of course, it's more efficient than the Internet, because instead of "logging on" for hours in the hope of finding something interesting, with the party line you just have to memorize the individualized ring of whomever it is you want to eavesdrop on.

Another superior feature is that, with practice, you can tell approximately how many other eavesdroppers there are, because with a party line the more phones that are off the hook, the less current goes to each phone and the harder it is to hear. When the Squire and I got back to his place, I phoned Maggie at the store.

"He saved my life, Maggie. It's the most amazing thing!"

"That's nice, Walt. I'll see you at home, dear."

"But, Maggie, don't you see, he knew it was going to happen because he'd already seen it. You understand? These things he's been seeing—some of them—are in the future!"

Maggie's voice was fainter now. "That's fine, dear. Bye-bye now."

"I beg your pardon?"

"I said that's fine, Walt. Bye now."

"I can hardly hear you, Maggie . . ."

"Just a minute, Walt. THIS IS A PRIVATE CONVERSATION. COULD YOU ALL PLEASE HANG UP!"

There was a series of clicks and Maggie's voice came up loud and clear again.

"We can talk about this at home, dear. Now hang up."

The Squire sighed. "I'd kinda hoped this coulda been our little secret, Walt."

"Oh. Sorry."

Yours sincerely,
Walt

Dear Ed,

Next morning Spike and I rose with the sun and went down to do chores. At this time of year, with everyone out on pasture, there aren't many chores to do. I just put out some feed for the chicken and there's one cow, Cupcakes, to milk. Instead of chasing her up to the barn, I decided to take the pail down to her under an apple tree by the pond. I sat down in the grass beside her and milked her out while she chewed and burped. The sun was beginning to warm my face through the morning mist. A gentle breeze rustled the leaves, bringing the fence-rows to life.

"How are you now, Walt?"

It was the Squire. "I feel great, thanks," I grinned. "You're up early."

"Yeah, it's too nice to stay in. This is the kind of morning it's fun to be a farmer. Makes everything look special. Well, how about that! Look there."

I rose quickly. "Good Lord, what do you see now?"

But when I looked, I saw it, too. The little field beside the pond had turned snow white overnight. It was supposed to be a hayfield, but now it was thick with blooms of buckwheat. I hadn't planted buckwheat there. Last year it was a plot of corn and everybody laughed because I decided to harvest the corn myself by hand. Actually the four pigs kept me company. They ate while I picked, and by Thanksgiving there was enough shelled corn in the barn to last Cupcakes all winter and the pigs weighed two hundred pounds. The field was a mess, so I just ran the disks over it last fall and scattered hayseed early this spring. But the Squire had an explanation.

"Old Fisher must have had buckwheat there sometime, years ago. The seed's been lyin' in the field all this time and, what with the pigs rootin' and the corn husks rottin', it was just the right conditions for nature to hand you a little surprise."

"That makes sense," I said. "I've had my weight on the wrong foot about this museum thing, haven't I? I've been afraid of surprises, afraid of things changing. I mean, it's good to honour the past, but you can't gather it into your lap and hang on to it."

The Squire nodded. "That's what the Miller McNabb tried to do."

"And that's the real curse, isn't it? Life goes on . . . things change. And the change isn't always bad. It could be a field of buckwheat or a stand of pin oaks on Calvin Currie's hill. They'll be there sooner or later, won't they?"

The old man grinned at me and poked me in the shoulder. "Be there sooner if you plant 'em, Walt."

That evening after supper, Maggie and I drove down to the Orange Hall in Larkspur for the Berry Festival Dance. The Price Family Orchestra was once quite large, but over the years it has dwindled in size and repertoire. They're down to three members and four tunes.

Maggie twirled over to me in her blue dress. "Come on, Walt," she coaxed. "They're playing our song. Let's waltz."

"'When You and I Were Young,' Maggie? That's not a waltz."

"It is the way *they* play it."

We danced around the hall. Maggie sang into my ear, and suddenly there were just two people in the world, floating on a gentle river of creaky violin music and thumping piano chords.

> I wandered today to the hill, Walter,
> To watch the scene below.
> The creek and the creaking old mill, Walter,
> As we used to long ago.

Then it was my turn:

> The green grove is gone from the hill, Maggie,
> Where first the daisies sprung.
> The creaking old mill is still, Maggie,
> Since you and I were young.

Maggie stopped suddenly, as if she'd forgotten a casserole in the oven at home.

"Oh, dear," she said. "Excuse me, Walt. I'll be right back."

"What's the matter? Is something . . . ?"

But she was gone. The Squire walked by me, followed closely by Willy. The Squire looked irritated.

"Willy, quit buggin' me!" he snarled.

"Aw, c'mon, Squire," pleaded Willy. "Next Wednesday. Demeter Downs Raceway. Our guest. You look over the racing form and, no pressure, we'll just see what comes to you."

The Squire waved him away. "It doesn't work like that. I can't turn it on and off like a light bulb."

"Okay, okay," said Willy. "Tell you what. We try Chicago again; it's perfect . . . we do the cattle, you do the futures."

The Squire stopped and touched his forehead. "Something's comin' to me now . . . flashing red lights. Cruisers. Bars on windows. G'day, Freddy . . . Don."

"Mrs. Lynch wants you to have a look at her bingo card, Squire," said Don solemnly.

"And when you're done there, could you have a peek at my Pick Six numbers for the Nevada?" said Freddy.

"No, I couldn't! Now back off, all of yas!"

The band struck up "The Crooked Stovepipe," and Freddy grabbed the microphone. The hall divided itself magically into groups of eight, and Freddy launched into one of his convoluted square dance calls.

"Ladies and Gentlemen," he announced. "This here's called 'Wingfield in the Straw.'"

> Four hands up, and away we go
> Around the hall with a do-see-do
> Walt quit the job and bought some land
> A hundred acres of rocks and sand.
>
> The rooster goes out, and the hen goes in
> The coons are killin' those chickens again
> Three hands round, the fourth is free
> So Walt and Maggie are at the K.F.C.
>
> Grand Chain!
>
> First couple off, second fills the void,
> Walt needed a ram, so he bought Pink Floyd
> Third couple off, let 'em all pass
> Floyd turned out to be a pain in the . . .

"How are you doin' down there?"

> Form a star with a right-hand cross.
> King did a bolt and gave Walt the toss.
> Swing her the half, and give her heck
> And Walt had a millstone round his neck.

When the dust settled, Mrs. Price brought us back full circle to the comparative calm of "When You and I Were Young." I found myself in a group with Freddy, Don and the Squire. The Squire raised his glass to me in a salute.

"Lovely evening, Walt. The kind you'll tell your children about."

"My children? Have you seen something?"

"Now, don't you start, Walt. You don't have to be Isaiah to see it. That healthy glow . . ."

"Yep," Don agreed. "And that smug look they get . . ."

Freddy nodded. "And when they plugged in the coffee urn back there, she ran outside and threw up."

Maggie appeared again in the half door of the kitchen. I excused myself and trotted over to her.

"Are you all right?" I asked.

"Just fine, Walt. Where were we?"

"'And now we are aged and grey.' Maggie . . . ?" She took my hand and put her cheek next to mine. "Did you have anything you wanted to tell me?" I asked.

"I was waiting for the test results to make it official," she whispered. "But it seems the only people who don't know are the doctor . . . and you."

"Well . . ." I said. "Surprise, surprise!"

"Imagine, at our age. Are you pleased?"

I held her closer and sang softly in her ear:

But to me you are fair as the day, Maggie,
When you and I were young.

Yours sincerely,
Walt

So that's the way it went. Dr. Winegard and his friends got their money back from the cattle venture and sank the whole wad into the mill property. They turned it into a restaurant called the Brass Key. The story of the Miller McNabb is printed on the placemats, and the key hangs in a glass case over the fireplace. Some say the curse is broken, but I don't know. A week after the opening, the chef quit and they had to bring in Donna from the Red Hen. She fought with the cappuccino machine for three days, then she threw it out the back door over the waterfall. It lies on its side in midstream at the bottom, and nobody will touch it.

The Seventh Line wanted to hold a barn-raising for Walt and Maggie, but you need good weather for that sort of thing. So they asked the Squire to pick the day. He went into a room by himself and shut the door. When he didn't come out, they got worried and peeked in. It looked like he'd gone into some kind of trance. Turned out he was on the phone, on hold with the Environment Canada weather office. Anyway they picked August the 10th, and it turned out perfect.

It was quite a sight. Men swarmed over the rafters like bees on a honeycomb. Willy and Dave scrambled up to the very top, nailed the ridgepole beam into place, then stood up on it, balancing beer bottles on their foreheads, making the girls scream. Maggie handed out hard hats to the ground crew. By the end of the day it was done, and they christened it with a barn dance that very night, with the Price Family Orchestra.

Maggie and Walt want to name the baby after the Squire . . . if it's a boy . . . but it turns out the Squire's real name is Baxter Fortescue. At school, the kids used to call him Back Forty. Anyway, if it's a girl, they think they might call her Hope.

Oh, and there's more surprises all the time. We just got word on the radio news that the new military junta in South America has collapsed in bankruptcy. No details yet, but authorities credit a brilliant but mysterious financial force known only as Spike.

Chapter Five

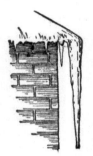

Wingfield

ON ICE

ANOTHER NOTE FROM THE EDITOR

After a lot of ups and downs, Walt was riding a wave now. He and Maggie had bread on the table and a bun in the oven. But no sooner had he accepted the idea that change was not necessarily fatal to his beloved Persephone, than another, more serious issue reared its head.

If a dog bites a man, it's not news; if a man bites a dog, *that's* news. At least that's what they say in the newspaper business. But if you run a small-town weekly it's not that simple. You have to be circumspect. Let me offer a case in point from today's paper:

> "Once again, the Humane Society was summoned after an encounter between J. Roberts of 84 Norman Street and Muffie of 86 Norman Street. Following a brief discussion, no charges were preferred, as it was ascertained that both parties' vaccinations were up to date."

It's a kind of code. The writer understands it; the experienced reader understands it; and our lawyers understand it. Here's another one:

> "During the lively discussion on the extension of
> the Town water line to the Scotch Settlement
> Road, Councillor Ramsay was quite clearly over-
> wrought. Mr. Ramsay is usually overwrought at
> evening council meetings and is sometimes over-
> wrought as early as ten o'clock in the morning."

Because of all the long-standing feuds that simmer along
the back roads of this community, you always have to remember that you're walking on eggshells. You just never know
when what you write will make, as Shakespeare would have
it, "ancient grudge break to new mutiny."

If you grow up here, the fractious nature of the community is just part of the furniture, and you don't even think
about it much. But to a newcomer like Walt, it can be disturbing. Not that Walt has been sensitive to slander lately. On the
contrary, nothing seems to bother him. He's been walking
around with a perpetual grin plastered on his face ever since
Maggie announced she was expecting.

——— *September 25*

Dear Ed,
I left Maggie sleeping this morning and stepped out onto the
verandah. The first hard frost had come during the night,
turning the cedar shingles and rail fences white. Wherever
the first rays of sunshine landed, steam rose into the air.

I've seen this all before—and if you've had a child I guess
you know this feeling—but it's as if I'm seeing it for the first
time. And it's so beautiful. I just can't wait for our kid to see it all.

Not that we're taking anything for granted. Maggie's
strong and healthy but she's thirty-eight years old, having her

first pregnancy. She had the amnio at week fourteen, and that was fine, but past the thirty-fifth week we have to have regular fetal assessments.

I don't know when Maggie will find the time. She hasn't slowed down on her chores, but it isn't that. It's the circle of women—cousins, aunts, neighbours, friends—who treat a pregnancy as a community project. The baby's room is full of socks and booties, blankets, quilts . . . soon there won't be any room for the baby. It's nice, but it's overwhelming.

And they're very prickly about protocol. There was so much competition over who would host the baby shower that Maggie had to arrange a series of smaller events to unruffle all the feathers. Freddy came over yesterday afternoon while Maggie was preparing for yet another prenatal get-together, baking enough chocolate eclairs to feed Napoleon's army. I was standing at the kitchen counter, grating lemons for a half-acre of lemon tarts. Even Freddy had been drafted and was grudgingly poking a single blueberry into each tart for decoration.

Maggie patted me on the shoulder as she went by. "They're just excited for us, Walt. They want to help."

"I understand that," I said. "But there's so many of them. You know, 'how many supervisors does it take . . . ?'"

"You can't fight The Sisterhood," said Freddy. "I've seen 'em in action. They bring in the next-youngest kid and look at the twist of its hair—that tells 'em whether the baby's gonna be a boy or a girl. They float a needle on a thread over the stomach of the pregnant woman and watch which way it turns. And that's just the stuff they let us guys know about. I'm tellin' ya—don't leave your pets out after dark."

Maggie laughed. "Oh, stop it, Freddy. You'll frighten Walt. He's used to quiet, harmless women . . . on the floor of the stock exchange. And besides, a lot of the sisterhood are very experienced. They say they can tell that the baby's head size and shape are good, its pulse response to movement is normal, and it makes the right number of kicks per hour."

"You know I don't believe in mumbo-jumbo, Walt," she said seriously. "I do believe in the ultrasound. When you were in the city yesterday, Dr. Brigham did an ultrasound and it said the same thing. I think one should always get a second opinion."

She stepped out on the verandah to snip Johnny-jump-ups for the tarts, and Freddy leaned over to me.

"You got pregnant at the wrong time, Walt. The crops are off, the pickles and preserves are down, and these women have got time on their hands. I saw a coupla them down at Dry Cry's the other day pickin' out the baby's first firearm."

In all fairness, it isn't just the women around here who regard a pregnancy as a public affair. I had the 4×4 at Ron's garage in Larkspur for the water pump at eight in the morning one day last summer and heard the following conversation over the snarl of impact air drills and the blare of Rock 95 radio:

"I think Helen's water broke last night."

"Yeah, I called Eric late and there was no answer."

"His car wasn't at the house this morning."

"I just did a lap of the hospital and it wasn't in the parking lot . . ."

"They'll have taken her to the Hillhurst Regional . . . she must have gone toxic like her sister."

And these were two bachelor mechanics in their early twenties. They'd correctly guessed that Helen Simpson was indeed in labour and had gone to the hospital, but because of an elevation in her blood pressure had been taken to the Hillhurst Regional, south of Highway 13.

Speaking of the water pump, it's had surgery four times now, and it's leaking again. I've watched Ron patch it enough times that I've sort of got the hang of it. Just takes a roll of Teflon tape and three hands. But this morning I decided I'd better get it fixed. Maggie's not due for a couple of months, but what if the baby's a "preemie"? I can't drive her to the hospital with the horses.

I was upside down in the engine compartment with a flashlight in my teeth, just getting the Teflon to a point where I could tighten it and make a seal . . . when it broke. Then the phone rang. I slithered back out and trotted over to the workbench for my remote phone. It was Freddy.

"How are you now, Walt?"

"Oh, I dunno," I said. "This damn water thing broke and I don't know what to do."

Freddy paused for a moment. "Are you gonna take her in, Walt?" he asked.

"I'm afraid to take her in," I said. "What if she seizes up on the highway?"

"You gotta take her in, Walt. Hang on, I'll be right over."

He hung up. I've never got used to the way people up here never say goodbye on the telephone. They just hang up. I went back to the 4×4 and stuck my head back down beside the radiator. The phone rang again. I squirmed out again and went back to the workbench. It was the Squire.

"I just talked to Freddy," he said. "He sounded kinda worried. He says this is it."

"It?" I snorted. "Well, maybe it is. She's been nothing but trouble since I got her."

"Walt," he said quickly. "Don't do anything, I'll be right over."

It's funny how they all get interested in a mechanical project at about the same time I'm ready to give up. The power windows don't work, the air conditioning quit last summer, the door hinges barely hold the doors in place. It just goes on and on. I took the phone with me on the next trip into the engine compartment. Sure enough, it rang again. This time it was Don.

"Walt?" he said. "I just talked to the Squire. He says you're talkin' kind of wild. Now, Walt, a lot of guys go through this; you're not thinking straight. You gotta take your time."

"Time?!" I scoffed. "Do you have any idea how much time I've wasted on this already? And there's no point being sentimental. I think I'm ready to drive her off a cliff somewhere."

The line went dead. A few minutes later, Don, the Squire, Freddy and the police officer from Larkspur arrived about the same time. Maggie appeared at the kitchen door with a tray of lemon tarts and leaned on the door frame.

"Well, I see nothing's changed around here," she sighed. "It still takes four supervisors for one man to work on a water pump. If we had a light bulb to change, we could get the whole Seventh Line down here."

Yours sincerely,

Walt

———— *October 10*

Dear Ed,

The Squire's real name is actually Baxter Fortescue, but nobody calls him that. I only know this because it's the name printed on the side of his mailbox. The Squire doesn't get a lot of mail. He does get a pension cheque once a month, but weeks go by without that little red flag going up. The only

reason he goes out to the mailbox is to pull bird's nests out of it. I've watched him in a constant struggle with the blackbirds since I moved up here. This year he installed a 'bang' stick on the mailbox. It's a contraption they use for scaring birds out of orchards. It's basically an over-sized air gun that goes off every fifteen minutes or so. The blackbirds soon got used to it . . . but it gets the postman every time.

There's an unopened letter on the shelf behind the Squire's wood stove that appears to be about fifty years old. That could explain why he doesn't get a lot of return mail. It's propped up between a share stock certificate from the long-defunct Persephone Oil Shale Company and a Hillhurst County quarantine notice for rabies, dated 1923. When I dropped in on the Squire yesterday for a cup of coffee, I pushed a copy of the newspaper across the table to him. He squinted at the page through his reading glasses.

"What am I supposed to be looking at here, Walt?" he asked.

"Oh, it's the Auction Register," I said, pointing to the classified section. "There's a listing here on the Prince of Wales Road for an Augustus Fortescue. I was just wondering if that could be a relation of yours."

The Squire studied the listing for a moment and gave one of his short nods. "You could say that. He's my brother." He handed the paper back to me.

"Your brother? I didn't know you had a brother."

The Squire leaned back and turned to the window. "Sure is dry for this time of year," he said. "You know that damp spot up at the north end of the pasture? That used to be a pond. I got a bullfrog up there . . . he's three years old and he's never learned how to swim. What do you make of that?"

It was difficult to know what to make of it, all right. You know, Ed, I used to think that everybody up here got along like one big happy family. I'm finally beginning to realize that every second house along the concession road is nursing an ancient feud that dates back to the Crusades. The Squire has a brother he doesn't want to talk about, but it isn't just that. Freddy and the Squire have an ongoing fight about a steer. Calvin Currie and Don haven't really spoken to each other for four years since a famous incident when Don built his new state-of-the-art dairy barn and invited all the farmers in the area to an open house. I was standing next to Don when Calvin walked into the barn and stopped to gaze up at the spiderweb of steel truss work that supported the high ceilings. Calvin's a big man, a little past retirement age, and he has what I call the old dairyman's flinch. Forty years of bending over at the waist in a damp barn has given him a back problem that makes him wince every time he has to look up in the air.

"So, Calvin, what do you think?" asked Don.

Calvin made a noise in his throat like he was choking up a bug.

"Think?" he snorted. "Think what God could do if he had the money!" And he walked stiffly over to the lunch table to pick out a sandwich. Don was still sore about it an hour later when the last of the guests were departing. He watched Calvin climb into his weather-beaten pickup and jerk the door shut.

"That old skinflint," he muttered. "He's so cheap—you know he gave up drinkin' tea because he lost his tea bag."

I suppose we should be grateful that they don't take up blunt instruments and kill each other. They think it's more sporting to wear an opponent down slowly over a half-century. We went to a funeral last summer for an old guy who lived up in Pluto Township all his life. He and his wife looked like a normal couple. You'd see them together at the occasional Pancake Supper. I thought they were a little odd because she always rode in the back seat of the car. Well, it turns out they hadn't exchanged a single word in thirty-eight years. They actually divided the house into two parts. She lived on one side and he lived on the other. She still cooked his meals, but they never spoke. There was a little sliding door in the wall between the kitchen and his room, and she would pass a plate of food through to him and shut the door. Thirty-eight years!

Back at the farm, I told Maggie about the Squire's brother. She was sitting at the kitchen table, making some duck stencils for the baby's bedroom wall.

I said, "I can't believe I've known the Squire for five years and I didn't know he had a brother. I thought we were close."

Maggie nodded and smiled. "Don't feel bad. I've been around farmers all my life and I've never heard men talk about personal things much. I've always thought the rule is, you can talk about anything except what is on your mind. All I know is, the Squire and his brother haven't spoken since before I was born. The Squire was the younger brother, but he got the farm. That's pretty unusual, so maybe that's what started it. That's how most family disagreements get going. Between neighbours it only takes a poor fence or a dog killing chickens. For people further away than next door, well, it could be almost anything."

"Did your family feud with anyone?"

Maggie rolled her eyes. "Oh, sure," she said. "Mother put candles on the altar at St. Luke's in 1965 and the Lynches wrote a letter to the bishop. Called Mother a Papist. That one's gone on for two generations."

"Mrs. Lynch? The lady beside the Orange Hall? I thought you liked her!"

Maggie looked at me in astonishment. "Walt, how could you like a woman who uses Dream Whip to make a cream puff?"

I didn't have an answer for that one.

Footsteps thumped on the verandah and Don and Freddy appeared at the screen door.

"Come on in, boys," said Maggie. "Coffee's on and I just made scones. Ask them about the Squire's brother, Walt. They probably know more than I do."

"What, Lucky Gus?" asked Don. "What do you want to know?"

"Well, for starters, why is he called Lucky?"

"Luckiest guy living," said Freddy as he slathered jam on a biscuit. "If that man shot at a pigeon and missed, he'd hit a moose."

"But he hasn't always been so lucky. I understand he lost the family farm to his younger brother."

"He did better than that!" exclaimed Freddy. "He got himself totally disinherited. The Squire was the one got chained to that hundred acres of sand hills and grey stone, and Gus was free to go off and make his fortune."

"Why was he disinherited?" I asked.

Don held out his cup for more coffee. "Gus ran off with a Catholic girl when he came back from the war," he explained. "It was a big scandal. The family was pretty staunch Orange Lodge. They cut him out of the will and wouldn't hear his name spoken in the house. What was her name?"

"Maureen Hoolihan," said Freddy with a knowing look. "And with a name like that, I wonder which foot she scratched with! Hmm?"

"Oh, yes. I remember," said Maggie. "Mum used to talk about her. They called her the Wildcat of the Pluto Marsh. She came out of one of those little shacks on the flats. They're all Catholics up there. She was like a wild animal. Red-haired, green eyes and ran around the country barefoot. My uncles were all warned."

"Ahh . . . did she have horns and a tail?" I wondered.

Maggie looked at me frankly. "Whatever she had, all the boys wanted it. But I don't know, it all happened before any of us was born."

"All right," I said. "I'm putting this together. So, Gus ran away and was disinherited. What happened after that?"

"He used his veteran's money to buy a really good farm down near the city and he never looked back," said Don.

"A good farmer, was he?"

"Nope," said Freddy reaching for the basket of scones again. "Terrible farmer. But the barn on that farm turned out to be just the spot where they wanted to build the clubhouse for the Woodbine racetrack."

"Aha," I said. "Lucky Gus."

"Lucky ain't the word for it," said Don. "I'd say he was carrying a tuba the day it rained gold."

"But this sale next month is not that far away," I pointed out. "It's just south of Highway 13. Which farm is that?"

"With all the money he got from the Woodbine farm, Gus bought three farms south of Highway 13. Now, the average guy only needs one farm to go broke. But Gus kept standing in the way of progress. One went for a gravel pit in the seventies and another went for a subdivision in the eighties. Now the last one's goin' for the Regional Hospital expansion. That's where the auction is. When that farm's gone, Gus'll have nothing left but the house and maybe twelve million dollars, poor fella."

"More good luck," I marvelled.

"Good luck?" snorted Freddy. "They used to say when Gus was down at Woodbine they never ran short of horse-shoes. They'd just get him to bend over and they'd pull one out of his—"

Maggie raised one her stencil knives in the air as a warning. "Freddy! You're not at home with the boys. And there'll soon be a child in this house."

Yours sincerely,
Walt

———— *October 15*

Dear Ed,

It is an old custom in Persephone Township that, when a girl is married, they send her off to her new farm with a dowry of linens and cookware and livestock. I was the beneficiary of this wonderful tradition. Maggie came with a complete set of Blue Willow china, a spool bed that all of her ancestors have died in since 1870, six more sheep . . . and, of course, her nephews, Willy and Dave. Unfortunately, the old custom carries a strict rule about exchanges or refunds.

In some ways, Willy and Dave are as alike as two peas in a pod: they both have a high energy level and low risk percep-tion. The only real difference between them is that animals love Dave and they hate Willy. Dave can load a herd of wild mustangs onto a trailer in the middle of a pasture armed with nothing but a carrot. Willy can't pull two rabbits out of a crate without causing property damage and personal injury.

Willy's been bitten by every dog in the township, including

Luke, his own blue heeler. Usually these incidents boil down to a simple case of ambush and counterstrike, but every so often he gets into a costly land war that drags out over a season.

One of these battles started last spring, when Willy picked up an old furnace oil tank from Isobel Meadows's place. Isobel has an almost-purebred dog we call a "borderline collie," named Pookie, who is really good with kids and has never bitten anybody. He does make a funny noise when he's excited. It's a rattling sound like a small electric motor starting up. Willy described the incident for us one day in the Red Hen.

"I was just tippin' the tank up into the back of the truck when I heard that noise . . . f-f-f-d-d-d-d-r-r . . . and felt hot teeth sinkin' into the back of my leg. I said, 'Oh, my goodness!' . . . and a couple of other things . . . and when I turned around I seen Pookie sneakin' under the hay wagon."

Isobel came out a few moments later and found Willy crouching under the hay wagon, taking wide, hard swings at the dog with a tire iron.

"Willy, what're you doing?" asked Isobel.

"I'm pickin' up that tank, Isobel. But first I'm gonna kill yer dog. He bit me."

"Pookie doesn't bite," protested Isobel.

"Oh, Pookie bites just fine," said Willy, rubbing his leg.

But the distraction was enough opportunity for Pookie. He disappeared behind the drive shed and Willy had to leave without squaring accounts. That was Round One. Round Two happened about a week later, when Willy was coming up the Seventh Line after breakfast at the Red Hen. Now, Pookie is not ordinarily a car chaser, but this day he hid behind the lilac bush by Isobel's mailbox and leapt out at the truck, causing

Willy to jerk the steering wheel violently to the left, emptying a cup of boiling-hot coffee into his lap.

"My mind started workin' really fast," recalled Willy. "I figured once the burns started to blister I probably wouldn't be able to run, so I kicked open the truck door and headed down into the ditch after Pookie."

I know the place he's talking about. It's a very steep ditch. Not the sort of ditch you should take at a gallop in a blind rage and hot underwear.

"I actually got my hand on Pookie's tail, but Pookie turned left and I was pretty well committed to the direction I was goin'—straight down through the crown vetch . . . you know that viney stuff with the purple flowers that the township sows along the roadsides to hold the banks. It grabs at your ankles like a bad dream, and before I knew it I was doin' a bobsled run without the bobsled. I was like the fella ridin' the tiger. I couldn't steer and I couldn't get off. I'd still be goin' today if it hadn't been for that barbed wire fence."

Isobel saw the truck sitting out in front of her house and went to investigate. She had to cut Willy out of the tangle of fence with a pair of pliers and drive him to the hospital for a tetanus shot. Willy stayed home for a couple of days, sitting in a pool of Rawleigh's Ointment.

The following Wednesday, Willy drove by Isobel's and swerved again, this time right instead of left. He snipped off Isobel's mailbox with the side mirror.

"I'm real sorry, Isobel," he said, when he explained the incident to Pookie's mistress. "I had to swerve on account of yer dog. Like, he was right under my wheels and I coulda had him . . . I MEAN, I MIGHTA HIT HIM . . . and that woulda been just terrible."

That episode cost Willy forty-nine dollars for a new mailbox and two hundred dollars for bodywork on the truck and a new side mirror. Pookie was well ahead on points going into Round Four.

Yours sincerely,
Walt

——— *October 20*

Dear Ed,

People up here have a long-standing tradition of using one tool to do several jobs, and the tradition extends to people's names. For instance, our farm is called the Old Fisher Place, but Fisher is the most common name in the township and that narrows it down to about four thousand acres. If you look in the phone book, you will find seven listings for A. Fisher at RR1 Larkspur. You're just expected to know by the numbers that they refer to Allan, Amos, Andy and the Anguses, that is, Angus B., Black Angus, Square-ass Angus and Tight-ass Angus. Andy Fisher often complains that, by the time he gets his mail, "It's all wore out."

My neighbour Don belongs to a veritable dynasty of Dons . . . there was Red Donald, Tall Donald, Donald the Bold, Mad Donald . . . going back seven generations. Don's oldest boy goes by the name of Young Donny. When I came here, he was a gawky kid of fourteen with high-water pants and a lot of acne. Now he's nineteen and he's filled out well. He's bigger than I am. In fact, I think he's bigger than Don. But he still calls me Mr. Wingfield . . . or sir . . . or both.

Recently, he's been dressing more carefully and has become somewhat bookish. Maggie tells me this has to do with the arrival of a new library assistant in Larkspur, a girl of his age named Kim Dodd. She has long black hair and a beautiful smile and goes about with a bare midriff that has given a real boost to business for Carl's Custom Collision out on the highway.

Donny can do anything with a car engine. He resurrected a '55 Chev pickup single-handed. He was helping me locate a short in the ignition system on the 4×4 a couple of weeks ago. He paused with the coil wire and the tester in mid-air and frowned as if some profound insight into alternating current had just occurred to him.

"Mr. Wingfield, sir," he said hesitantly. "You're pretty old, aren't you? I mean you're my dad's age . . ."

"I guess so," I said.

"But you married Mrs. Wingfield just about a year and a half ago. How'd you do it, sir?"

"What do you mean?"

Donny screwed up his face and shut his eyes for a moment. Finally he blurted out. "I mean . . . how'd you get her to marry you?"

I finished scrubbing the battery cable clamp I was working on. "Is this about Kim at the library, Donny?"

He grinned sheepishly. "Yes, sir, Mr. Wingfield." I smiled and turned back to the battery cable.

"So, you're having trouble telling her how you feel? Well, we all have trouble finding the right words at times. But when it comes right down to it, there are really only three words that a woman wants to hear . . ."

"Cables are backwards," offered Donny.

"No, not those words," I said, and the clamp went Kapow! in my hand. I stepped back and Donny relieved me of the cables and took over. I decided to focus on the answer to his question and let him handle the electrical work.

"Women love a grand gesture," I explained. "Something that says you're not afraid to tell the world how you feel."

Donny thought about this for a few minutes. Then he straightened up and grinned at me. "A grand gesture. Yeah . . . thanks, Mr. Wingfield . . ." It appeared that he had finally made up his mind about something, and I was humbled to be a part of such an important moment in his life. Just how important I was still to find out.

There's a new herbicide on the market this year called Grim Reaper. Farmers love it because, as they say, "It just kills everything!" Shortly after our conversation, Donny filled his father's field sprayer with Grim Reaper, went out to Don's high field on the town line, overlooking Larkspur, and wrote the words "I love you Kim Dodd" in acre-sized letters in a freshly planted crop of winter wheat. It was about a week before the herbicide took effect, making the letters turn stark brown against the beautiful green background. Maggie and I first noticed them when we were driving by on the highway and the sun came out on the hillside. The next thing I knew, Don was standing in my kitchen without a flicker of humour on his face.

"The boy says it was your idea, Walt."

"My idea . . ." I stammered. "I was just . . ."

"I figure every letter'll cost me a ton of winter wheat. I suppose I should be glad he wasn't sweet on that other girl at the library . . . Henrietta Przbylowski. Do me a favour, Walt. Next time he asks you for advice, just keep it to yourself!"

He turned on his heel and left without another word.

Yours sincerely,

Walt

Dear Ed,

The feuds and internecine strife around here are starting to really worry me. And they're striking closer to home. I thought I knew the Squire, but clearly I don't. I made one innocent remark, and now Don isn't speaking to me. And then we heard that the new couple from the city, Professor Burns and his wife, got a real jolt. You remember he wrote that letter you printed objecting to a new factory hog barn planned for the township on the basis that it was inhumane for the pigs. Yesterday, he went down to get the mail and found a pig's head in the mailbox. It's just unbelievable.

If you're bringing life into the world, it should be into a garden. I'm not naive when it comes to this community. I didn't expect to find the Garden of Eden up here, but I did think I had found a place where neighbourhood meant something, a society of, if not love, at least tolerance and trust. Now I'm finding it's overgrown with discord and hatred. Is this a place to bring up a child? You might as well go back to the city, where anonymity gives the illusion of tolerance . . . where you can pretend to live peacefully with your neighbour because you don't know enough about him to think the worst of him.

Perhaps I'm being a bit shrill. The fact is, any garden needs work. Some of these old feuds will just have to be weeded out. It doesn't need a miracle worker. It just needs someone who will take the time and who knows what to do.

I have a book on my shelf that I found very useful at the firm, when I was responsible for a large staff of people. It's called *Making Peace in Your Workplace*. It's just chock full of good ideas. I've been flipping through it recently and I found a really good example. It's called the Borlov Technique. It goes like this:

Here the mediator's task is to find some object
that has warm associations for both parties and
use it as a focus for conversation . . .

It's so simple, and yet so effective. Dr. Borlov was the
famous United Nations mediator who had a brilliant career . . .
until angry natives in Djakarta speared him to death in 1965.
But there's a lot of really good stuff in this book. I read some
of it to Maggie one night in bed, when she was having trouble
drifting off.

"Walt," she said. "If you want to do something, why don't
you see if you can get the Squire to go with you to that auction?"

It was a good suggestion. The day of Gus Fortescue's sale,
I dropped in on the Squire. He was propped up on the sofa,
reading *The Blazing Guns of Lost River Mesa.*

"How are you now, Walt?" he asked cheerfully.

"I'm fine, thanks," I said, taking a chair and plopping the
picnic basket on the table. "Look, I thought I'd drive down to
your brother's sale today. It's a beautiful day, Maggie's packed a
lunch for us . . . ham and egg sandwiches, pumpkin pie, a couple
of Newcastle Browns . . . Why don't you come with me?"

He sat up and rubbed his chin. Then he shook his head.
"That's kind of you, Walt. But I don't think I will. Thanks
for asking . . ." He glanced at the picnic basket. "Can I keep
the lunch?"

"Sure," I said. It was none of my business, but I pressed on
a little further. "You know, the notice says that they're having
the sale because of ill health."

"Mm-hmm," he nodded. "I saw that. I wondered which one
of them it was. I always figured Gus was too lucky to get sick."

"You don't know?"

"I know as much about them as you do, Walt. The last communication I had was that letter from the Catholic woman he married."

I stood up and walked over to the wood stove and looked at the envelope. "So that's what that is. But you never opened it."

"Nope. You might let me know whether it's Gus or her that's poorly. The only time I ever hear anything is if someone tells me."

About fifteen miles south of Highway 13 I turned in the drive of Gus's farm. You can always tell farms that are getting a transfusion from some outside source. A half-acre front lawn with a sprinkler system, asphalt on the driveway, raised flower beds, a flagpole . . . Gus's farm looked like the cover for the Thanksgiving issue of *Country Guide Magazine*. I joined the registration lineup, which was set up in a renovated summer kitchen that served as a second entrance to the house. A middle-aged woman with unusually blue hair and a smoky voice wrote me down in her book and handed me a card with my auction number on it.

"All the way down from Larkspur, Mr. Wingfield," she observed.

"Yes, I believe Mr. Fortescue came from Larkspur originally. Is he here today?"

"Gus is here, all right," she replied. "But he doesn't get out of the house now at all." Her voice dropped confidentially. "He has the cancer, you know. That's why they're having the sale. Actually his wife is right there. Maureen?" she called. "Mr. Wingfield here is from Larkspur."

A tall, graceful woman with white hair came across the room and extended her hand.

"Mr. Wingfield. How do you do?"

I shook hands with her and explained that I lived across the road from Mr. Fortescue's brother. She smiled.

"Baxter. Yes, of course. Please come in and meet my husband."

I followed her in through the summer kitchen down a large hallway to the front room. There, sitting in a soft chair by the window, was a tiny man wrapped in a quilt. He had a shock of white hair and an oxygen tube attached to his nose. He was watching the crowd on the lawn through the window. Behind him on the mantelpiece stood a number of framed black-and-white photos of a slim young man in the uniform of the Simcoe and Grey Foresters Regiment from World War II. Mrs. Fortescue touched her husband on the shoulder and he turned to look at me. He had the Squire's bushy eyebrows and high cheekbones, made even more prominent by the sickness.

"Augustus," she said. "This is a gentleman from home. Mr. Wingfield has the farm across the road from Baxter."

The old man made an effort at a smile. "How are things on the Seventh Line?" he asked in a hoarse whisper.

"Very well," I replied. "A bit dry, like everywhere else."

"You must be on the old Fisher place. Next door to the Haddocks."

"Mr. Wingfield is married to Mary Haddock's daughter Maggie," said Mrs. Fortescue.

"Yes, I am," I said in surprise. "How did you know that?"

Gus answered for her. "Maureen knows all about the families up there. She studies up on them like they was related to her."

"I was very fond of the old farm," she said. "Are any of the elms still standing? The ones in the laneway?"

"The Dutch elm disease got all but one, I'm afraid. I guess it must be the last one on the Seventh Line."

"I remember the elms," sighed Maureen. "Such graceful trees. The Baltimore orioles came to them every year and built nests and sang like opera singers. So noisy and full of life. I was so fond of the elms."

"The Sq . . . ah, Baxter," I corrected myself, "he wraps the trunk of that elm every year with sticky tape. It seems to stop the beetles. He's kept it going for years. I'll tell him you were asking after it, Mrs. Fortescue."

"Please call me Maureen," she said.

Gus coughed. "Lot of fuss over a tree. There's elms all over the place here. You never cared a fig for them."

"Drink your juice, dear," she said, placing the paper cup with a straw beside his pale hand. "You have to keep your fluids up." She turned to me. "We'll let him rest."

Outside, Maureen and I stood together under a large black walnut tree and listened to the patter of the auctioneer. I was surprised she had taken so much time with me on what must have been a stressful day for both of them.

"You know Baxter well, do you?" she asked.

"I thought I did. But I'm embarrassed to say I didn't know he had a brother until I saw the notice in the paper about the sale."

"That would be like him. They don't have any contact with each other, you know."

"Yes," I said. "That's one of the reasons I wanted to come today. It seems a shame, considering your husband's illness . . ."

"Yes, it is. How is Baxter doing, then?"

"He's fine. His memory comes and goes a bit, but basically he's fine."

"That's good. Please say hello to him for me . . . Goodness me . . . Look at that."

The auctioneer was taking bids for a white wooden porch swing with two rusty chains draped across it.

"That came from the home farm back in Larkspur," she explained. "It hung on the verandah. We used to rock in it for hours and hours. Oh, my. It's been lugged around from place to place all these years, but no one got around to putting it up. And there it goes. Excuse me, Mr. Wingfield, but I should get back to Gus."

She glided away across the yard to the house, nodding at people as she passed. She touched a woman on the arm and smiled; people made way for her. This was the Wildcat of the Marsh?

"Forty-two is bid," said the auctioneer. "Do I hear forty-five? Forty-five an-a-bid-a-bid-five-an-a-bid-a-bid-five-an-a-bid-a-bid-five?"

As he babbled away, I looked at the ancient porch swing and thought about its travels over the years. And then it occurred to me. Here was an object with warm associations for both parties. Dr. Borlov would certainly approve. I stuck up my hand and the auctioneer took the bid. After a brief canvass of the crowd, he knocked it down to me for forty-five dollars.

I drove back to Larkspur with the porch swing in the back of the 4×4. When I turned into the Squire's lane, I found him rolling up a hose on the front lawn. He straightened up and tossed the roll of hose beside the steps.

"I think the irrigation season is closed for the year, don't you?" he said. "Well, what do you know since we last spoke?"

"Gus is not well," I said. "He has cancer and I don't think he's going to last much longer."

The Squire took a breath and nodded. "That's too bad," he said. "I guess his luck's finally run out."

"I spoke to Mrs. Fortescue and she asked me to say hello to you."

The Squire looked at me sharply. "Oh, yeah? That's nice."

"And I have something for you from the sale. She thought it belonged back here at the farm."

I opened the back door of the 4×4 to show him the porch swing. The Squire blinked at it for a moment, looked at the ground and shook his head. When he looked up again, his face was hard and flushed. When he spoke, he used a tone I had never heard from him before.

"It's none of your damned business, Walter," he said, his voice thick with anger. "No business of yours at all. Now stop your meddling and leave me alone!"

He trudged away up the verandah steps and disappeared inside. The door banged shut behind him.

Yours sincerely,

Walt

———— *December 5*

Dear Ed,

At the beginning of December we got our first cold snap and the ground froze hard. But there still wasn't a puff of snow. Then the goat died. Mrs. Pankhurst was one of the oldest members of the staff. I brought her in during my second year to handle security for the sheep operation. She has presided over the farm ever since as an enforcer, dispensing justice with her hoofs and horns. I once asked Freddy how old she was.

"Geez, it's hard to tell with goats, Walt," he said. "But you see that one over there, the real bony one with the long beard that's havin' trouble walkin'? Well, this one of yours is the mother to that one over there."

Mrs. Pankhurst kept herself in fighting trim with regular workouts that included smashing her head against the barn door, which I eventually had to reinforce with quarter-inch steel plate. Visitors to the house would ask if I had a pile driver running in the barnyard, and I'd say, "No, that's just the goat."

Violence was in her nature, and it came as a surprise to me that she died of natural causes . . . sort of. She picked the lock on the stable door in the middle of the night and got into the feed room, where I store the sweet feed for the horses. At my age, I know better than to mess with mince pie after midnight, but Mrs. Pankhurst has been a risk-taker all of her life. She stuffed herself until her pancreas exploded and she died with a smile on her face.

This presented a problem. Because of the deep frost, burial on the property was out of the question without some heavy machinery. Dead stock companies won't pick up sheep or goats anymore, and you can't take them to a landfill site. Most people around here just haul the carcass back to the bush for the coyotes, but it's an indictable offence under the Dead Animal Disposal Act.

I was reflecting on this when I got a call from Freddy.

"I'm just sitting here watching the soaps," he said. "Why don't we run her down to Scotty's mink farm in my truck? I need to get out for a drive anyway."

Maggie turned from the sink.

"Scotty's mink farm?" she protested.

"Well, I know it's not what we usually do," I replied.

"Chopped up and fed to the minks? It's not right to treat her like that."

"I know it isn't. But what am I supposed to do?"

Maggie has always felt that long-service employees should be laid to rest under the apple tree by the lane. If an animal dies in the middle of winter, she holds it in cold storage out in the pump house for spring interment.

"But she won't fit in the pump house."

"Go ahead, then," she conceded. "I guess there's nothing else for it. Oh, look. It's starting to rain. You be careful out there. It'll be slippery."

When Freddy arrived, we loaded the dear departed onto the bed of the pickup and Maggie placed a blanket over her. Freddy and I steamed off towards Larkspur. Out on the highway, Freddy glanced in the rear-view mirror.

"Uh-oh," he said. "Here's trouble."

I glanced back and saw a police car looming up out of the mist.

"He's not interested in us, Freddy. You weren't going that fast."

Freddy scowled. "They're always interested in a farm truck. This thing wouldn't run without all the Vise-Grips holding it together. The sticker's expired . . . I haven't got the new insurance certificate on me . . . and we're carrying dead stock without a licence, aren't we? This should be interesting."

I glanced in the side mirror. The cruiser lights were now flashing. Freddy steered carefully off to the side of the road with one hand while his other hand searched frantically under the seat for his safety belt. He found it and clicked it into the buckle. We both looked in the mirror and recognized the officer as Constable Bradley, a fairly recent addition to the Larkspur detachment.

"By gollies," said Freddy. "Look who we get today. Let the words of my mouth and the meditation of my heart be always acceptable in Thy sight." He rolled his eyes skyward and gave a quick sign of the cross.

Freddy speaks differently to this constable than to any other member of the force. I asked him about this once, and Freddy explained that the first time he was stopped by Constable Bradley his opening gambit had been: "Nice to see some sun for a change."

Constable Bradley replied, "The Lord makes his face to shine upon the unrighteous as well as the righteous." That day, the unrighteous received a seventy-five-dollar fine and lost three points for failing to yield.

Constable Bradley came to the driver's window. The rain was freezing to the brim of his hat.

"Good morning, sir. Do you have any idea how fast you were going?"

Freddy said, "I don't know, Officer. But it must have been fast. I had 'er right on the mat. We're on the Lord's business, Officer. We're taking a sick goat . . . to the vet."

Constable Bradley glanced in the back of the truck and saw the shape under the blanket. "Let's have a look here," he said, moving away from the window. Freddy scrambled out of the truck after him.

"Oh, Lord, be careful, Officer," he said anxiously. "We just got her quieted down. We don't want her to get violent again."

Bradley lifted the blanket and looked at Mrs. Pankhurst. "This goat is dead," he said.

"Oh, no!" gasped Freddy. "Gollies, I pray not, Officer. Grab that side mirror, Walt. Just give her a tug and she'll come off. Now hold her down, Officer." As the puzzled officer placed his hand on the goat, Freddy puffed quickly on the mirror and held it to Mrs. Pankhurst's nose and then showed it to him. "See, a little foggin' . . . she's breathin'," he assured the officer. "Real shallow, but she's still goin' . . . praise the Lord."

Bradley was nonplussed. "She's stiff as a board," he said.

"They go that way with the tetanus," said Freddy gravely. "But Dr. Jim has brought her back before, and God willing, he can do it again . . . if only we aren't too late . . ."

Bradley reflected for a moment, in a way that suggested he was not often given to such moments. "Do you want me to give you an escort into town?" he asked.

"That would be very good of you, Officer," said Freddy. "Time is precious to us."

The officer got back in his cruiser and skidded away with the lights still flashing. And Freddy gave hot pursuit in the direction of downtown Larkspur. I just looked at Freddy and shook my head, but he grinned at me like a pirate.

"Geez," he said. "This is gettin' more complicated than that soap opera I was watchin'. I hope it turns out better."

The wind was howling now. Branches lay across the road and a patch of black ice sent the truck into a short skid. "Careful, Freddy," I warned. "It looks pretty slippery."

We turned into the Larkspur Veterinary Clinic just as the good doctor was getting out of his car, coming back from lunch at the Red Hen. Seeing the flashing lights and sensing an emergency, he jogged over to the truck.

"Morning, Officer," said Dr. Jim. "What have we got here?"

Freddy stepped in quickly. "We thought it might be the tetanus again, Dr. Jim. Do you think you can save her?"

"Tetanus?" asked Dr. Jim with a frown. He looked at the officer and then at me and then he bent over to lift the blanket on Mrs. Pankhurst. Freddy and I held our breath. He straightened up and nodded his head.

"Yes . . . tetanus . . . I recognize the symptoms. Let's get her inside and we'll see what we can do."

As Freddy and I struggled with Mrs. Pankhurst, Bradley stood watching with a puzzled expression. "What causes tetanus, Doctor?" he asked.

"Oh, it can be a variety of things, Officer," replied Dr. Jim patiently. "Often it's contact with rusty metal. I had to attend to a cow this morning that had contact with a rusty farm truck out on the highway. In that case, tetanus was instantaneous . . ."

Freddy carried his end of the goat between the constable and the vet, gently nudging Dr. Jim towards the door of the clinic. "Ah . . . thanks fer all yer help, Constable," he said. "We sure wouldn't wanna interrupt you any further in the course of yer duties. God bless you for helping us out here this morning . . ." Bradley shrugged off Freddy's thanks and turned to go. Freddy hustled us towards the clinic, keeping one eye on the cruiser until it was safely out of sight. Then he dropped the goat. "Geez, that was a close one," he sighed. "I could just feel the dungeon door closin' on me this time. As the fella said, 'give me liberty or give me—'"

"Tetanus?" offered Dr. Jim testily. "I don't know what you two clowns are up to, but I've got some livestock to see to. There's a storm warning out. They've closed the highway north out of Larkspur. I want to finish up and get home while

I can." He went back into the clinic, shaking his head in disbelief as he went.

"Well, looks like the road's closed to Scotty's," sighed Freddy. "We'll have to get a coffee and rethink our strategy. Let's throw her back on the truck, Walt."

All the usual suspects were gathered in the Red Hen, declaiming loudly about herbicides and pinto beans. Cigarette smoke and bacon fumes hung along the ceiling. Freddy and I had just got our coffee when the lights went out and the exhaust fans over the grill whirred to a stop. Donna, the waitress, moved to the blackboard above the cash register.

"Larkspur's power supply is gettin' more unreliable than Venezuela," she announced grimly. "We're on the blackout menu, boys. The special's changed from hot beef on toast with gravy to cold ham on bread with applesauce. You can have coffee . . . if you have it now."

The door opened and Don appeared, ice plastered down the front of his overalls. He didn't sit down, and the room went quiet.

"There's a bad storm coming in," he announced. "They say there's three separate fronts and they all got freezing rain. They figure it's gonna go on for a coupla days at least." He set his hat, turned and walked out again.

There was dead silence for a moment. Then a general scraping of chairs and zippering of coats as people rose and left. In a few minutes the café was empty, cold and dark. Outside the Red Hen, the falling sleet stung our faces as we looked at the sky. It had turned a weird purple colour. There was a distant rumble, like an approaching snowplow.

"By gollies," murmured Freddy. "That's thunder. You don't often hear that in the winter."

We looked in the truck bed. Mrs. Pankhurst was now encased in a clear coat of ice. She looked like the captain in the *Wreck of the Hesperus.*

> Lashed to the helm all stiff and stark, with her face
> turned to the skies,
> The lantern gleamed on gleaming snow and her
> fixed and glassy eyes.

"Well, geez, ain't it the truth?" agreed Freddy. "And then there's that other poet who said:

> If we stand in the rain at ten below without a
> decent coat,
> It won't be long, I fear, before we look like this
> here goat.

By the time Freddy and I got home, the roads were slick with ice and treacherous. Mrs. Pankhurst was frozen solid and welded to the truck bed, so Freddy just let me out at my gate and I walked down the lane to the house. Slid is more like it. The entire length of the lane was one vast sheet of ice.

For two months of the year, Persephone Township is like the south of France. The sun beats down upon the fragrant meadows, and gentle zephyrs waft through the trees. This is when most of the real estate is sold around here. For the other ten months, it's like . . . well . . . Persephone Township.

The winters are just ferocious. And the wind . . . I grabbed a tree at the halfway point to rest. We have our own species of conifer here, called the Persephone pine. They have branches only on the east side. I will admit that the township is not bad for bugs, though. I've only seen one mosquito on the farm in five years, and it had out-of-province plates.

I looked back out to the road, which was deserted. Ice-crusted twigs and branches dropped to the roadway from the maple trees in a steady clatter. Three days of this? It's impossible to move around; we'll be afraid to leave the house. Everywhere you turn in this township it's like being mugged. The people are hostile. Practically no one is speaking to me . . . Ed, I can get all this in the city!

When I finally gained the verandah and fell in through the kitchen door, Maggie was on the telephone. She said "Oh, my," several times and rang off.

"That was Elma," she said. "She says it's really bad south of us. Hydro poles are snapping like toothpicks under the weight of the ice. Her cousin Harry is a lineman, and he says we'll be without power for at least a week. Maybe more if the weather keeps up like this."

"A week!" I exclaimed. "What do we do? Are you going to be all right?"

"Oh, I'm fine," she assured me. "Nothing's happening. I think you'd better get togged up and go over to Don's. Young Donny's away this week and he'll have no one to help him in the barn."

As she spoke, a series of cracks like gunshots sounded outside the house, and we both turned to the window as the main branches of the maple on the front lawn crashed heavily to the ground. Ice chips smashed everywhere, making a sound like breaking glass.

I wrapped barbed wire over my boots and made my way gingerly down the road to Don's place, shielding my face from the wind and picking my way around fallen branches. I found

Don chopping ice off the door of the root cellar, where he had stored his y2k generator after the millennium scare wore off. I wasn't sure if he was still speaking to me, so I tried a fairly neutral opening.

"Is there ah . . . anything I can do?" I asked.

"Yeah," he nodded. "The fans are all shut down and ammonia builds up real fast in there."

"You mean the cows could suffocate?"

"Them and us both. We gotta work fast here."

State of the art is a terrific thing when you have electricity. When the fans are going, you'd never be aware that the slatted floors are located above a vast liquid manure tank. But when the fans shut down, a barn like Don's takes on all the ventilating properties of a quart sealer with a dead mouse in it. The smell of ammonia was thick enough to make my eyes water. We plugged the generator into the electrical panel, fired it up and watched as the fans slowly brought the barn back to life. After fifteen minutes, we could breathe again and I turned to go, when Don caught me by the elbow.

"As soon as we get the milking done, we've got to get the generator over to Bill Barnett's. I promised I'd be there by five o'clock."

We made it by six. Don put chains on all four tires of the tractor for the two-mile trip over to the Town Line. We didn't pass another vehicle on the way, which was fortunate because at times we were travelling sideways and needed both sides of the road.

Bill's cows were bawling because they were used to being milked by 4:30 p.m. By now, it was pitch dark. The three of us milked in the dim light of a storm lantern. We did all the feeding with a flashlight. Then Don and I hurried back with the generator to freshen up his cows again. At midnight we got a panic-stricken call from a farmer with a chick hatchery. His backup heat system had failed, and five thousand day-old chicks were in danger of freezing to death.

When we got there, Don had to take the panel apart and rewire it with a plug for the generator. We spent the rest of the night repairing the farmer's backup system. At daylight we staggered into Don's barn and found Don's wife, Elma, and the two younger kids sitting in the feed room in their coats.

"I figured they might be here," he said. "It's pretty murky, but at least it's warmer than the house. We have a fireplace, but it's electric."

"Look," I said. "We've got a wood stove . . ."

"No, I couldn't do that to you. Maggie's expecting the baby . . ."

I assured him she wouldn't mind one little bit. Elma and Don started the milking together, and I strapped on my barbed wire boots and made my way back to the farm, where I met Maggie on her knees on the verandah, piling wood into a wheelbarrow.

"There's no power anywhere within thirty miles," she sighed. "And there won't be for at least a week. All the roads are closed and they're calling for more freezing rain. The only buildings with a backup system are the school, the hospital and the arena, so they're setting them up as relief shelters. At least the phones work, so we can talk to each other."

I helped her to her feet and took over the wood job.

"I hope you don't mind," I said. "I invited Don's family here for the night. They don't have heat . . ."

Maggie nodded and patted me on the shoulder. "That's

fine, dear. Four more doesn't matter at this point. That makes seventeen, now."

I went into the house and saw them all. Isobel Meadows was there with her new baby. She was very upset because she'd had to leave without her dog. Pookie had disappeared at the beginning of the storm and hadn't been seen since. There was Professor Burns and his wife. They'd built that odd-looking house up on the hill, the passive solar, geodesic, energy self-sufficient New Earth place. Apparently they bailed out after about three hours. Everybody was playing board games around the kitchen table.

I was surprised to see Mrs. Lynch coming out of the larder.

"You sure got a full house, Mr. Wingfield," she said cheerfully as she bustled by.

"Yes. Well, we're delighted to have you. We'll try to make you comfortable."

Mrs. Lynch put her hand on my arm and smiled. "Maggie, dear," she said. "I was just going to make up some cream puffs for you, but I see you're out of Dream Whip."

Maggie's eyes twitched, but she managed to return the smile. "You're right, I am. Maybe we'll just have to settle for some fresh cream."

When Don, Elma and the kids arrived, Don and I napped on couches for an hour before Willy and Dave burst in. Willy looked around at the clusters of people in various rooms.

"Hey, what have we got here?" he cackled. "The Christian Science Reading Room?"

I asked them what they had been doing.

"Errands of mercy, just like you," said Willy. "We've been chopping wood for the weekenders—"

"That's good of you," I said.

"—'cause they're the only people with wood stoves anymore. All the farmers are movin' in with them, and we gotta keep the precious farmers warm, don't we? Hey, cream puffs! Hi, Isobel, how're ya doin'?" Suddenly, he whirled and scanned the room. "Where's that dog?"

Isobel burst into tears.

"She had to rush here with the baby," said Maggie. "The Burnses have been down to look, but they couldn't find Pookie."

"That's too bad," said Dave. "It's not fit for man nor beast out there. I think we've got the wood problem covered for now, but there's beef cattle all over the place with no water for over a day now."

"There's lots of ice," I said. "Can't they just lick the ice?"

Don shook his head. "A cow needs twenty gallons of water a day. You can't get that licking ice."

So, while Willy and Dave went off to join the township crews clearing trees from the roadways, Don and I went off again with the generator, watering cattle and milking cows. This time, Professor Burns joined us. He pitched right in and helped carry pails, fork manure, wash cows' udders, you name it. We returned to the house for a supper of beef stew and bread baked in the wood stove. Then, too tired to sleep, the three of us went out to the haymow in the barn and sat in the open doorway above the barnyard, which gives a commanding view of the Seventh Line. We saw weird blue flashes of light on the horizon. We learned later it was from high-voltage transmission towers crashing to the ground. The only other lights to be seen were from snowmobiles buzzing here and there. It seemed odd that people still had the energy for snowmobiling after all the commotion.

Don explained to me. "That's the Kinsmen Snowbunnies

out checking the houses. They're delivering candles and food to people and telling police about the ones who need to go to the shelters. It's dangerous work making a snowmobile run on that ice." After riding the tractor around on it, I had to agree with him.

Two sets of flashing lights approached on the Seventh Line from the south. It was Dave on a four-wheel-drive monster tractor, the "small one" they use for blowing snow. Hooked behind Dave's machine was the Persephone Township Moose Bus, with its front wheels a few inches off the ground. This is the wretched old pink school bus they take to Kenora every fall for their annual hunting expedition. With the help of a tow truck lift, the boys had cobbled together an all-terrain personnel carrier. He turned into the lane, and we met Dave on the verandah.

"That's quite a people-mover you've rigged up there, Dave," said Don.

"Thanks! Say, have you seen Willy? He went off on his own a while back. Said he'd catch up with me."

Maggie pointed to the living room. "He just came in a minute ago, looking like Nanook of the North. He's getting warmed up by the fire."

We looked in and saw Willy bent over by the wood stove, whispering something to Isobel Meadows. He opened his coat sheepishly, revealing a shivering and bedraggled Pookie . . . with a strip of duct tape wrapped around his snout.

"F-f-f-d-d-d-r-r-r," growled Pookie.

"Ah, isn't that sweet," said Dave. "He's got Isobel's dog! Hey everybody! Willy rescued Pookie!"

Willy glared at Dave. "Ahhh . . . shaddap!" was all he could say.

Yours sincerely,
Walt

Dear Ed,

On the morning of the third day, the sun rose in a clear sky and the temperature fell twenty degrees. For the first time I stopped to survey the devastation. My farm looked like it had been bombed from the air. Trees were down everywhere, and those still standing were stripped of their branches. Out in the orchard, all of the old apple trees lay crumpled under the weight of the ice. My new page-wire fence along the road had been crushed in a dozen places by fallen debris. Even the old mulberry tree had been pounded flat. It made me think of lines I'd memorized at school:

> A little fire in human hearts
> Will light the world and all its parts.
> But fire blazing uncontrolled
> Leaves the world in ashes, cold.
> A little ice is like a balm,
> It cools the world and makes it calm.
> But ice on ice with no respite
> Will crush the world and kill the light.

On the radio, we heard the mayor of the restructured community of Hillview announce a state of emergency. Now, when you do this in the United States, it triggers an immediate reaction. The government coffers for disaster relief open, the National Guard moves in, and the president flies over in a helicopter. It's not quite the same in Canada. Government offices are usually closed, journalists move in, and the prime minister flies south to the Caribbean.

In Ontario, our latest attempt to develop an emergency

response procedure stalled in the definition stage. The committee just couldn't agree on what constituted an emergency. Finally someone said, "Come on, people, let's start with the obvious—what's the worst thing that could happen here?" Hank Burford, the minister at the time, said, "An NDP victory."

Anyway, the mayor called the Department of Defence in Ottawa and was connected to a colonel who said the army could be sent, but the township would have to pay for it. Now, the complete property tax income for the township wouldn't cover the colonel's photocopying budget for the year, let alone the rental of the Queen's Own Rifles for a week. So the mayor hung up the phone and left the office, but, fortunately, he ran into a camera crew from *CBC Newsworld*. He explained the situation, and the army arrived about an hour after the next newscast.

When the soldiers got here, they were terrific. They fanned out across the neighbourhood, checking every house for signs of life. An armoured personnel carrier stopped outside Mrs. Coutts's house on the Town Line. The officer saw an oil lamp glowing on the kitchen table inside. He knocked; Mrs. Coutts came to the door and opened it a crack.

"Canadian Forces, ma'am," said the officer. "We're here to help."

"Oh, yes," said Mrs. Coutts.

"Do you need food, ma'am?"

"No."

"Do you need any water?"

"No."

The officer looked around and saw a pile of maple logs in front of the house.

"Well, there must be something we can do. Can we split that pile of firewood for you?"

Mrs. Coutts peered around him at the wood and thought about that for a minute.

"Yes," she said, finally. The men leapt into action, split three cords of wood and stacked it on her verandah. When they were done, Mrs. Coutts peeked out the door again and became downright chatty.

"Why, thank you, boys. That's very kind of you to do all that for me," she said. And she gave them a cup of tea.

"Just part of the job, ma'am," said the officer. "How long have you been without power?"

Mrs. Coutts thought about this for another minute.

"Seventy-two years," she said.

I was helping Don with the milking again this afternoon and suddenly found myself very short of breath. I asked Don if he would mind if I stepped outside for a minute. To my surprise, he came out with me and we both sat on the tailgate of the truck. It turned out he was having trouble breathing, too.

"The trouble is, that little generator will run the ventilating fans, but it don't have enough juice to run the compressor, too," he complained. "So I have to turn the fans off to get enough pressure to run the milking machines. In twenty minutes, the place fills up with ammonia again and I have to throw the doors open. That's a great way to give the cows pneumonia, because they're used to a warm barn. So, either I'm suffocating or I'm standing in a cold wind. I don't know what to do."

I looked up to see Calvin Currie turning in the lane in his old Dodge pickup. He drove up to the barn beside us and switched off the engine.

"Hi, Calvin," I said.

"How're you now, Walt?" Calvin gave me a quick nod and eased himself stiffly out of the cab. He turned and fished around in the front seat for a moment, looking for something.

"I think you need a bigger generator, Don," I said. "I wonder if there's anyplace . . ."

"Can't be found," said Don. "I've called everywhere. And they say they've got to rebuild the power grid all the way up from Highway 13. It could be weeks before we're back up and goin'."

Calvin emerged from the truck cab and heaved the door shut with a bang.

"You know, Don," he said. "A milker only needs ten or twelve pounds of vacuum pressure, and years ago, when the power went out, we used to get that from the farm truck."

"How'd you do that?" asked Don.

"There's enough vacuum in the carburettor to run the windshield wipers, right? So, if you run a small diameter hose, about an inch maybe, from the air cleaner on the truck to the milk line, you can get enough pressure to run a milker, maybe even two with that souped up '55 Chevy yer boy's got there. Then you can milk and run the fans at the same time. You get me?"

"Don," I laughed. "You're going to have to ask Donny if you can borrow the car tonight."

"One-inch hose . . ." said Don, carefully. The two men eyed each other.

"Yeah," grunted Calvin. "I brought a roll of it with me. And a coupla adapters . . ." He lifted the plastic shopping bag he was carrying. "If it's any use to you. Maybe you got the problem licked already. I was just goin' by and wondered if you'd thought of it."

"You were just goin' by, were you?" asked Don. Calvin doesn't use the Seventh Line except during the summer, when he's checking cattle on the pasture across the road from me.

"Yeah, I got some fence down over here . . . I'll have to do something about it in the spring."

In fifteen minutes, Calvin's vacuum system was installed and running two milkers. Don could now milk and breathe at the same time, and I could see that his working life might return to something approaching normal. Calvin grinned.

"What do you think of that?" he said, to no one in particular.

Don nodded. "Yeah. I guess it works . . . Thanks for the idea."

"You got a nice barn here," said Calvin, squinting at the truss system above him.

"Oh?" said Don skeptically. "I thought you didn't like it."

"What's not to like? Lovely place to work. I would have put one up myself if I could."

"Then why didn't you?"

Calvin sat down on the concrete manger. "I couldn't do it," he said. "But that don't mean I don't like your barn. It was different for us. When Mary got the Parkinson's, that left me on my own. I had to redo the house for her, pay for a nurse, wheelchair and stuff. I had to make that old barn pay every day, all year. I couldn't think twenty years out the way you did. It was just different, you know? No, this is the way to do her, if you can swing it." He sighed and nodded to himself, looking around at the barn.

We talked for a little while and Calvin eventually went on

his way. Don didn't say anything for a long time. While we were washing the milking equipment in the sink in the milk house, he finally broke the silence.

"You know, that old guy's smarter than I give him credit. He's looked after a sick wife for ten years with twenty cows and a cream cheque. He doesn't owe a dime to anybody. And he could make a water pump out of juice cans and a coupla rubber bands. Maybe I'll get him back here and see if he can hook up the stereo system."

The thaw we were all praying for didn't happen. The fourth and fifth days we got wind and snow. The snow hid the black ice in spots, making the footing even more treacherous for man and snowplow. The roads drifted so badly we wondered if they'd ever get cleared. If we wanted to get into town, we had to organize a convoy for safety—if one car got stuck, then the others could shovel and tow it free.

But the thaw in the human condition was remarkable. Gradually our seventeen house guests departed, having managed to arrange food and heat in their own houses. There was a lot of laughing and hugging and even some tears with the farewells. Young Donny was back in his father's good graces, not just because of the '55 Chevy. It seems some aerial footage on the national news picked up Donny's message in the winter wheat and the chamber of commerce for Larkspur wants to talk to Don about next year.

Don and Calvin Currie have become fast friends, a roving pit crew specializing in low-tech solutions to difficult problems. For example, the stoves and the furnace in the Orange Hall in Larkspur run on natural gas, which was still in service, but the system was useless because the gas valves are triggered by electricity. So is the fan motor on the furnace. Calvin guessed that a twelve-volt battery with a small transformer would run the relay switch on the gas valves. And Don rigged up a chain drive for the furnace fan using a stationary exercise bike. Young Charlie Teeter's training program for the provincial cycling championships was all shot by the storm, so they recruited him to provide the muscle power on the bike. Calvin joked that with Charlie pedalling they could pump enough hot air to run an election campaign.

News travelled fast. The masters of the Orange Lodge threw the doors open to the public as yet another relief shelter. They set out sleeping bags and cots and prepared to serve hot dogs and soup to all comers. Everybody came, but they weren't looking for food or shelter. They were looking for company. With no TV or video games at home, the kids rediscovered the old bowling alley in the basement. Mrs. Lynch started playing the hall piano.

When the ladies of the community were informed they could operate the hall gas stoves again, they announced an impromptu supper of the combined auxiliaries of the Anglican and United Churches . . . Freddy calls it the Ladies Artillery. Everyone dashed home to salvage food that had been left outside to freeze.

As the daylight faded, candles were lit and kerosene barn lanterns glowed from the ceiling. I sat beside Mrs. Lynch on the piano bench and listened to the place humming with the sound of human community . . . of something like harmony . . . except for the Squire, of course. I saw him a couple of times across the room, but he didn't look my way. I sat beside Mrs. Lynch on the piano bench as she paused between tunes. She looked around the hall and her face softened.

"You know, it was like this when I was a little girl, before the electrification," she said. "The winter was long and cold and dark, and it took nearly all of your energy to keep warm and fed. But then, it was the only time you really saw people. The farm work was all done and the roads were good, packed with snow. It was the visiting time. Oh, yes, it was just like this."

"Do you suppose the people in those days really got along any better than they do now?" I asked.

"They had their battles, that's true. I don't think that ever changes."

"I mean, here we are sitting in the Orange Lodge, an anti-Catholic organization dedicated to the nursing of ancient grudges. No wonder people don't get along. It's institutional."

"Oh, nobody pays any heed to that business anymore," she scoffed. "This year they cancelled the Orange Parade because one of the Orangemen was sick and the other one didn't want to march alone. Who cares if you're Protestant or Catholic these days?"

"Lots of people, apparently," I said, nodding towards the Squire.

"What?" she exclaimed. "Not the Squire. Oh, no, you're very wrong there, Walt. The Squire has no problems with Catholics. Why, he wanted to marry a Catholic girl."

"He did? Who was that?"

"Let me think. Her name was Maureen Hoolihan. Lovely girl. Such a shame. She ended up marrying his brother, and we don't see her anymore."

Just at that moment Freddy appeared at my shoulder and grabbed my elbow. "We got trouble here, Walt," he whispered. "Pookie broke the ceasefire. He took the seat out of Willy's pants this morning and got away clean. Willy's just come in and he's packin'."

We found Willy and Don in the coatroom at the hall entrance. Don was blocking Willy's passage into the hall, and Willy was fuming.

"It ain't right, Willy," Don was saying. "There's kids here."

"This town ain't big enough for the two of us," declared Willy. "I was carryin' a flat of eggs for Pete's sake . . . for the nursing home. Then I hear that noise . . . F-f-d-d-r-r-r-r. I just squirmed up like a spider on a hot stove lid. You could have plugged my ass end with a turnip seed, I tell you."

"What have you got there, Willy?" I asked.

Willy opened his jacket to reveal a short electric cattle prod in one pocket and a can of ether in the other. I just shook my head.

Willy was adamant. "I'm not gonna start anything . . . but a man's got a right to defend his person."

"It'll probably be okay, Don," I said. "Pookie's tied up to Isobel's chair way up at the other end of the hall."

"All right, you can go in," said Don. "But stay down here, Willy. Let's keep a lid on this thing."

The buffet tables sagged under the weight of strip loin steaks, smoked salmon, seventeen salads, scalloped potatoes, coq au vin, breads, cheeses, fruit and an exotic array of desserts. The combination of candlepower and over a hundred warm bodies sent the temperature and humidity in the hall up sharply. Charlie Teeter had stopped pedalling and was loading up two plates with carbohydrates. Calvin and Don had rigged up a simple clockwork winding mechanism to run the ceiling fan over the buffet table. You pull a chain attached to a ratchet that tightens the spring beside the fan. It's ingenious, and the fan runs for about fifteen minutes. It was just whirring to a standstill when Willy, Don and I went through the buffet line together.

"Many's the poor family has to make do and call this a meal," laughed Willy, helping himself to a large portion of beef tenderloin. I was just pouring myself a glass of Chateau Margaux when I heard the minister from St. Luke's behind me.

"It sure is stuffy in here," he complained. "Oh, ye winds of God, bless ye the Lord!"

He reached up and pulled down on the chain of the ceiling fan. The ratchet turned, making a rattling sound like a small electric motor starting up. "F-f-f-d-d-d-r-r-r-r-r-r-r-r—"

What happened after that was something of a blur. Willy whirled and fired. A wild jab with the cattle prod sent the poor minister headfirst into a Savannah Cream Cake. A blast from the ether can passed over the chafing dish and sent a sheet of flame the length of the buffet table. Women screamed. The piano stopped. When the smoke cleared, Willy was lying in a pile of potato salad. The minister sat on the floor, dabbing at sticky red fluid drenching his shirtfront.

"My God, I've been shot!" he exclaimed.

Freddy knelt down beside him and handed him some napkins. "You're okay, Reverend," he said soothingly. "That's just raspberry purée. It comes out after a couple of washes."

Don frog-marched Willy to the coatroom and disarmed him. Freddy threw Willy a towel and trotted back out and up onto the stage to calm the crowd.

"Okay, folks," he said. "Okay. There's nothing more to see here. Go back to your suppers and we're gonna have us some entertainment. Mrs. Sniderman? Come on up here. Mrs. Sniderman's gonna sing 'Marble Halls' for us, folks. Mrs. Lynch, pound out a verse to get her going, will ya?"

Mrs. Sniderman is a big woman . . . as Freddy says, big enough to burn diesel. As a soprano, she has tremendous stamina. She sang "Marble Halls," "How Great Thou Art," "Softly and Tenderly Jesus Is Calling" and appeared to be just getting warmed up. Freddy leapt up on stage again.

"Thank you, Mrs. Sniderman," he said, clapping enthusiastically. "I'll bet they heard that down in Lavender. Now we'll get back to you, but the first thing you want in a variety night is some variety."

He pulled a crumpled sheet of paper from his back pocket and consulted it. "What have we got here? We got a great show for yas here tonight. The Marshall Sisters are the synchronized swimming champs for Hillhurst County . . . and they do some step-dancing, too." He grinned at the crowd. "I guess we'll go with the step-dancing, huh?

"Then George McCormick's gonna come up here and do his ear stand . . . and if you haven't seen this, you're in for a real treat. It looks pretty much the way it sounds. He'll need a door frame. Then either we could have seven-year-old Roberta Przbylowski to do her intermediate program on the trampoline . . . or I could play the accordion. You know the difference between the accordion and the trampoline, don't you folks . . . ? You take off your shoes before you jump on a trampoline!

"While everyone gets ready, I shall recite a poem written especially for this occasion, entitled 'The Ballad of the Great Ice Storm.'"

Along the line of western hills the thunderclouds
    will form
Till even the guys at Environment can see she's
    coming on to storm,
But she'll have to pack a helluva whack and chill
    us to the bone
To come anywhere near the awful storm that iced
    up Persephone.

It struck on Thursday afternoon and swept across
    the region.
Honest folk fled to their homes; it even emptied
    out the Legion.
The ice built higher on every wire, falling branches
    found their mark,
And supper found us without heat and sittin' in
    the dark.

"Now isn't this an awful sight," I said, surveying
    that scene.
There ain't a tree left standing twixt here and
    Road 13.
You cannot walk a single block, the sidewalks are
    like glass,
And if you put a foot down wrong, you fall flat on
    your face.

Oh, what can you do when the rain comes down
    and freezes cold and white?
And the price of beer and candles has tripled
    overnight?

> Well . . . you learn to curse in rhyming verse and
>   plot some way to fly
> And yank the motor outa' that great Zamboni in
>   the sky.

I glanced over at Maggie and saw that she was holding her sides and rocking with laughter. She looked as though she would . . . and then I realized she was . . .

"Oh, Walt!" she gasped. "The baby! It's coming!"

Mrs. Lynch and I helped Maggie into the Regalia Room, where the banners and stuff are stored for the Orange Parade. A cellphone appeared out of nowhere and I tried to call the doctor. I couldn't remember the number.

Maggie took a breath and said very clearly: "Four, three, five, five, oh, five, eight." I pressed the numbers carefully and got that all right. The message said that the doctor was at the Regional Hospital south of Highway 13. More numbers and we finally connected.

"Doctor, the baby's coming and it's early!" Maggie says that I was shouting at this point.

"Early is a relative term, Walt," replied Dr. Brigham patiently. "The date I gave you was an educated guess. Maggie's in good health. We know this from the office visits. You just keep her warm and comfortable and we'll see how things develop."

"But we've got to get her to the hospital!"

"I'm afraid Larkspur Hospital is pretty much out of commission right now," said the doctor. "Most of the patients have been moved here to the Regional. I think you might be better to sit tight right where you are until I can get there."

"We're in the Orange Hall. Is that safe?"

"Safe is a relative term, Walt. You roll the dice every time a woman goes through childbirth, and ninety-five percent of the time it's completely routine. You just stand there and catch it. Now, if you're at the Orange Hall, you have a retired obstetrical nurse living right next door. Gertrude Lynch. Do you think someone could find her?"

"Mrs. Lynch? She's with Maggie right now."

"Excellent," said the doctor. "Good. I want you to tell Mrs. Lynch that I'll need pulse, blood pressure and temperature for the mother, dilation, fetal vitals . . . that sort of thing."

I put my hand over the phone and said, "Mrs. Lynch . . . the doctor needs Maggie's purse and her mother's thermal underwear and her fighter beetles . . ."

"For Pete's sake, gimme that," said Don. His big hand closed over the phone, and he handed it to Mrs. Lynch.

"Yes, Doctor," said Mrs. Lynch. "Her pulse is seventy-eight, temperature normal, cervix dilated five centimetres . . . yes, I'll just slip over and get my things now."

She passed the phone back to me and went briskly back to Maggie.

"Walt, it sounds like everything's progressing very well," continued the doctor. "I don't think I need to be there at all."

"But what if something goes wrong?" I protested.

"The army's right here, Walt. In the unlikely event there's a complication, I can be there in a helicopter in fifteen minutes."

In less than a minute, Mrs. Lynch bustled back into the room with a bag, checking a list she had made. "Yes, I've got everything here . . . except . . . oh . . . ! I'll need a roasting pan . . . We've got one in the hall kitchen. Marjorie?"

"A roasting pan?" I said. "Doctor, please! You've got to get here somehow!"

"Walt," said the doctor soothingly. "Maggie's in good health and in good hands. Frankly, if it's a choice between a normal childbirth with Mrs. Lynch attending and me climbing into a Canadian army helicopter built in 1964, I like Maggie's chances a lot better than mine. Now, I have to slip away, Walt. Call me if there's any change." And he rang off.

Mrs. Lynch was sitting next to Maggie, listening to the baby's heartbeat with a fetoscope. Maggie was quite pale and her forehead was covered with sweat. But she was quiet for the moment.

"And how are you, dear?" said Mrs. Lynch. "Are the pains stronger now? How far apart are they?"

"About four minutes, I think," whispered Maggie. "I think they're coming again."

Mrs. Lynch took her by the shoulders and said, "Get a deep breath into you, dear, that's it."

Maggie breathed deeply and her eyes widened. "I think I'm gonna . . . throw aaaaaaagghh!"

Mrs. Lynch grabbed a wastebasket and plunked it in front of Maggie as she retched.

"There you go," she said. "You just honk into that, honey. That's your body's way of getting ready to do battle." She turned to me and spoke in crisp words that would have sent a platoon of men scampering out of a trench into gunfire. "You want to get her two wet towels, Mr. Wingfield . . . one hot and one cold."

"I can't sit down," moaned Maggie. "I can't sit."

"That's good," approved Mrs. Lynch, helping Maggie to her feet. "Walking's the best thing for you, if you can do it. C'mon, dear, take my arm and we'll look at these pictures on the wall. What do we have here? Oh, my goodness, there's the massacre of the Protestants at Castle Kerry. Not as restful as the new labour room at the hospital, is it?"

She was terrific. She took Maggie's vital signs and the baby's heart rate every half hour and checked the dilation of the cervix. She got Maggie to breathe through the contractions. I timed each one and counted out loud for her so that she knew when they were coming to an end, and when they finally stopped and she called for a cloth I mopped her brow, first with the cold cloth, then the hot cloth, sticking a Popsicle in her mouth and smearing her lips with lip balm.

So it went until one o'clock in the morning, the contractions getting closer and closer and more and more powerful, until finally Maggie dropped to her knees and crushed my hand in hers.

"I can't do this anymore!" she wailed.

"That's what we like to hear!" cheered Mrs. Lynch. She turned to me with a knowing smile. "They always say that when they're ready to pop." She helped Maggie back onto the cushions. "Yes, you're going to have a little baby now, Mrs. Wingfield. You've done a wonderful job, and it's just going to take two or three more pushes and we'll be all done. It's all right to push now. Are you ready . . . ? Now . . . PUSH!"

Maggie pushed with all her might. The baby emerged on the third try.

"There she is!" cried Mrs. Lynch. "Look at her, the little purple bundle of grief that she is. You have a little girl. There's your Hope, Mrs. Wingfield. And she's just perfect, so she is."

Mrs. Lynch cut the cord, tied it off and gently laid the baby on Maggie's chest. After a minute, she wrapped her in a warm towel and placed her in the roasting pan. Then she handed her to me.

They tell me babies can't see anything at birth because their eyes don't focus. But I have strong doubts about this theory. The baby's eyes opened wide and stared straight at me, such a look of skeptical appraisal as I have ever received from anyone in my life.

I heard voices and then a cheer from the main hall. I opened the door a crack and saw a sea of faces. They were all still there. I stepped out with Hope in the roasting pan and held her up for everyone to see. There was another cheer.

"It's a g-g-girl," I stammered. "Her name is Hope."

Fortunately, they cheered again, because I couldn't say anything else.

Yours sincerely,
Walt

—— *December 15*

Dear Ed,

The next week was, let's say . . . busy. If you think a newborn is a handful at the best of times, try having one when the power's out, supplies are scarce and to get to the road you still have to crawl on your hands and knees up the lane. Never mind, it's been the best week of my life.

Everyone has helped. Mrs. Lynch has been over every day. She even brought her last can of Dream Whip to make cream puffs. Now, Maggie is a woman who will never eat crow—but she ate the Dream Whip.

Yesterday afternoon Hope was napping, Maggie was on the phone, and I was piling wood on the verandah, when I heard a crack like a cannon shot. The great elm tree in the Squire's lane crashed to the ground. As it went down, it took the power line, a fence and the Squire's pump house with it. Maggie came out on the verandah. She looked at the fallen elm tree, but she clearly had something else on her mind.

"That was Maureen," she said. "Gus is dying, and she can't get hold of the Squire because his phone is out. She says Gus wants to come home. The hospital's in chaos right now, and there's nothing more they can do for him there, anyway. He just keeps asking her to take him home to the Seventh Line."

I couldn't make any sense of this. There were so many questions. The Squire wanted to marry Maureen, but she went off with Gus. Why would Gus want to come home?

"I don't know," said Maggie. "But I think we've been wrong about all of this. She said something odd on the phone. She said she knew it might be hard for the Squire, but she feels she's been a disappointment to Gus in many ways and just this once she wants to 'do the right thing by him.' She said it twice."

I looked over at the Squire's house. With all of the trees now gone between us, it seemed a long way off. The porch swing I'd bought at the auction was sitting at my feet. I remembered how Maureen had said, "We used to rock in it for hours and hours."

The walk over to the Squire's was treacherous, but it wasn't the walk I was worried about. I picked my way up the lane and across the road, climbed over the fallen elm tree and up the walk to the Squire's front door. The Squire was waiting in the doorway.

"Hell of a mess out there, isn't it?" he said.

"I'm sorry about your poor old tree," I replied.

"Yeah. We won the battle and lost the war. At least those damned elm beetles didn't get it. It took the power line down with it, too. Did you see that? I'm going to need an electrician; that is, if we ever get the power back. And look at all the—"

"Maggie just got a call from Maureen. Your brother is dying and he wants to be brought home here to the house."

"Home? After fifty-five years he calls this his home?"

"Maureen wants to know if you will allow it. I can't imagine it will be for very long. We'll have nursing care around the clock, and you know everybody is here to help. Maureen said she is anxious to spare your feelings, as well."

"What would she care about my feelings? She walked out of here all those years ago and never looked back."

"Are you sure about that?" I asked.

"Oh, she sent me a letter to explain it all." He tossed his head in the direction of the wood stove.

"But you never opened it . . . Don't you think you should open it now?"

The Squire was silent. Finally he motioned me to come in. He stood looking at the envelope on the stove for a long time. Then he carefully picked it off the shelf and ran his thumbnail along the seal. He removed the letter gingerly, unfolded it and stared at it for a moment. Then he handed it to me and looked away.

"Would you read it?" he asked gruffly.

I took the letter. It was written on robin's egg blue paper in a poised, elegant hand and dated November 17, 1945. I read the words out loud to the Squire:

> Dear Baxter,
> I'm writing this late at night because I can't sleep
> and I want to say what is in my heart.
> I have had many second thoughts since
> Gus asked me to marry him. He's a fine man,
> but I can't seem to forget the time you and I

spent together, in spite of all the difficulties with your parents.

I know it's important for you to obey your parents' wishes, but I also know that I love you, and if you love me, too, then I feel everything else will work itself out somehow.

If you say the word, I will tell Gus I'm sorry, that I can't marry him next Friday. It may be hard for him, but I know it will be for the best.

Hoping to hear from you.

All my love,

Maureen

I folded the letter and handed it back to him. "I'm so sorry," I said. He took it, raised it slowly to his face and sniffed the paper. Then he folded it back into the envelope and replaced it on the shelf of the wood stove. Finally, he spoke.

"You tell Maureen that Gus can come home."

Back at the house, Maggie and Hope were waiting at the kitchen door. I told her what had happened.

"It seems such a waste," I said. "Why on earth would he not have opened that letter?"

"There's a difference between not needing to know and needing not to know," said Maggie slowly. "My guess is he thought the letter said one of two things . . . and he couldn't really live with either."

Late the next afternoon, an ambulance appeared on the road from the south. Maggie and I bundled up the baby and made our way over to the Squire's. The elm tree blocked the lane, but they backed up the ambulance as far as they could. The back door opened and the stretcher emerged. I caught a brief glimpse of Gus's gaunt face, eyes wide open and fixed on the house. Then shoulders and hats obscured my view as they carried him forward.

He didn't make it. He died before they could get the stretcher over the fallen elm. Maureen knelt at his side for a few minutes, her hand on his. Then she made the sign of the cross and allowed herself to be helped to her feet. She looked around at the crowd of neighbours, smiled faintly and took a deep breath.

"There . . . it's done," she said. "He saw the house. Poor Gus. Thank you so much. Thank you all so much." She looked up to the verandah and saw the Squire. "Oh, Baxter. There you are. What a commotion we've made for you this afternoon. Here, Mr. Wingfield, take my hand. I can't stand on this treacherous ice."

I helped her over the last of the elm trees and up the steps to the Squire. He took her hand and they stood looking at each other for the first time in over fifty years.

"I just read your letter yesterday," said the Squire.

"Yesterday?" said Maureen.

They looked at each other for another long moment, and then the Squire held the door open for her and they went inside together. I made my way back up the lane to Maggie and Hope. We stood and watched as the ambulance slowly backed out of the laneway onto the Seventh Line, paused and headed back south.

"What do we do?" I asked her. "What will become of them?"

"Who knows, Walt? We'll just have to make sure she knows she's always welcome here."

"Yes, we can do that. What do you think, Hope?"

Hope made that gllliggggccchh sound that babies make so that we can fill in the words for them. Across the road, the small group of Gus's mourners lingered beside the fallen tree, the way people often do outside a small country church after a service. It was a scene in black and white that made me think again of fire and ice.

Sometimes it's hard to tell the difference between the two. For the Squire and Maureen, their fire acted like ice—it made their lives cold for half a century. For the folks around here, the ice acted like fire—it warmed them and brought them a bit closer. But it also had the same effect as a forest fire—it cleared the ground for a fresh start. A fresh start and a new Hope.

Yours sincerely,

Walt

A NOTE FROM THE EDITOR

The Great Persephone Ice Storm cleared the ground, all right.

For one brief, shining moment, peace and harmony prevailed across the township. Which was great news for everyone, except the newspaper. I was dismayed to realize how much I rely on hatred and discord for my livelihood. When the lion lies down with the lamb, it means a sleepless night for the editor.

There were some lasting changes to the landscape. When they restored the power to the Town Line, the crews were in such a rush they accidentally put a pole in Mrs. Coutts's yard and hooked her up to the grid. When they realized their mistake, Mrs. Coutts told them not to worry—she was sure it would come in handy. That "terrible ice storm" had taken down the pole for her clothesline.

The mayor received a cheque for thirty thousand dollars from the Federal Disaster Relief Fund. The town fathers used the money to buy a Zamboni for the arena. Ernie Pickets has been doing the job for years in a pair of snow boots, hauling a perforated oil drum. He was thrilled he'd get to drive it, and he was the one who suggested entering it in the books under Ice Relief.

Professor Burns went down to his mailbox and found a smoked ham in it, with a note saying, "Thanks for the help. You're a good neighbour."

But in some ways, things are just the same. The day after the lights came back on, the Seventh Line celebrated by organizing an ice fishing expedition in the Persephone Township Moose Bus, with Freddy at the wheel. Constable Bradley pulled them over for speeding, belching smoke and impersonating a school bus. And Pookie didn't change. He still harbours bloodthirsty designs on Willy's lower regions. But that didn't stop Willy from asking Isobel out to the Ice Storm Dance for the Heart and Stroke Fund. He got her a costume as the Ice Princess, and he went as her knight in shining armour.

Walt said he'd never suspected Willy had such a sense of romance. But Freddy said, "It isn't the romance, Walt, it's the tin pants."

Chapter Six

Wingfield's

INFERNO

ANOTHER NOTE FROM THE EDITOR

I just received a letter from our insurance company, advising me of a hefty hike in our premiums. They offered only this by way of explanation:

> Dear Sir,
> Please be advised that we are reviewing your insurance coverage in light of the increased risk factors that are associated with running a weekly newspaper.

It's odd, because I thought the weekly newspaper business was getting safer. In this country we haven't lost a printing press to violent insurrection since 1826. That was the year a bunch of hooligans destroyed the newspaper office of that radical, William Lyon Mackenzie. Even then, a jury awarded damages to Mackenzie, which helped him set up shop again, made him famous and enabled him to start an insurrection of his very own ten years later.

Turns out the "risk factors" this fellow is talking about have nothing to do with violence or property damage. He's just trying to protect himself after the McKelvey incident.

Dry Cry McKelvey used to have a monopoly on hardware and building supply in Larkspur. Last winter a big national outfit set up shop outside of town with the slogan "We've got your lumber." "Not for long, you don't," said Dry Cry, and set out in the dead of night to torch the place. But it had just snowed, and he slipped on the handicapped access ramp. The snow put out his torch, and the fall put out his back. So he sued the company for not exercising due diligence in snow removal. He won and now the insurance company thinks all our premiums should go up.

We're not all Dry Crys in this community, but try explaining that to an insurance company. I figured I'd check with Walt. If anyone knows anything about managing risk, it would be him. He's been juggling the farm, his work at the brokerage firm and, for the last nine months, a baby.

——— *September 21*

Dear Ed,

My biggest problem these days is sleep deprivation. I've always been sympathetic to those new fathers sitting in the Monday morning meetings with that thousand-yard stare. Now I know how it feels—it's brutal.

The other day my partner, Alf Harrison, said that he thinks I came back from maternity leave too soon. I wondered what gave him that idea. He said that I drifted off during the Comco Pension Fund meeting, so he gave me a nudge and said it was "my turn." Apparently I picked up his cellphone and told him I was going to warm it up then we could all "go sleepy-bye-byes."

It's not the actual sleeping time. It's the sleep interruption that plays havoc with your circadian rhythms. Hope gets a lot of colds, and every time they go straight to her ears. We have some drops for her, but the only thing that gives her effective relief is yelling for about an hour.

But a couple of weeks ago we passed a milestone. Maggie finally broke down and left Hope in the hands of someone else for the evening. For the first time in nine months, we went out on a date. Gertrude Lynch was wonderfully helpful during Maggie's confinement, and when I called she said she was happy to babysit.

"But you know you'll have to get rid of that dog, Walt," she warned.

"Spike?" I asked, somewhat taken aback.

"He isn't safe around the baby. You know what they say: 'The house is filled with perils untold, when the child is new and the dog is old.'"

The vet warned me about this, too. But Spike has been with me almost from the beginning here. He was originally Freddy's dog, but there were problems. He wandered, he chased deer, he stayed out all night, and finally Spike just couldn't stand it anymore. One day he followed me home, and he's been here ever since.

But, of course, a baby changes everything. Animal psychologists say it's because the dog suddenly finds itself no longer the centre of attention. It gets jealous and may eventually even attack the child. But Spike's always been so gentle. I asked Maggie about it while we were doing dishes.

"Have you ever known dogs to attack babies?"

"It doesn't come up, Walt. Where I come from, dogs live outside. Right next to the barn they have a nice, cozy doghouse, which they have to share with the husband from time to time. But they don't seem to mind."

Maggie has never warmed to the idea of an inside dog, although I remember two beagles named Amos and Andy that Freddy attempted to housetrain while Maggie was still living with him. For quite a while I thought their names were Geddoff and Geddout.

"I know you're fond of Spike, dear, but it's a real question," said Maggie. "Hope's starting to get pretty mobile. We can't watch her every second."

I sat down on the floor and had a heart-to-heart chat with Spike over his supper bowl.

"Look, old bean," I said. "I know I've been busy and we haven't got out as much as we used to. And I guess I've been preoccupied and missed a couple of doggie supper times. But you wouldn't hold that against Hope, would you?"

Spike looked at me with those mournful eyes and said, "Woof."

The trouble is, I don't know what woof means. So I decided I'd better just keep an eye on him.

Anyway, when we got back from our date, I checked in with Mrs. Lynch on the verandah while Maggie was inside, crooning over a sleeping Hope.

"How did you manage?" I asked her.

"I managed, Walt. But I was right. You'll have to get rid of that dog. That's an accident just waiting to happen."

I didn't say anything to Maggie but I kept a close eye on Spike and Hope for the next few days. Then, last night, we went out again. This time Freddy came down to babysit. As soon as we got home and shut off the engine we could hear it from right across the yard—Hope howling, Freddy shouting, Spike woofing. We rushed inside and found Hope standing red-faced in her playpen. Freddy and Spike were glaring at each other in the middle of the room. You could cut the tension with a knife.

Freddy's shoulders dropped with relief when he saw us. "Jeez, am I glad to see to see you guys!" he said, "Welcome to Fight Night."

Maggie scooped Hope up in her arms and soothed her.

"There, there, darling. What's the matter?" she cooed. Then she turned on Freddy. "What is the matter with her! What happened here?"

Freddy shrugged. "I reckon she's probably hungry after all this time."

"Didn't you feed her? We left the formula in the fridge for you."

"Feed her?" sputtered Freddy. "I couldn't get anywhere near her. Spike wouldn't let me."

Apparently Spike only said what he always says—"woof." But in this case woof meant, "If you want to touch the kid, you go through me."

Freddy watched Spike retire to his corner and flop down, exhausted.

"That dog's been on the job all night," he said. "Never moved once. If Hope had the St. John's Ambulance and the Secret Service looking after her, she wouldn't be any safer than she is with that dog."

So I guess we don't have to worry about Spike being jealous. I've been watching the two of them this past week. There's starting to be a little bare spot in Spike's fur behind his left ear. It's where Hope hangs on to him as they roam around the house.

Hope makes a lot of little sounds, and we're perched on the edge of our seats, waiting for her first word. I must confess I've been campaigning at mealtimes with her favourite raspberry Jell-O to get her to say "daddy" first. I hold a spoon just a few inches from her mouth, look her directly in the eye and say, "Da da da da! Can you say that, Hope? Da da? Can you say 'daddy'?"

Maggie caught me at it today.

"That's not fair," she complained, and sat down on the other side of Hope's chair. "'Daddy' is easier to say than 'mummy.' But you can say it, can't you, darling? Say 'mum mum . . . mummy'!"

"Dada . . . daddy!"

"Mum mum . . . mummy!"

Hope looked from Maggie to me and back again. Then she gave a little hiccup and said quite clearly: "'pike!"

Lots of babies have been raised by animals: Mowgli by wolves, Tarzan by the apes. Rumour has it that Dry Cry McKelvey was brought up by turkey vultures.

Yours sincerely,

Walt

—— *October 15*

Dear Ed,

Now that I'm a family man, I thought I should have a look at disability insurance. You know, $5,000 if you lose a hand, $10,000 for an eye, $25,000 for an arm and a leg . . . cheerful stuff. And, if you prefer not to dispose of yourself bit by bit, there's always accidental death. That particular "black hole" is worth more than the sum of your parts.

I still have a disability policy at the firm, but I thought it should be updated. So this week I had lunch with the insurance guy we always deal with in the city. He promised to write something up, but he warned me that it would involve major changes.

"You're on the farm now, Walt," he explained. "If we write a new policy, I'd have to move you into a new classification. Right now you're A-2 Office Worker—pretty low risk."

My office staff is low risk all right. I hardly ever see them move. I wondered what kind of worker could be considered A-1. Probably senators.

"So, what classification am I now?" I asked.

He riffled through his black book. "Let's see . . . it looks like you'd be F-18. That's parachute testers, bomb defusers and farmers. And fighter pilots. It's more expensive."

He wasn't sure how much more, but he'll let me know. I expect it'll be considerably more, because, for the first time ever, he bought lunch.

I was curious about all this, so I went down to see Don. He and Freddy were having a coffee break on his verandah. Freddy wouldn't carry a nickel of insurance, but I figured that since Don has a wife and three kids, he would probably have some kind of plan that would work for me.

"If you don't mind my asking, what do you pay for disability insurance?" I asked.

"Nothin'," said Don. "Can't afford it. And I don't know who can. I keep a bit of life insurance through the federation, and I take out crop insurance most years, but my real insurance is those seven guys out there."

He waved at the neighbouring farms dotted around the slopes of the Pine River Valley.

"I know if I get laid up and can't get the crop off, those fellas will be on my fields tomorrow. And they know I'd do the same for them."

"Yep," said Freddy. "Count on your neighbours, Walt. You're better off to stick with your old policy, the one with the

Office Worker classification. Then, if you get hurt bad, we'll drag you inside the house and drop a filing cabinet on you. Hey, what are friends for?"

I was pondering this on the train home from the city. The trip offers more time for reflection than it used to, because the last twenty miles cross about a dozen bridges and culverts that have been downgraded to a fifteen-mile-an-hour limit—for insurance reasons, of course. This drops the average speed of the trip to thirty miles an hour, which is actually one mile an hour slower than when the line was built in 1856.

It was still light when the spires of Larkspur appeared on the horizon. While I was away the fall plowing had begun, turning the fields of the Pine River Valley to slabs of chocolate. Combines munched through cornfields, billowing dark clouds of dust behind them. I stepped off the train and breathed in the smells of home: ripe apples, freshly turned earth and burning leaves. I had a few minutes to spare before Maggie picked me up, so I sat down on the war memorial in front of the station to enjoy the evening. A light ring of white mist surrounded the Orange Hall like a halo. Little plumes of it steamed out of the vents under the eaves. With a start, I realized that the Orange Hall was on fire!

Fortunately, our 911 service has recently been upgraded. I grabbed my cellphone and dialled. A voice promptly responded.

"Hello?" I said. "The Orange Hall is on fire . . . No, I don't know the numerical fire code, but you know the building—it's at the four corners of Wellington Street and the Town Li . . . well, it used to be the Town Line. Now it's Regional Road number . . . oh, what is it . . ."

"What town is that, sir?"

"Right in Larkspur."

"And where is Larkspur?"

"Larkspur? It's north of Highway 13, about five miles west of Demeter—"

"And what province is that, sir?"

"In Ontario, for Pete's sake! Where are you?"

At that moment the 4×4 swung into the parking lot and Maggie jumped out.

"Walt, I need to use the phone," she said and took it from me. She dialled seven numbers and had to wait only a few seconds. "Sparky," she said into the phone. "The Orange Hall's on fire! Get the boys!" Then she handed it back to me. "Well, this is a fine how-do-you-do," she sighed.

"Thank goodness you got here. Who knows how long it would have taken me to give directions to someone coming from Nova Scotia."

"Well, the volunteers are on their way but I don't know if it'll help much," said Maggie. "You know what we call the fire department, Walt—the Larkspur Basement Savers."

I've heard this before. Don't get me wrong; the Larkspur Volunteers are a great group. No matter what the weather, they are on the scene within minutes. They train and fundraise relentlessly. But still, their success rate isn't all that good. Let's just say their save percentage wouldn't keep them playing goal in the NHL. They're more in the league of the Ancient Mariner, who, you may recall, "stoppeth one of three."

The fire truck skidded to a halt in front of the hall. Sparky McKeown leapt from the cab, barking orders in all directions. Sparky has been the fire chief for years and years. In fact, he's been chief for so long no one can remember when they started calling him Sparky. He has lots of experience fighting fires. The trouble is, quite a few of them have been on his own farm.

The drive shed went first, then the dairy barn, then the house. There were the usual rumours. As Freddy put it, "Try as you like, you cannot save old farm buildings by loadin' them up with insurance."

Anyway, I don't think anyone could have saved the Orange Hall—it was too far gone. The volunteers did what they could to contain the fire. They hooked up hoses and soon had two streams arcing through the air. Two men actually went into the building for a few brief minutes and came out again, one carrying a large painting of William the Third crossing the Boyne River, the other following with an armful of brightly coloured flags from the Regalia Room. Gertrude Lynch, whose house is right next door to the hall came and stood beside us.

"Why are they rescuing that junk?" she complained. "What about the piano?"

"It's too far back," said Maggie. "The floor might collapse under them."

As she spoke, there was an ominous crack, then a sickening crash as the piano hit the bowling alley in the basement. Two hundred and twenty strings of piano wire gave up the ghost with a sound like an original composition by R. Murray Schafer. Then the steel roofing at the rear buckled and an angry spike of orange flame shot up through the gap. A window exploded and the curls of white smoke along the eaves changed to thick black clouds. I heard a sound like an engine revving up and realized it was air rushing in through the window to feed the fire. The two spouts of water shifted away from the hall and began playing on Gertrude's house. One brave soul remained on a ladder against the front of the hall, prying off the wooden sign that read LOL Number 26, Larkspur 1954.

The Orange Hall was burning down. Scenes from the last five years flashed across my mind: Old Jimmy step-dancing under the chestnut tree in the dark. The Price Family Orchestra playing all night with babies in baskets parked along the edge of the stage in front of them. Our wedding dance was here. We were at the Berry Festival Dance when Maggie told me she was pregnant. She gave birth to Hope in the Regalia Room. And it was all going up in a whirl of flame.

"The lights have been on in this hall every night for fifty years. It's going to leave a big hole," said Maggie quietly.

"Well, I guess, thank goodness for insurance, after all," I said.

Maggie looked at me. "It's the Orange Lodge, Walt. It's not insured."

Shadows and emergency lights played on the sea of faces staring at the collapsing building. Not a person spoke. Gertrude Lynch stood on the front walk of her house and dabbed at her eyes with a handkerchief. Finally, Maggie touched my arm.

"C'mon, Walt. Let's go home."

Yours sincerely,
Walt

—— October 20

Dear Ed,

King is my oldest horse; I bought him from Freddy four years ago, and he was ready to retire back then. I don't know exactly how old King is, but people often comment about the deep worry lines on his face. I tell them it's because he remembers the Cuban Missile Crisis.

I don't know how old Feedbin and Mortgage are either, but they are very long in the tooth. You tell a horse's age by looking at its teeth. As the horse ages, the front teeth get longer and the back teeth are worn down to almost nothing. It's the opposite of how you tell the age of a hockey player.

Old they may be; slow they are not. The first season was a nightmare, trying to work up the little field in front of the house. It was like water-skiing behind a boat with no driver. My neighbour across the road, the Squire, came over one morning to make an observation in my very first year on the farm, just a few months after I first met him.

"I was looking at the big circles in your crop from my bedroom window and thought maybe you were getting visits from alien spaceships," he said.

"No, it's just the horses," I said. "When they take off, they always do a big circle in the field and head back to the barn. I'd like to teach them to make sharper turns, but first I'd have to get them to go a bit slower."

"You need a bigger space to work in . . . like Saskatchewan," he chuckled.

"Is there a bigger field where I could practise?" I asked.

"I've got that twenty-five acres across the road. Maybe you'd like to rent it?" he offered.

"I don't know. There sure are a lot of stones on it."

"You gotta have the stones, Walt. They knock the dirt off the implements when you're goin' around the field."

"Oh," I said. "I didn't know that. But I notice on Calvin Currie's fields the stones are all in piles."

"Yeah, Calvin just got them in last week. He hasn't got them spread yet."

The horses never really did settle down, and I came to regard the whole investment as a dead loss. Then, out of the blue, Feedbin had a secret affair and produced a filly. Somewhat hopefully, I named her Dividend. She seems to be a natural pacer, and I made a brief attempt at training her to harness with an old two-wheeled buggy I got from the Mennonites. I took her out on the unopened road allowance at the end of the Seventh Line, where I thought we would be fairly safe. But she got going so fast I couldn't hold her, and we sliced off a row of mailboxes trying to negotiate the turn onto the 25 Sideroad. One of the mailboxes belonged to a guy from Alberta—a big, tall man with a moustache and a stetson. I was helping him set up a new mailbox the next day when he made an observation about Dividend.

"You know, I can help you put some brains in that horse if you want to leave her with me some afternoon. She'd be a lot safer to handle."

"Oh, really?" I said. "What can you do in an afternoon?"

"I can explain to her what we mean out west when we say 'whoa'."

When I asked him about his technique for working with a problem horse, he talked about a second set of reins and a surcingle and a running martingale down through the thin-gummies . . . Now, I know about reins and bridles, but when people start talking about surcingles and martingales, they might as well be speaking medieval Italian to me. However, the man seemed to know what he was doing, so one day I led Dividend over and left her with him. When I picked her up that evening, she was a changed horse. I could lead her around with a piece of string. If the buggy ever comes back from the Mennonite repair shop in Elmira, I think I might try her in harness again.

In the meantime, she still enjoys a breakout. Last week Maggie was going to let me sleep in after my stint in the city. But she appeared at the top of the stairs shortly after seven and announced that Dividend was joyriding again, out on the road.

Dividend's breakouts all follow the same pattern. She goes to the south end of the road allowance and waits; when I show up in the 4×4, the chase is on, back to the barn. Sure enough, as soon as she saw the 4×4, her tail went up and she took off out onto the road. She's amazing to watch like this. It's like she's on a set of tracks. Her whole body stretches out and the dirt flies out behind her as she hammers down the road. And she never breaks into a canter. This morning she was really humming, and when we got back to the farm she shot right past the gate without even glancing at it, and then right past Freddy's gate, too. That left nothing between her and the highway. I stepped on the gas, got out in front of her and honked the horn until she ran down into the ditch and turned around. She whinnied cheerfully and pounded off back down the Seventh Line. I was relieved to see Freddy standing at his gate this time, but he didn't stop her. He just stood there and watched as we flashed by. I stepped on the gas, chased her down once more and got her turned around.

This time, Freddy waved her in. She streaked down the lane to the barnyard past the drive shed, where Freddy and Maggie's two nephews, Willy and Dave, were repairing a giant corn picker. They both looked up as Dividend went past, and Dave trotted over to swing the barnyard gate shut.

"You don't normally see something going that fast without slicks and a brake chute," he said.

Freddy walked over. "Did you see her out there, fellas?" he asked. "Three times the length of the concession, and look at her. She wouldn't blow out a candle."

"Look at the ass-end on her," agreed Willy. "Where you been hiding this one, Walt?"

"This is Feedbin's filly," I replied.

"Feedbin's filly, huh?" said Dave. "That's where this one gets her speed, then."

"Apparently, Feedbin wasn't that fast," I said. "I understand she was retired after one season."

"Oh, she was fast enough," said Dave. "Feedbin had all the speed in the world. The problem was, she always broke stride. You see, in harness racing, if a horse breaks into a canter, it has to pull over and yield to other horses until it gets back on stride. Most horses have to be trained not to break stride, but some have the gene that makes them natural pacers, and they're worth their weight in gold. So, who was the father to this one?"

It was anybody's guess, but I always suspected a scruffy black stallion that Freddy brought home from the track during my first year on the farm. He got out a few times.

"E-mail?" said Dave. "Well, that explains it, then. His great-great-great grandfather was one of the great natural pacers in this part of the world—Clipper Ship."

"Oh, yeah," agreed Freddy. "That was the start of a breeding line where every generation seemed to get a little bit faster than the one before. What was the colt they got out of Clipper Ship?"

"Pony Express," said Willy. "And then Pony Express sired Overnight Courier."

"Yeah that's right," said Freddy. "And then Overnight Courier begat Telegram. And Telegram begat Fax Machine, who begat E-mail, who begat . . . Say, Walt, we need a racing name for this filly. Jeez, what goes faster than e-mail?"

"I don't know," I said. "How about Paycheque? Gone before you see it."

Dave stroked Dividend's neck admiringly. He gave me a sideways look and said, "Say, Walt. Why don't you leave her up here with us for a bit? She's got a lot of jam, and she needs someone to work with her. Preferably someone with no dependants."

That was fine with me. Dave has this way with animals. If St. Francis of Assisi were a dirtbike racer—that'd be Dave. A few days later I bumped into him outside the post office in Larkspur and he looked preoccupied.

"How's the training going?" I asked.

"Awful, Walt," he said. "I can't figure it out. When you put the bridle on her, she just stands there and shakes. Did she have something bad happen to her? Any train wrecks when you had her out?"

I said, "Just the business with the mailboxes. And she was going so fast that time I don't think she even noticed."

Dave mulled this over. "Anybody else work with her?"

"That guy from Alberta; he had a few hours with her teaching her how to stop."

Dave nodded. "Oh, yeah, the Mountain Man. What did he do?"

I tried to explain the harness arrangement as if I knew what I was talking about: the second set of reins that went through the bellyband and the running martingale . . .

"A Flyin' W!" cried Dave in horror.

"A Flying W—that's what he called it. Why what's the matter? What is that, anyway?"

Dave winced. "Jeez, Walt. Those reins don't go to her mouth, they go down to her front feet. If the horse runs away and doesn't stop when you say whoa, you yank her front feet out from under her and knock her flat on her face."

"Oh, my goodness, that's awful!" I said. "He told me he was just going to make her safe."

"Well, she's safe, all right," said Dave, shaking his head. "She's so safe she don't know what she's for anymore. Jeez, Walt, I can't believe you did a 'Flying W' on a filly from the line of the great Clipper Ship."

And with that he walked away to his truck.

Yours sincerely,
Walt

—— October 27

Dear Ed,

This hasn't been a good week for livestock. After the business with Dividend, I noticed that our egg production had dropped drastically. I went down to the barn one day last week and looked in all the usual places, but there wasn't a single one. I asked Maggie if she thought maybe the short nights and the cooler weather would make them stop laying.

"No," she said. "Nothing's wrong with the hens, Walt. We've got a thief, one with four feet. My guess is that it's a skunk."

"I thought security was pretty tight in here. So, I guess I should get one those wire traps from the Humane Society, huh? Would that work for a skunk?"

"Yes, it would trap the skunk," she agreed. "Then what?"

"Then I take it somewhere far away and release it, right?"

"Not if you want to sleep in the house," she said.

"Ah, yes . . . I see."

I love challenges like this. It's like those case studies they put in front of you at business school to test your skill at problem solving. I made my own humane trap, consisting of a long smooth board, a tall sawhorse, an egg and a garbage can. The board was hinged like a seesaw at the sawhorse, and I fixed an egg to the end of the board with an elastic band. As the candidate stepped out to the end of the board, it would tip, and he would slide down into the garbage can, which, of course, has a lid. I set it up.

Next morning I checked it out. The trap was sprung. But there was no candidate. The garbage can was lying on its side and the egg was gone. It was a skunk all right. The aroma hanging in the air told me that it had fired a warning shot at the garbage can.

But I don't give up easily. I was confident I could think my way through this. I just needed to find a way to temporarily immobilize the skunk. Horse tranquilizer! I'll inject horse tranquilizer into the egg. It works fast. The skunk gets the egg, falls into the trap and then just goes to sleep. I went to the vet to get some.

"What would you use it for, Mr. Wingfield?" asked the doctor. I explained my plan while he listened with one eyebrow raised. When I finished, he thought for a moment.

"It's an interesting approach," he conceded. "It should tranquilize the skunk, all right. Then what?"

"Then I take it out to the escarpment somewhere and dump it. What do you think?"

"You could do that," he said. "But you don't want to be too long about it. This stuff is time-specific. You've got five hours, at the most, before the skunk wakes up—scared and mad."

Five hours seemed like plenty of time. I just had to know exactly when the trap was sprung. And that part was easy. I'd just sit up in the barn until I heard a kerfuffle and a thump. I filled a syringe with horse tranquilizer and injected two eggs with it, since I might have need of a backup—and trundled off to put my plan to the test.

So, that's how I came to be sitting motionless in a dark corner of the barn on a very pleasant Saturday evening in late October, waiting for the sound of a homemade skunk trap being blundered into. I really didn't mind the waiting. It was such a pleasant Saturday evening, unusually pleasant for late October. And, anyway, it gave me a chance to think about stuff. I got a letter from my insurance company telling me that they don't insure farms and that I have to find another carrier. My broker tells me this is happening a lot these days. He said I was lucky because some farmers can't be insured at all. It's too expensive. The Orange Lodge couldn't afford it. More and more low-income home owners and even drivers are just doing without it. Who's to blame? Who's the skunk here?

You can't really blame the insurance companies. If people are going to sue for damages when a cup of coffee spills in their laps—well, the money's got to come from somewhere. And no matter what you want to say about lawyers—and who doesn't?—it's not really their fault. They're just representing the interests of their clients.

So who is the skunk? Is it the courts who award the damages? Is that why judges are all in black with those white collars and stripey things? Sitting in the gloom of the barn, listening to soft rock on the talk-free FM station, was making my mind wander.

I glanced at my watch. It was three o'clock in the morning and my eyes were starting to close. Maybe tonight wasn't the night. I started to think maybe I should have a little nap. It looked as if we might not get any action this night, anyway, and it couldn't hurt if I just rested my eyes for a bit, even just for a few minutes. I made my way up to the house in the dark, let myself in quietly and stretched out on the sofa.

When I woke up, it was getting light outside. I grabbed the remote and turned on the television. It was 7:05. I'd slept for four hours! I pulled my boots on and trotted back down to the barn. It was beautiful outside. The morn in russet mantle clad walks o'er the dew of Calvin Currie's pasture. A really lovely late-October Sunday morning.

Better yet, the trap was sprung, the egg was gone, and the skunk was in the garbage can, sleeping peacefully. This was okay. The earliest this could have happened was three in the morning. That still gave me an hour. I reached in, grasped the skunk gently but firmly by the scruff and lifted it out of the garbage can.

The thing I had forgotten is that on a Saturday night in late October, everywhere in Canada—except in Saskatchewan—we change over from daylight saving to standard time by moving our clocks . . .

The skunk woke up.

Skunks have only one natural defence. But it's a beauty. That night I slept in the barn. But Maggie was very sweet. Next morning she came out to the barn, with a clothespin on her nose, and brought me breakfast—warm toast and a lovely soft-boiled egg, just the way I like it . . .

Of course, she used the other egg. I'm pretty sure it was an accident. I made it out of the barn as far as the horse feeder and then decided it was time for another nap. This time, I got about ten hours of the most restful sleep I have ever known.

Yours sincerely,

Walt

———— *November 2*

Dear Ed,

There's an old rock elm stump in my lower pasture that has been rotting very slowly since the elm blight swept through this area forty years ago. Snows cover it in winter; wild grape vines and scotch thistles shroud it from view during the summer. But in the melt and frost of the shoulder seasons, it emerges pretty much unchanged, stubbornly refusing to rot down and disappear. I was reminded of that stump this week when I paid a visit to the offices of our local regional government of Hillview.

The recent restructuring of the old township councils into a regional government created a lot of upset, partly because so many councillors, clerks and road crew were declared redundant and bounced out of their jobs. People like Harold MacNabb, the man who has served as Persephone Township's clerk-treasurer, Fair Board secretary and bartender at the Legion since . . . well, since before Mackenzie King was born.

Anyway, a week after the fire, I got a call from the secretary to the Chief Administrative Officer for Hillview, inviting me to a meeting to discuss the rebuilding plans for the Orange Hall. It was my first visit to the new admin centre on Wellington Street—an air-conditioned chrome and glass tower that really stands out. On the third floor, the secretary ushered me into a large, handsomely decorated office. A figure in a leather armchair was talking on the phone with his back to me. As I entered, the chair swung around to reveal Nine Lives Harold, the old clerk of Persephone.

"Well, now, Mr. Wingfield. Won't you sit down?"

I was so startled I forgot to congratulate him on his appointment.

"Very good of you to take the time to see me, Mr. Wingfield," said Harold. "I know you're a busy man, so I'll come right to the point. Your name has come forward as a candidate for the steering committee to rebuild the Orange Hall. Council has instructed me to ascertain if you'd be willing to serve."

"They have?" I asked in surprise.

I have crossed paths with Harold twice before, and on both occasions I went home empty-handed, with a vague sensation of having been blindsided by a Ministry of Transportation snowplow.

"Why would they want me for the committee?" I asked cautiously.

"In point of fact, we was thinking of you for chairman."

"Chairman! I don't know what to say . . ."

"We were hoping you would say yes. The committee needs someone with a solid understanding of finance and the expertise to run a public building campaign. Clearly, you possess both. So, what do you think?"

"Well, I'm flattered to be asked," I stammered. "It's a very worthwhile project and a great challenge . . ."

"A challenge? Oh, it is that," he agreed warmly.

"When would we start?" I asked.

"That would be your call, Mr. Chairman."

I hadn't actually said yes, but by the time I got to the elevator I seemed to have lost the opportunity to say no. When I arrived home, Hope was sitting on Freddy's lap on the verandah, a watchful Spike close by. Freddy was instructing Hope in the art of calling wild turkeys.

"Can't start 'em too soon, Walt," he said cheerfully. "Those turkeys are great eatin' when they're barbequed. You gotta get a young one, though."

"Oh," I said. "I guess the old ones are pretty tough, are they?"

"No, they're good eatin', too. But the old ones generally have a computer chip planted just here under the wing. And those game wardens will track you right to your freezer. Always remember that, Hope."

I told him about being appointed chairman. Freddy frowned.

"Jeez, Walt, isn't that kinda public? I got a fieldstone foundation wall at the back of my barn. You could bang your head against that for as long as you like and no one need know but you and the cows."

Freddy has always been a cynic when it comes to public service. At that moment we looked up to see Don mounting the steps of the verandah.

"You guys doin' coffee here?" he asked.

"Maybe something stronger," said Freddy. "Guess who Harold just nabbed to chair the new Orange Hall Building Committee."

Don has actually served on council. I knew I'd get a more measured response from him.

"Did he pull a gun on you, Walt?"

Just at that moment Maggie drove in with a load of groceries. Freddy handed Hope to me and scampered down the steps to help her with the bags.

"Let me take a couple of those, Maggie," he said. "Maybe the chairman here could get the apple juice."

Maggie glanced up at me. "Yes, I heard," she said. "It's all over town."

"Well, what do you think?" I asked.

She straightened up and paused. "Well, I'm just surprised, that's all," she said. "You've always been perfectly nice to him."

"Oh, come on, people," I said. "It's easy to be cynical, but lots of committees work just fine, and, you know, they *can* get things done. They just have to be run properly, that's all."

Maggie tossed Freddy two bags of diapers. "If the fence needs painting," she said, "give me a paintbrush and let me paint the fence. But don't expect me to sit through a meeting of the Fair Board and talk all night about how we're going to paint the fence. It just puts me out of temper." And she breezed past me into the house.

However, she allowed the appointment to stand. I convened the first meeting of the Steering Committee at the home of Gertrude Lynch, since she's also on the committee and lives right next door to the site. A little before eight last Tuesday night, I tapped on Gertrude's door. I was a few minutes early but I found the committee already assembled around Gertrude's arborite kitchen table. Harold rose, smiling his affable smile, and shook my hand.

"We'll put you right here, Mr. Wingfield . . . that is, Mr. Chairman." And he ushered me to the chair at the end of the table. Besides Gertrude and myself, there are two other committee members—those former township councillors who were so interested and unhelpful with my museum proposal—Ernie and Wilfrid. They also happen to be the last two Orangemen in the community. Ernie's been president of the Fair Board, the Federation of Agriculture, Soil and Crop, the Plowmen's, the Curling Club . . . they say that during his lifetime he has run for everything except cover.

"Evening, Mr. Wingfield," boomed Ernie. He always talks to you as though you're at the other end of a hayfield.

Wilfrid is the secretary of the Orange Lodge. Judging by his age, he could write much of the lodge's history in Canada from personal experience.

"Evening, Mr. Windfall," he croaked, not attempting to get out his chair.

"Wingfield," I corrected him.

Wilfrid looked at Ernie. "What did he say?"

"WingFIELD," repeated Gertrude.

"Oh, I feel fine, thank you," said Wilfrid.

I let the matter pass and brought the meeting to order.

"First, I'd like to thank you all for agreeing to accept this challenge," I said. "Tonight is going to be a fact-finding exercise, and I'm going to get right down to business, but—"

"Don't need to spend much time on it," announced Ernie flatly. "Just bulldoze the place and put up a couple of nice bungalows."

"Well, sure . . ." I said as patiently as I could. "That's one possibility, but we're here to explore a range of opportunities. I want to pass something around the table that I found in the township archives yesterday."

I showed them a photograph of the lodge building under construction just about fifty years ago. It's a wonderful picture. There must be fifty people assembled on and around the building, all of them grinning from ear to ear and just so pleased with themselves. You can tell how proud they are of what they accomplished.

As it passed around, I said, "Imagine what it must have felt like, creating something like that from nothing."

"I know what it felt like, Mr. Wingfield," said Harold, "because I was on that committee. That's me there—the handsome young fella at the front. I guess Wilfrid might have worked on the committee, too, but you were already retired, weren't you, Wilfrid?"

"What's that?" said Wilfrid, his eyes snapping open.

"Battery's gone on his hearing aid," said Ernie. He leaned over to Wilfrid's ear. "NEVER MIND, WILFRID. WE'LL TELL YOU WHICH WAY TO VOTE." Then he put his finger on the picture. "That's my dad, there. He hauled the cement up from the train station with a wagon and a team of horses. Worked for more than a month and never got a cent out of it, unlike some people."

This remark jolted Gertrude upright in her chair. "If you're referring to my father," she said, "he did all the finish carpentry but the only money he took was the cost of hinges and doorknobs."

Ernie snorted. "He tarted the place up, using money we didn't have for stuff we didn't need."

"There was provision in the budget for cupboards," said Gertrude.

"The budget was for hooks and shelves. My dad always said you don't need cupboards if you have nothing to hide. There were more doors and hinges in that place than in a New Orleans cathouse!"

"You have the advantage of me there, Ernie," said Gertrude evenly. "I've never been in a New Orleans cathouse. And your father couldn't be expected to understand the need for cupboards, because he was born in a barn—"

"Now, now," I said, leaning between the two of them. "We're not here to dig up old feuds and reopen old wounds. Come on, people, a plague on both your houses!"

"What did he say?" asked Wilfrid.

Ernie turned to him. "I dunno. SOMETHING ABOUT BOTH OUR HOUSES!"

Wilfrid nodded happily. "Well, I agree . . . a couple of nice bungalows."

"Look," I said. "We're rushing the fences here. Our first task tonight should be to establish exactly what our resources are. What is the financial position of the lodge? Can either of the lodge members speak to that?"

"What did he say?" asked Wilfrid.

"DOES THE LODGE HAVE ANY MONEY?"

"Oh, sure," said Wilfrid. "When I went to the bank two weeks ago, there was $361.96. It'll be higher now with the interest paid since then."

"Well, I knew we'd have to fundraise," I sighed. "Just makes the job a little more challenging. We'll have to get a mortgage of some kind. All right, then, apart from finances, are there any other obstacles we might face?"

Harold raised a finger and said, "Can't build on the lot as it is."

"Oh," I said. "Why is that?"

"It's too small for today's regulations. It would have to be rezoned."

I made a note of that. "Okay," I said. "We've got to finance the entire amount and apply for rezoning. Anything else?"

Harold's finger went up again. "The insurance company will have some concerns."

"But I thought there was no insurance."

Harold shrugged. "You can't get a mortgage if it's not insured. And they won't give us insurance unless we put in a new septic tank."

I added the septic system to the list. "Is that it?" I asked, glancing automatically at Harold's finger. It twitched again.

"They'll want a new well," he said apologetically. "And a paved parking lot with lighting, stormwater drainage and, of course, handicapped access."

It went like that all evening. By ten o'clock it was time to sum up. It appeared that, to satisfy the requirements of the bank, the township and the insurance company, we were looking at spending about a million dollars altogether. After I said this figure out loud, a dead silence hung over the room. It appeared that any enthusiasm that might have come into the room earlier that evening was rapidly draining away. An injection of energy and optimism was urgently needed.

"I know that looks like a daunting sum," I said, "but the trick is to break it down into smaller chunks—then it all looks more manageable. For instance, from each man, woman and child in the community it comes to only . . ." I did a rapid calculation on my pocket calculator. "Let's see . . . ten thousand dollars each." The silence deepened and I plunged on.

"The important thing is not to get discouraged. You know, five hundred years ago, the people of Florence in Renaissance Italy had a town square, and it had a tall tower with a huge bell nicknamed the Cowbell. Whenever something really important happened, the Cowbell rang and all the people would come down to the square to hear the news and decide what they were going to do. Our modern democratic system has its roots in that town square in Florence. People gathered there to debate the big issues and to vote in their leaders. They held festivals there with food and games and entertainment.

"That's what the Orange Hall is to us. It defines us as a

people just as surely as that town square defined the Florentines. And it is just as vital a community resource. Don't you see how important it is?"

I could see them nodding to each other, and I leaned back in my chair. It appeared that I was reaching them.

"We're agreed, then," said Ernie.

"Well, thank goodness," I grinned at him. "I think we've made a start."

Ernie shook his head. "No, I didn't mean you . . . I'm saying we agree with him." He waved at Wilfrid, who stirred to life once again.

"Yeah, I think we should bulldoze the place and put up a couple of nice bungalows."

I drove home in the dark. It had turned chilly and the wind was wild. It whipped up swirling towers of dead leaves in the headlights, and the clouds sailed like ghostly galleons above me. I was still talking to myself when I walked in the door at home. Maggie and Freddy were sitting in front of the fire. Hope had an earache again, and she was fussing.

"She won't settle," said Maggie, handing Hope to me. "Let me sleep for a couple of hours, will you, and then I'll take over again. Freddy, would you stay and visit with Walt? Someone will have to talk him down after his committee meeting."

She went upstairs and Freddy went over to my liquor cabinet.

"So, you look like you've been wading through the tar pits," he said cheerfully.

I just shook my head in exasperation. "Do you know anything about Dante's *Inferno*?" I asked him.

"Is that the new pizza place in Port Petunia?"

"Well, it's Italian," I laughed. "But it's not a restaurant. It's a book, a very long poem about a trip that a man takes through the nine circles of Hell."

"You have had a rough night," said Freddy. "Can I pour you something?"

"A couple of fingers, thanks. When the pilgrim finds his way down to the seventh circle, he sees all the tortured souls stretched out on the burning sand, swatting away at the flames and complaining about the heat. Then he recognizes the faces of people he knows: moneylenders, stockbrokers and insurance agents. He asks his guide what makes these people such terrible sinners. And he's told that it is God's will for man to make his living through creativity and industry . . . from the sweat of his brow. These people make their living off the creativity and industry of others. Worse than that, by doing so, they stifle human achievement."

Freddy clinked glasses with me. "Stifling creativity is this country's biggest growth industry," he said. "If that's what the seventh circle is for, they're gonna have to build an addition onto it."

"I suppose. The thing is, fifty years ago, it would have been perfectly simple to gather up building supplies, muster the will of the community and just rebuild the Orange Hall. But now, at every turn, there's some new constraint that adds to the costs, and it adds and it adds until you simply can't do it anymore. We're paralyzed. We're trapped in the seventh circle of the Inferno."

"Well, with winter coming on, I guess there's worse places to be," said Freddy.

"Yeah, but remember what it said over the gate at the entrance to Hell: 'Abandon hope, all ye who enter here.'"

Hope sighed and blinked slowly. It looked like half my audience was about to nod off.

"No one's going to abandon you, Hope. Not while I'm around," I whispered as I set her in her crib and tucked the blanket up under her chin. As she drifted into sleep, I sang:

> I'll be there for you.
> There's no risk I wouldn't take,
> No sacrifice I wouldn't make.
> I'll take the world on for your sake,
> And, dear, each morning when you wake
> I'll be there for you.

Yours sincerely,
Walt

—— *November 5*

Dear Ed,

The ancient Greeks said, "Those whom the gods love, die young." It would appear the gods are very fond of chickens. I've never raised a bird to middle age around here. And they all die in debt. As risky enterprises go, I have found that poultry farming is right up there with Third World mining stocks and airline companies. Maggie's pretty blunt about it.

"You could find a less expensive hobby, Walt. How about Formula One racing or cocaine?"

But this year I ventured forth again. I read about the Araucana, a cross between a South American game bird and a domestic chicken. It's very hardy and it lays blue-shelled eggs that are supposed to be cholesterol-free.

They're expensive, but I figured I could save a lot if I got hatching eggs and incubated my own laying flock. Trouble was, after the first batch, I ended up with twenty-four roosters and one hen. I ask you, what are the odds of that?

Anyway, I put them under low light in a large pen, but as soon as they got their feathers they started attacking and killing each other. Every morning I had to pull a couple of carcasses out of the pen. It was awful. It was like a leadership convention for the Conservative Party.

I found that if I let them out to free range at first light and gathered them up again after dark I could keep them from tearing each other apart. But that meant every night I had to search the apple trees with a flashlight and a feed sack for sixteen roosters.

So I decided to sell them. One morning I put one in a cage out at the road, with a sign saying "Rare South American Rooster. Five bucks." It was gone by noon. Same thing the next day. And the next. But after two weeks I shone the light up into the trees and still counted sixteen roosters. It turned out they were flying home as soon as they were let out at their new digs.

Not a bad business, really. I even had some repeat customers. But Maggie pointed out there were risks here, too. She had an ancestor who had a similar marketing strategy with horses. He trained them to come home as soon as the cheque cleared the bank. Apparently he built a flourishing trade, was known to everyone and sought after by quite a few.

"And what happened to him?" I asked.

"Well, my grandmother would only say that 'the platform collapsed under him at a public ceremony.'"

I've been thinking about those sinners in the seventh

circle, and I think Dante was right. When insurance companies began, they were supposed to facilitate human achievement by cushioning it against the effects of catastrophe. But look what's happened. Our fall fair and four others around us had to be cancelled this year because the Fair Boards couldn't afford the liability insurance. The playground equipment at the school is gone. No one ever got hurt on it, but the Board of Education's insurance company found it failed to meet "modern safety standards."

And now it's becoming quite clear that we can't rebuild the Orange Hall.

I dropped in to the Red Hen Restaurant this week. When he was the clerk for Persephone Township, Harold maintained a regular table at the Red Hen. He spent hours here, receiving petitions, bestowing favours and playing euchre anytime there were four gathered together. Now that the townships have been amalgamated and everything is centralized, absolutely nothing has changed. Gertrude Lynch was sitting with him today, but I decided she might as well hear what I had to say.

"Good morning, Mr. Chairman, won't you sit down?" said Harold, in that maddeningly affable way he has.

"You can cut out the 'Mr. Chairman' stuff, Harold," I said coldly. "I resign. You knew full well there wasn't the slightest chance of getting that hall rebuilt before you appointed me. You just wanted someone else to shoulder the responsibility and take the blame when the committee came up empty-handed. We have a name for that back in the city—when you send someone off looking for something you know they're not going to find—we call it a unicorn hunt. I don't know what you call it here."

"We call it a unicorn hunt. And, if I may say so, Mr. Wing-field, it's harder and harder these days to find hunters of your calibre."

I blinked and groped for a response, but none came. Seeing me speechless, Harold continued, with that bland smile fixed firmly on his face.

"I understand your frustration," he said genially. "And, of course, you're right: there was never a chance the hall could be rebuilt. But you can't just tell people that. They have to be shown the conclusion's been arrived at by due process, and the project has died a natural death."

Once again, Harold was three steps ahead of me. I felt like every time I opened my mouth with this man it was just to eat up some of the bread crumbs from the trail that he was laying down in front of me. In the meantime, Don and Freddy appeared at the door of the Red Hen. They saw me sitting with Harold and came over to check on me.

"Is this a private autopsy, or can anybody grab a scalpel?" asked Freddy.

"Be my guest," I said, and they both sat down. "This is turning into an ad hoc committee meeting anyway. The thing that baffles me is that there was no financial provision for the hall, no operations budget, no maintenance fund . . . it seems to me, if it hadn't burned down, it would have fallen down eventually. What was everybody thinking?"

"Oh, no, Walt," said Gertrude. "We had great plans for the hall. Last year we applied for a Heritage grant to completely restore it. It would have been just like new, but there would have been a beautiful plaque commemorating my father . . . and, of course, the others. But, alas, you can't restore a building that doesn't exist."

"Indeed," said Harold. "I wrote the application. It was comprehensive, if I do say so myself—more for a reconstruction than just a renovation. It was a beautiful application, and a cruel turn of fate that thwarted it."

The Orange Hall wasn't a dangerous place. The well water was fine for watering the grass and washing the floors; everyone knew you didn't drink it. The septic system was okay for emergencies, just not for heavy use; everyone knew you went to the bathroom before you went to the hall. The Clarke brothers handled handicapped access. They're two big, brawny guys who can whisk a wheelchair up the steps as smoothly as Clark Gable sweeping Vivien Leigh up the grand staircase. They look a bit like Clark Gable, too. A number of young women have been known to twist their ankles in the parking lot just to gain handicapped access to the hall.

"It's just so frustrating," I said. "You need the building to get the grant, and you need the grant to get the building."

We all sat in silence for a moment, and then Freddy finally spoke.

"What if it hadn't burned down?" he wondered.

"Well, I can speak to that," said Harold. "You wouldn't need the rezoning because it would be a renovation of a non-conforming pre-existing use."

"Yeah, but what about the water and the septic?"

"You would still have to do that, but the timeline wouldn't be as demanding. And, of course, there was provision for it in the grant application."

Don raised his hand off his chin. "What about the other stuff—parking, lighting and the handicapped access?" he asked.

"Nonconforming pre-existing use covers a broad spectrum . . . lots of wiggle room on that stuff." Harold smiled knowingly. "Besides, I made sure there were funds for that in the budget for the grant. It was a lovely application."

Gertrude wrinkled her forehead and looked at Harold. "Well, then, if it hadn't burned down, and we got the grant, what else would we need?"

"Let me see . . ." said Harold, thinking carefully. "We'd need . . . a building permit. I have one right here . . . if it hadn't burned down."

"Yes," I interrupted impatiently. "And if pigs had wings they'd be eagles. Could we get back to reality here? The fact is—it did burn down."

Freddy looked up at the ceiling fan. "Did it?" he asked.

"What do you mean, 'did it.' Of course it did."

"I dunno," said Freddy doubtfully. "There was a lot of smoke. Kinda hard to see."

I glanced at Don in exasperation. But he wasn't paying any attention to me. He was looking at Freddy.

"Yeah," he said. "Smoke damage always makes that stuff look worse than it is. Hard to say how much structural damage there might have been."

"You know, sometimes it's amazing what a cleanup and a good coat of paint will do," agreed Gertrude.

I couldn't believe this. "Cleanup? Coat of paint? There's nothing to paint. It's a pile of ashes!" I exclaimed.

Don finally looked at me. "You know that," he said. "And we know that. The question is, who else knows that?"

"Who else? Why everybody. It was in the paper, for Pete's sake!"

"He's right," said Freddy. "What's the circulation of the paper these days?"

"Pretty high in the summer," said Harold. "But a lot less

at this time of the year with the weekenders gone. Maybe . . . fifty-seven. And most of those are at the bottom of the bird-cage by Friday. But that's a good point. We'll have to get Ed to print a retraction."

I said, "You can't be serious. The chairman of the Heritage Commission is our own member of parliament. Surely he must know—"

"Not necessarily," said Harold. "Windy Hallett's been under the weather recently."

"Oh? With what?"

"Rideau Fever," explained Freddy. "A lot of fellas come down with it when they move to Ottawa and get the govern-ment car and the expense account."

"We don't see much of Windy anymore, that's for sure," agreed Harold. "A lot of people are saying that."

"I can't believe this. Are you seriously suggesting we defraud the government by filing a false application?"

"'Defraud' is a strong word, Walt," said Harold mildly. "The application is already filed, and it was bona fide when we filed it. In the meantime, a small hiccup has occurred that creates a bit of a gap between perception and reality. I think the committee is suggesting we put perception on hold for a while and let reality catch up."

"You are!" I said rising from the table. "You're seriously suggesting we mount some kind of massive conspiracy to pretend that the Orange Hall fire never happened!"

Gertrude pursed her lips and flashed a look at me. "We could try to, Walt. Or I suppose we could let those two dod-dering old Orangemen bulldoze the lot and put up 'a couple of nice bungalows' while we sit around the Red Hen Restaurant picking the flyshit out of the pepper."

"That sounds like a motion," said Harold. "Would you care to put that to a vote, Mr. Chairman?"

Of course I was outvoted, and I probably should have resigned. But I didn't. Not only that, but, as I'm still chairman, I'm expected to lobby our member of parliament, Winston Hallett, the chairman of the Heritage Commission, to speed along approval of the grant. Well, that's okay. The sooner reality catches up with perception here, the easier I'll breathe.

By the way, Ed, if you're keeping score . . . fraud is also in the seventh circle of the Inferno. At least I'm not getting any lower. Not yet.

Yours sincerely,
Walt

———— *November 8*

Dear Ed,

Hope is still getting these ear infections, and yesterday Maggie and I drove her into the doctor's for a consultation. I thought we'd come away with another round of antibiotics, but this time the doctor showed us a diagram of an infant's inner ear.

"What we're dealing with here is a rather stubborn otitis media, an inflammation of the middle ear. Now, there are two schools of thought on this. One is that, in most cases, the infection will respond to the antibiotics and eventually clear up. On the other hand, there are stubborn cases, of which this may be one, where surgery is the best course."

"Surgery?" I said, alarmed.

"Yes," said Dr. Brigham. "We install little tubes, called myringotomy tubes, that drain the infection from the eardrum."

"But you say there's a chance with the antibiotics it could just go away."

"Most of the time it does," agreed the doctor. "There is some risk involved whichever way we decide to go."

"What kind of risk?"

"It's really a matter of the child's hearing. The tubes themselves can cause scarring and reduce the range of hearing . . . slightly. On the other hand, if the infection doesn't respond to the antibiotics, becomes severe and spreads, it could result in a condition called mastoiditis. It's rare, but it does occur. In that case, we would have to operate immediately, and there is a good chance the child could lose her hearing entirely."

"What do you think we should do, Doctor?"

"In this sort of case, I lean towards the surgery. But there doesn't appear to be any immediate danger. Why don't you think about it, and we'll see you next week. In the meantime, let me know if you see any change . . . fever, irritability, any redness or swelling."

We went out to the parking lot and walked over to the 4×4. Maggie, who had said almost nothing during the interview, now asked me why I was being quiet.

"I just don't know what to do," I said. "How do we know which is the right choice?"

"If there's any danger she might lose her hearing, we have to do the surgery, don't you think?"

"But he said the tubes might reduce her hearing."

"He said 'slightly.' What is it, Walt?" She came around to face me.

"I don't know," I sighed. "Both options have risks. For Hope, I want the other option—the one with no risks. I just don't want to pull another Flying W."

"Life is full of risks, Walt, you know that. It's the same as the business with the Orange Hall. If you try to make life risk-free, you end up not living it."

Freddy pulled up beside us in his truck.

"Say, Walt," he grinned. "I think you should come up and see what Dave is doing with your horse."

Maggie patted me on the arm. "You go ahead, Walt. I'm going to get on the Internet and see what I can find out about otitis media."

When we got to Freddy's, Dave was doing a warm-up lap with Dividend on Freddy's dirt track out behind the barn. He had her hooked up to the sulky, and she looked terrific with the breeze streaming through her mane and her head high; I've never seen her happier. There was something odd about her bridle—she didn't seem to have one. I asked Freddy how he had done it.

"He started off riding her," explained Freddy. "No bridle, no reins, nothing—just around the corral. After a while he put the bellyband on her. Then he hooked up the shafts of the sulky to the bellyband and just let her stand there. And then he started riding her with the sulky behind. And then, finally, he got off her and sat on the sulky. As long as she has nothing touching her head and no lines or reins, she's fine."

"How does he steer?"

Freddy raised his eyebrows. "He whispers to her," he said.

Dave and Dividend picked up speed as they passed in front of us. Freddy clicked the stopwatch.

"We're not out of the woods here, Walt," he warned. "We have to get her to do this at the track."

"You think she should race?"

"Look at her, Walt. It's what she's born to do. Not to

mention the fact that this horse is fast. You were complaining that this community doesn't have money. This is a horse that could turn around the Larkspur gross domestic product—in a heartbeat."

"Really?" I said. "So, Dave can drive her at the track and just whisper to her, right?"

"Yeah, and we'll tell all the other drivers and the twelve hundred people in the stands to please keep quiet—Dave has to whisper to his horse. It's no good, Walt. She might as well be deaf out there."

"So, what can you do?"

Freddy glanced at Willy. "Show him," he said.

Willy uncoiled a garden hose and showed me a bottle of horse liniment.

"We're trying an ancient herbal therapy—it's called Absorbine Junior. A few dabs on her back. Makes her itchy. She wants to race anyhow; now, she's itching to race. She does her race lap and gets a shower with the hose. Itch gone. We do it a few times. The horse learns the sequence: itch, run the race, shower. And it's all positive reinforcement. She likes the itch; she loves the race; and she really loves the shower. And the best part of it is, it's actually legal."

By this time Dave was well into Dividend's race training lap. They rounded the clubhouse turn and thundered by us. Freddy clicked the stopwatch and sent Willy into action.

"Okay, Willy, hose her down quick!"

Dividend turned on a dime and trotted over to Willy who stuck his thumb on the end of the hose and doused her, head to tail and back. Dividend shook her head and whinnied in girlish glee. Dave jumped out of the cart.

"What does the stopwatch say, Uncle Freddy?"

Freddy held it up, and his hand started to shake. "It says . . . it says . . . oh, my sufferin' sainted sister. It says that our dirt farmin' days of poverty are about to end! Now, boys, we want to be real, real careful with this horse. We don't want to try to bring her along too fast. I mean, we wouldn't want to, like, put her in the first race at Demeter Downs next Saturday."

"Nooo, we sure wouldn't want to do that," agreed Dave. "Would we, Willy?"

"Heavens, no. How about the fourth race?"

I wished them good luck and turned to go, but Freddy stopped me.

"You're coming too, Walt," he said.

"I'm not much of a racing fan, Freddy," I protested. "I'll leave it in your capable—"

"No, Walt, this is about the Orange Hall application. You can't track down Windy Hallett at the office. But he never misses a Saturday at Demeter Downs in Port Petunia. He has a box in the stands, and as far as the business of the constituency is concerned, that's where it all happens. We'll pick you up at seven Saturday morning."

Yours sincerely,
Walt

———— *November 12*

Dear Ed,

Saturday was classic late autumn. One moment the sun shone bravely, lighting up the last patches of crimson and gold on the hills. The next moment, heavy grey clouds scudded in off the lake and the hills turned dark again. The forecast was "changeable," which, of course, is weathermanese for "we dunno."

It was one of those days that could go either way. I understand Napoleon said something to that effect heading into the
Battle of Waterloo. I just hoped I wasn't heading into my own
Waterloo as I prepared to lie to my member of parliament,
speak in support of a fraudulent grant application and encour-
age the Heritage Commission to incriminate itself.

When we got to Demeter Downs, we got Dividend into
her box stall, and Willy and Dave went to work, rubbing her
down and wrapping her forelegs, preparing her for her debut
on the track.

Freddy pointed up into the stands. "There's your target,
Walt—that box up there with the red and white bunting.
That's the constituency office during the racing season, and
I see old Windy himself just blew in."

Winston Hallett is approaching the end of his second
term as the member for Hillhurst County. He's never been
considered cabinet material because he's a bit of a loose cannon.
They put him in charge of a few harmless things, like the
House Committee on Ethics in Banking, and they made him
chair of the Heritage Commission.

With some trepidation, I climbed the stairs, joined in the
line of petitioners and waited my turn. I waited through the
first race and the second and third races. The trumpet was just
sounding for the fourth race when I finally got my chance.
Hallett was a rotund man with a shiny bald pate and a fringe
of snow white hair around his ears. He grabbed me enthusiastically in a warm handshake.

"How are YOU! Come on and sit down, young fella!"

It gave me the feeling that we actually knew each other
from somewhere, but I couldn't think where that might be.
"Hi. I'm Walt Wingfield," I introduced myself.

"Oh, I KNOW, I know, I know. You're from . . ."

"Larkspur," I prompted.

"Oh, I know, I know, I know. Tell me, how are things down there? How's my old friend John Drinkwater?"

"John?" I said. "Not very well, actually. He died last September."

"No! Oh, that's too bad. I hadn't heard about that. And how about my old pal Ross McNabb—still in the beef business?"

"Ross died about two years ago, in fact."

"Oh, my . . . and his wife, Vera . . . is she still . . . ?"

"Yes, still dead," I said.

Windy picked up his field glasses and looked out over the track. "Well, here they come." The horses were coming around for the start of the fourth race.

So far so good. Evidently, Windy was a couple of laps off the pace when it came to current events in Larkspur. Of course, that didn't mean he hadn't heard about the fire.

The starting truck was bringing the horses around in formation, gathering speed as they approached the start line. It wasn't hard to pick out Dividend. Dave's Department of Highways orange vest and pink dirt bike helmet stood out sharply from the row of designer racing silks on the other drivers. They swept past the grandstand; Dividend looked terrific, head high, eyes bright; she was having the time of her life. Suddenly, the sun broke through the clouds and all things seemed positive. I took a deep breath and popped the question.

"Have you heard anything about the Orange Hall in Larkspur?"

Hallett looked at me sharply. "Of course I have," he said.

"You have?" I ventured. Bread crumbs, I thought. Just drop a bread crumb and see how he takes it.

"It is a beautiful building," he said finally.

"It is? I mean, yes, it is. We have an application in for a Heritage grant to do a restoration. Has it crossed your desk yet?"

"Oh, for sure. I was just looking at that last week. Lovely stonework in that building."

"Actually it was a . . . I mean, it is a wood frame. Golly, it must have been . . . it went up like a . . . I mean, they built it very quickly."

"And folks feel pretty good that you're fixing it up, do they?"

"Oh, absolutely. And the committee's going like a house on . . . that is, the idea has really caught fire . . . caught on. What I mean is, everybody is very enthusiastic."

Hallett turned back to me with a puzzled frown. "Now, hang on just a minute, did you say 'fire'? I just remembered . . ."

A chill wind rustled the bunting; a dark cloud snuffed out the sun; a couple of big raindrops thudded on the roof of the box.

"I just remembered . . . I have a little money on a horse in this race named Firebrand; I don't want to miss it." He raised his field glasses to watch the race.

The horses were turning to the back stretch. I saw Dave's pink helmet in the middle of the pack. Dividend was moving ahead fast, and the announcer was calling her name. Now she was in front. She was winning. The rain drumming on the roof of the box drowned out the announcer's voice, and I lost sight of the horses. Then it brightened again and the horses came back into sight, rounding the turn for home.

I couldn't see Dividend. One by one they flashed past the grandstand. No Dividend. She'd just disappeared in that shower . . . Aaah! Shower! She's had her shower; she thinks the race is over. She's probably headed home.

"By gollies, looks like there's a runaway," said Hallett, pointing to the backfield.

I snatched up his field glasses and scanned the track. I picked up a flash of orange and pink near the stables and saw Dividend trotting gaily through the backfield towards the parking lot, pursued by a posse of trainers, stewards and grooms. The parking arm was blocking the exit onto the road. Surely, I thought, that would stop her. It didn't. She crashed through, lost one wheel of the sulky on a fire hydrant and the other on the bumper of a parked car—a police cruiser. Dave bounced along on the gravel behind her, his arms waving and his mouth wide open. He was not whispering now.

Windy was waving his race ticket.

"How about that?" he crowed. "I picked a winner! Firebrand came home in a romp. And I thought I might get burned. Ha, ha, ha! Looks like you brought me good luck, Mr. . . . uh . . ."

"Wingfield."

"Oh, I KNOW, I know, I know," he assured me, grabbing my hand and pumping it again. "Thank you so much. Now, I'm going to look into that grant application just as soon as I get back to Ottawa. We'll see if we can't move it along for you." The next petitioner moved into the box. "And how are YOU, young fella? How are things in Glockamorra, mmm? Oh, I KNOW, I know, I know . . ."

And with that, my audience with the great man was over.

Thankfully, Dave and Dividend are both going to be all right. Even the sulky wasn't a total writeoff. They were able to use the shafts as a temporary splint for Dave's leg.

Yours sincerely,
Walt

———— *November 16*

Dear Ed,

Three days later we were back at the doctor's. He said Hope's okay for now, but we shouldn't wait too long to decide what to do. It seems the symptoms of otitis media vary a lot, and sometimes it's hard to diagnose how serious it is.

On our way back through Larkspur, I noticed a group of people standing in front of the Red Hen Restaurant—Harold, Gertrude, Freddy and Don—so I pulled over to the curb. It looked like another impromptu meeting of the ad hoc committee.

Harold looked up as I opened the car door. "Morning, Walt," he said cheerily. "We've got some good news . . . and some other news."

"Oh?" I said. "What's the good news?"

"I got a call from the Heritage Commission this morning. They say the grant's been approved for the full amount. They're sending us a cheque. It's going to arrive today."

"Today? That's terrific! The full amount? Today? I can't believe it. Listen, everybody. I'm sorry I was so negative about that 'perception–reality' thing. I'm just hopelessly old-fashioned, I guess. I had some paranoid notion we'd find ourselves at the centre of an Auditor General's investigation. What's the other news?"

"Windy Hallett is delivering the cheque personally," said Harold. "He's coming down by train. He wants to kick off his re-election campaign by having his picture taken in front of the Orange Hall."

"I knew it!" I shouted. "We'll be caught. We're all going to jail! I told you this was crazy!"

If Harold was concerned, he showed no sign of it. "We've been discussing it, Walt. He's just coming to have his picture taken."

"In front of the Orange Hall, which, may I remind you, does not exist."

"Certainly that does present a challenge."

That seemed to me to be the understatement of the decade.

"It gets dark about 5:45," said Maggie. "It would help if it was dark."

"Yeah," said Don. "And it would help if he didn't have his glasses."

"And it would help if he was drunk," added Freddy.

"I suppose," I said. "But we can't count on any of those things. Who's going to meet him at the station?"

"He appears to assume it will be you, Mr. Chairman," said Harold. "We were thinking maybe you could pick him up in your 4×4. He'll be on the 4:15."

"Really? I was actually thinking of leaving town on that train. Anyway, why would I pick him up in the car? We can walk to the hall from the station; it's just across the bridge."

Maggie took me by the elbow back to the car and handed Hope to me. "Bring him over in the 4×4, Walt. It will be all right. In the meantime, you take Hope down to the farm and get her settled. I'll come down and spell you off when you have to leave."

This often happens to me up here. I listen to the same

conversation as everyone else and I watch them all lift off in the same direction in a common cause, leaving me—the last starling on the fence—without the faintest idea what just happened.

When I drove into the station parking lot, there was a light drizzle falling and the weather had turned cold. The train pulled in right on time. Windy stepped down onto the platform.

"And how are YOU, young fella? How are your two front feet?" he asked heartily, pumping my hand.

"Hi, Mr. Hallett. I'm Walt Wingfield."

"Oh, I know, I know, I know . . . you're my lucky fireman, ho, ho, ho." This time he did actually seem to remember me. I got him settled in the 4×4. As we pulled out of the parking lot, I took a deep breath.

"Listen, Mr. Hallett, there's something I should probably explain to you before we . . ."

And then I saw the fire truck sitting at the bridge with its lights flashing and men in yellow rainsuits standing about. One of them walked over to us and tapped on the window. It was Don.

"G'day, sir," he said, leaning in the window. "We got us a little problem with the bridge here, and we're gonna have to send you the long way round to get to the hall. Just follow the signs and keep to the left."

I turned left and we followed Mill Street, which goes steeply downhill to make the loop around Dry Cry's store, the fuel depot and a row of old factory buildings that are finally being renovated to house various local arts and crafts. Another knot of people in rain slickers stood in the middle of the road and waved us to a halt. A face appeared at the window. It was Freddy.

"Hi there, your honour. We were thinking that, while you're in the fair town of Larkspur, you might just take a minute to have a tour of our newest industry—the Pine Springs Micro-Brewery. Just opened last month."

"Oh, by gollies, I read about that in the papers," said Windy. "I think we have a minute, don't we, Mr. Wingfield?"

I shrugged and said, "Sure, by all means."

We got out of the car and Freddy led us over to the door. Freddy steered Windy inside and began the cook's tour of the brewery.

"You know, they have sixteen different varieties they make right here on the premises. But you can't get them in Ottawa yet. Made with the finest local ingredients. One hundred years of brewing experience . . . about one month with an actual licence."

"Sixteen varieties, you say?" marvelled Windy.

"Yeah," said Freddy handing him a tall glass. "Here's the first one. It's called Strongarm."

We were there for over an hour while Windy sampled all sixteen. We poured him back into the car at 5:30, just as the light started to fade. We followed the River Road for another few hundred yards, and then I heard the unmistakable sound of the steam calliope coming from the fairgrounds up ahead. Sure enough, as we rounded the bend, we saw people at the gate. I smelled popcorn and hot dogs and saw a row of black-and-white dairy calves being led in the gate by young kids. The Larkspur Fair seemed to be in full swing. Suddenly, Gertrude Lynch appeared beside the car.

"Why, Mr. Hallett," she cried. "What a wonderful surprise! You're just in time for the opening ceremonies. Everyone will be just thrilled to see you on the platform."

Windy made straight for the grandstand, where Isobel Meadows was receiving her crown as the Fair Queen. He huffed up the stairs, put his arm around Isobel and gave her a big kiss. The crowd cheered. A voice called out for a speech, and Windy was happy to oblige.

"I want to thank yas all for coming out," he hiccuped into the microphone. "You know, it's a great thing when you have a group of hard-working volunteers to put on a good little fair like they do here in . . . in . . ."

"Larkspur," prompted Gertrude.

" . . . Larkspur! I remember the day when I brought my pig to this fair when I was just the same age as these young people down here in front of the stage. I polished up that pig with buttermilk until he was so bright you pretty near needed a pair of sunglasses just to look at him. And I was so proud when I got a white ribbon for third place, it was like they crowned me king, so it was . . ."

Windy rang all the changes . . . agriculture is the backbone of the country, the government can and will do more to help the small producer, and if you ate breakfast this morning you should thank a farmer. Then he lambasted the firearms registry which, by the way, he voted for in his first term.

"You know the difference between a boat anchor and the gun registry, do you? Well, you would normally tie a rope on the boat anchor before you throw it overboard, ho, ho, ho!

"I think you all know I'm not a man to forget his friends in the constituency. My opponents have called it dipping into the pork barrel. Well, I call it bringing home the bacon!

"You know," he said, passing a hand over his face and looking serious for a moment. "It was a terrible thing when they gave women the vote. But, God help them, they've done it, and we're just going to have to . . . what's that you say?"

Gertrude was tugging on his arm now and guiding him off the stage. "They want your picture with the Fair Queen and the grand champion calf," she said. "Come and help, Isobel. This way, your honour."

Isobel took his arm and smiled sweetly at him as she guided him down the platform steps. "Oh, Mr. Hallett, you'd look so much handsomer without your glasses. Here, let me hold them for you." Windy missed the last step on the grandstand and stumbled into the side of young Donny's prize calf, who took no notice and went on chewing its cud. Windy bounced back into the arms of two spectators.

"My, that's a wild calf you got there, young man," he sputtered. "Can you not get her quieted down?"

He grabbed the calf's ear for support. It shook its head and moved forward six inches, and there was an audible crunch of broken glass. Isobel looked crestfallen as she handed him the broken frames.

"I'm so sorry, Mr. Hallett. Donny's calf stepped on your glasses."

"Not to worry, my dear, I have another pair at home. But they're not as nice as the pair on you. I mean, your glasses, ho, ho, ho!"

We took the picture and supported Windy back to the 4×4. By now it was dark.

"Gertrude," I whispered. "If the bridge is closed, how do I get him across the river?"

"They've rigged up the old cable ferry for you, your honour," said Gertrude. "Keep bearing to the left and you'll see the old crossing."

"Left again?" mumbled Windy. "If we go any further left, we'll end up sitting with the NDP."

Down at the river crossing, a hooded figure stood on the deck of the cable ferry, his hand on the winch, waving the 4×4 onto the barge—an aged man whose hair was white . . . who was, in fact, the Squire. He raised an arm in salute.

"I come to lead you to the other shore," he called.

We crossed the river in a blanket of fog, in silence broken only by the creaking of the old winch and Windy singing softly to himself.

> Yes, we will gather at the river,
> the beautiful, the beautiful river . . .

We bumped against the shore, and I drove off the ferry onto a rough track that wound up the side of the hill. At the crest, we emerged from the fog and drove out under the stars. There was a light. And there in front of us was the Orange Hall. In three hours, the community had rebuilt the hall.

When I looked closer, I saw that it was just scaffolding shrouded with plastic; they'd put up scaffolding in the shape of the hall. I hurried Windy around to the front, where the light was coming from a row of floodlights, illuminating the facade. Here, there was a gap in the scaffolding and an actual structure—part of a wall, a set of steps and a doorway with the old sign fixed above it: LOL Number 26, Larkspur 1954. It wasn't the Orange Hall, but it did look familiar. A small group of people waited to welcome Windy. At the front was Harold.

"So good of you to come, Mr. Hallett," he said in his most courtly manner. "Everyone is so pleased and excited to see you. Now, just stand up here and we can take your picture."

I was right next to the facade now. I looked down and saw some printing stamped at the corner of the plywood—Larkspur Little Theatre. That's why I recognized it! It was the set from last summer's production of *The Perils of Persephone*. It was just a plywood set piece.

"We must go inside and have a look," insisted Windy.

Harold moved in front of him. "No, no, no, Mr. Hallett, we can't do that."

"Oh," said Windy. "And why not?"

For the first time, Harold wavered. "Because . . . because . . ." He turned to me. "Mr. Chairman, tell him why not."

The inspiration came like a bolt out of the blue. "Because of insurance," I said triumphantly. "Yes, insurance! Why we'd need hard hats, steel-toed boots, safety glasses, breathing masks . . . The safety railings aren't installed and, of course, waivers would have to be signed . . ."

Windy instantly relented. "Ah, yes, insurance," he said. "Say no more. I understand. We'll just have to make do with a picture. I have the cheque here. Who should I give this to?"

"To everybody," I shouted. "C'mon, everyone, crowd in here. Harold, Don, Gertrude, Freddy . . ." They all crowded in around me, and the flashbulbs popped.

When I got back home, the house was dark; Maggie and Hope weren't there. I found a scribbled note from Maggie on the kitchen table. It read: "Elma is driving us to Emergency at Hillhurst Regional Hospital. Mastoiditis."

I called Spike and herded him quickly to the 4×4. Hope would need him. At the hospital, we found them in the recovery room. I spoke to the doctor briefly. He said the surgery had been successful, but we'd have to wait until Hope came out of the anesthetic to know whether she was all right.

Maggie was worn out, asleep in the chair beside the bed. Spike settled beside her on the floor and put his head on her foot. I sat with Hope and sang softly to her, the lullaby she might not ever hear again.

> I'll be there for you.
> There's no risk I wouldn't take . . .

But I couldn't finish it, because it wasn't true. The fact is, I wasn't there for her. I didn't take the risk. I just abandoned Hope . . .

Spike looked at me reproachfully. "Woof," he said. Hope's eyes blinked open. "'pike!" she cried.

I breathed a sigh of relief and sent a prayer heavenward.

Yours sincerely,
Walt

A NOTE FROM THE EDITOR

So that's how it went.

Over the next few weeks, the new hall was framed, roofed and bricked, and the gap between perception and reality was closed. Walt stepped off the Hall Committee about the same time Ernie and Gertrude came to blows over the cost of the new cupboards.

Shortly after the election was called, I got Windy's campaign brochure in the mail. "Winston Hallett's Vision for the Future: It Doesn't Get Any Better." Politicians aren't normally given to such brutal candour.

Freddy, Willy and Dave aren't giving up on Dividend. They're trying to breed her for the next addition to the line of the great Clipper Ship. They just need to find a stallion fast enough to catch up with her.

I have a picture on my desk. It shows a big crowd of maybe fifty people standing in front of the new hall, watching a crane hoisting a heavy cast-iron bell into a square tower on the south peak of the roof. They found it when they were cleaning up the debris in the basement. Gertrude said it was donated when the old hall was built, but at the time, they didn't have the money to put up a bell tower.

Now that it's finally on the building, they ring it for every important event, like a fiftieth wedding anniversary or someone bowling a perfect game or a winning lottery ticket.

People call it the Cowbell. In the absence of any fine sculpture or great architecture, it helps remind us who we are. Of course, the insurance company has told us they don't insure bell towers and if it falls off the building and kills somebody, we're not covered.

It's unfortunate, but we're just going to have to live with that risk.

Chapter Seven

Wingfield

LOST AND FOUND

ANOTHER NOTE FROM THE EDITOR

The other day, I was looking through some of the publications that pile up on my desk when I caught this item on page four of the *Western Soil and Crop News*: "Federal Minister Urges Farmers to Expand Beef Herds." Right opposite that story, on page five, there was another headline: "Vegetarianism on the Rise."

Next I picked up the *Free Press and Economist* and read: "Worst Drought in 25 Years Strikes County." A little further down on the same page I spotted: "Water Bottling Company Set to Pump One Million Litres Per Day from Pluto Marsh Starting August 10."·

The mentally active reader should be able to connect the dots. Unfortunately, I'm not sure how many of those I have. That's why I have to write editorials. And that's why I keep printing the "Letter from Wingfield Farm."

Going into his sixth season on the farm, Walt was starting to show all the signs of a man who was getting fairly experienced at country life. He even asked me at one point how long I thought he would have to live on his farm before people would stop referring to it as "the old Fisher place." I explained as gently as I could that he would pretty much have to die in bed in the farmhouse before the residents would make that adjustment.

He shrugged and seemed to accept that this was probably the case. And then I got this letter from him.

——— *June 15*

Dear Ed,

One of the reasons I prefer the train to travelling by car is that you actually get to look out the window and watch how the landscape changes. This spring, the weekly reality checks have been particularly harsh. I have watched the landscape get drier and more parched. As the train crosses Highway 13 and labours up into the sand hills of Persephone Township, it gets worse. A reddish-brown haze hangs in the air, and even the old cedar trees look exhausted by the heat.

As I stepped off the train, I spotted the 4×4 sitting by itself in the station parking lot. Maggie and Hope are usually waiting to pick me up, but today there was no sign of them, only this note tucked under the windshield wiper.

"Hello dear. The cows are out. I would have called you but . . . you know . . . !! Love, Maggie."

On principle I like to be unreachable by the brokerage when I'm at the farm. One of the main reasons for owning a place in the country is the peace and quiet, after all. I did start carrying a cellphone when Maggie was expecting Hope, but I've been trying to get rid of it ever since. As I keep telling Maggie, the trouble with being reachable is that people reach you, all the time. I'm actually surprised the phone is still working, considering the number of things I've thrown it against. Generally I just leave the damn thing at home or turn it off. It drives Maggie crazy.

So, the cows were out. I subscribed to the *Green Farmer* last winter, a magazine that promotes grass-fed beef. It's supposed to be the healthy alternative, and, of course, if the cows eat grass you don't have to buy grain for them, and that cuts your costs significantly. An article I read recommended a breed called the Belted Galloway. I asked Don if he knew about them.

"Yeah," he said. "They're black at each end and they got a big white belt around the middle. People call them the Oreo cookie cow . . . I guess you eat the middle first."

I handed Don the article. "It says here that Galloways are directly descended from the ancient Hebridean auroch, and that they can live outside in the harshest conditions all year round. They're a quiet, docile breed, too. That's good, isn't it?"

Don glanced briefly at the pages. He said, "Walt . . . you get the odd quiet cow, but there is no such thing as a quiet breed of cow."

They looked quiet enough when I bought them. They were in a barnyard on a little farm south of Highway 13, but when the truck delivered them to the farm, we opened the trailer doors and they streaked out into the pasture and disappeared. For the next few weeks, all I saw was a flash of black and white as they flitted from one clump of cedar trees to the next. They moved like pronghorn antelope. After a few weeks they got so they would come up to the barn once a day, but they aren't what you would call quiet cows.

I put Maggie's note in my pocket, climbed into the 4×4 and drove out of Larkspur, scanning the fields for any sign of beef-on-the-run.

Of course, one of the key factors in successful grassland farming is actually having grass. The snow went away in a rush in March, and we got a few rains in April. But it stayed dry and cold until the end of May, when it turned dry and hot. By the middle of June the grass just stopped growing, and we've been supplementing the cows' diet ever since with a ration of grain. Obviously, this erases both the health benefits and the economic advantage.

I drove down the Seventh Line towards the farm and saw the Squire standing at his mailbox, peering into the distance. I pulled up beside him and he looked around.

"How are you now, Walt?" he asked.

"Oh, fine," I said. "I understand my cows are out. Has anyone seen them?"

"We've all seen them. Seein' them ain't the problem. Keepin' them in sight is the problem. Fifteen minutes ago, they were at the back of my place along Calvin's line fence. Hard to say now." His gaze returned to the horizon. I heard a motor and glanced in the mirror. Freddy's truck pulled up abreast of the 4×4 with a decrepit old horse trailer in tow. Freddy jumped out and kicked the battered door shut behind him with a boot heel.

"Dry enough for you?" he asked.

"Sure is," I said. "Would you mind giving me a hand? My cows are out."

"You're behind the curve, Walt. We've been chasin' them black-and-whites of yours all afternoon."

"I'm sorry about this. How do you think we'll get them back?"

The Squire shrugged. "When it's this dry, cows would have to be pretty stupid to stray too far from the hand that feeds them every morning with the big red bucket."

"Well, they're not handing out any bovine scholarships these days, Squire," said Freddy.

"There must be some way to get them to settle down," I fumed.

Freddy said, "You might want to pick up one of those Ritalin blowguns the teachers use in the schools nowadays. But don't get your knickers in a knot. We have the advantage of technology on our side—we have digitized the cattle drive."

"How's that?" I asked.

"The biggest problem when yer chasin' cows is knowin' where everybody is and what they're doin'. Communication, right? Years ago we tried walkie-talkies. Too much noise. You can't hear nothin'. Now we have cellphones."

"But it's the same thing with cellphones, Freddy. You can't talk to everyone at the same time, and if you're moving you can't hear yourself, let alone anyone else."

"That's where the technology has caught up." He tapped his cellphone. "Nowadays, we can text."

A dirt bike with no muffler zoomed up beside us and skidded to a halt. Willy and Dave grinned at me like two pirates riding a leaky frigate on the Spanish Main. There were now three vehicles abreast on the road, blocking traffic, and it looked like we had the quorum required for a sideroad meeting.

"We're here to help, Uncle Walt!" said Willy.

It's getting so that I flinch when I hear those words. As the Squire says, having those two help is like having four good men not show up.

"Gentlemen," said Freddy, in a voice of command. "Stand by to text. The Squire and I will stay here at the mailbox as

Command and Control. You boys go out and do recon. Willy's on the bike and Dave can take Predator."

"Who is Predator?" I asked.

Dave slid open the back door of the trailer and led out a very tough-looking buckskin horse, already saddled.

"The funny thing is," said Dave genially, "you just got those new cows, and I just got this new cow pony. Is that a coincidence or what? And I've got this dandy little holster right here on the saddle for my cellphone. Leaves my hands free to rope and shoot."

A cellphone rang. Freddy, Willy and Dave looked at each other blankly. It rang again and the Squire started. "Oh, it's me!" he said, and pulled a Blackberry out of his breast pocket.

"I got it for Christmas. It's more fun than a barrel of monkeys." He looked at the call display and saw a message. "A report coming in from one of my scouts . . . Calvin Currie says the cows went right across his place and jumped out onto 25 Sideroad."

"So here's Plan A," said Freddy. "Willy, you whip around the block and see if you can get on the other side of them and drive them this way. Dave, you get down here to the corners and turn them up the Seventh Line towards us. We'll stay here and funnel them through Walt's gate."

Willy nodded. "We're wired, we're mounted, we have a plan. What can go wrong?"

Dave swung up on the horse and took off south to the corners in a shower of small stones. Willy darted away north in a cloud of black smoke. The bike made a sound in the distance like an angry bee trapped in tinfoil.

"Shouldn't they be wearing helmets?" I asked.

"Yeah, helmets," agreed the Squire. "And a first aid kit . . . and bail money."

We stood there waiting for a couple of minutes, and finally the Squire's Blackberry beeped. It was a message from Willy. The Squire squinted at it.

"ICM," he read.

Freddy brightened. "He says, 'I see 'em'!"

The Blackberry beeped again, this time with a message from Dave. "He says 'ICM2,'" said the Squire. "This is good." He poked the keyboard with a reply. "Where RU?" A few seconds later the reply came back: "Plan A OK. GTG."

Even I knew that meant "got to go." It sounded like the cows were coming our way. Freddy parked his truck and trailer up against my gate to block the road. We manned the ditches on either side and watched for the cows to appear on the road from the south. Nothing happened. The Squire's Blackberry finally beeped. The Squire studied it for a moment and called to us.

"It's Willy. He says, 'SOL on Plan A.'"

"SOL?" I said. "What does that mean, Freddy?"

"Ah . . . d-d-did not work."

"They took a detour through Calvin Currie's orchard. That's not good! Those apple trees could be hazardous."

"Oh yeah," I said. "I guess green apples are bad for cows. They can choke on them, can't they?"

"They're not good for the cowboys either. Low limbs. Here's another one from Dave. He says . . . 'GGGG' . . . ? What the hell is he—"

"Jeez," said Freddy.

"Oh, right," said the Squire. "He says, 'Cows are fast, but I R faster!'"

My God, I thought. Is he texting at a full gallop through that orchard? The Squire kept reading the messages as they came in.

"'I'm on 'em like a duck on a June bug . . . like a fat boy on a cupcake . . . like . . . '" And then there was silence for two minutes and then another message from Willy. "'Dave hit low limb. Phone lost in tall grass. IM following cows.'"

"Well, jeez," said Freddy. "What do we do now?"

"Make a call to Dave," I suggested. "Let the phone ring and he'll find it in the grass."

"Good thinking, Walt," said the Squire. "Now I know why they made you chairman." The Squire's call was interrupted by the call-waiting signal. It turned out to be a man from Nigeria who needed a loan. The Squire says he hears from him almost daily. By the time the Squire had extricated himself from that, there was another message from Willy, only it was Dave using Willy's phone. The message read, "Willy hit same branch. LOL. FIFO."

"Okay, I know LOL means 'laugh out loud.' But what is FIFO?"

Freddy thought for a minute. "My guess is . . . 'friggin' idiot fell off.'"

The Squire shook his head. "I can't raise Dave. It says 'The customer you are trying to reach is out of service.' How can that be . . . ? Oh wait, here's a note from Willy. 'Predator found Dave's phone. Does warranty cover phone stepped on by horse?'"

"Jeez," cursed Freddy, taking the phone from the Squire and poking the keyboard. "'Where R those cows?'"

The reply came back: "No CM. Bring stretcher."

An hour later, we had gathered up Willy and Dave, found

Predator and loaded up what was left of the dirt bike onto Freddy's truck. Back at the mailbox, the Squire was still waiting patiently for us.

"Another productive afternoon on the Seventh Line," he observed drily. "Two men hobbled, two machines destroyed, a horse that will need therapy and—gollies, has anybody seen the cows?"

"Well, I'll be roped and branded," said Freddy, glancing over to my barn. "There's your cows right there."

I turned and saw the Galloways in the barnyard. Maggie and Hope were sitting on the fence, watching the cows clean up the last of the grain in the feeder. I trotted over to join them. It turned out Maggie had seen the cows coming back up the road by themselves, and when she and Hope went out to the field with the big red bucket they all jumped the fence and ran up to be fed.

"How long ago did this happen? I wish we'd known," I said.

Maggie smiled. "Well, dear. The trouble with being unreachable is that people can't reach you."

Yours sincerely,
Walt

———— *June 25*

Dear Ed,
Our third wedding anniversary is coming up on August 15th. For our first anniversary, I asked Maggie if there was any place in the world she would really like to see. She chose Tuscany.

The elderly lady who works with Maggie at the dress shop, Mariella, grew up in a small town in central Italy, and Maggie had heard all about the hill towns of Tuscany from her. I guess Maggie was fascinated by the idea that there were dry sand hills somewhere that could actually produce great food. On the trip, I bought Maggie a gold bracelet with red carnelian stones in it. She loved it because the stones had little designs etched in them: a goat, a horse, a cat, a chicken and a hound dog that looked just like Spike.

When I gave it to her she said: "It's just lovely, Walt. It's like having the farm on my arm."

The "farm on the arm" is what we called it. But when we were getting ready for bed the day of the cattle drive, she noticed it was missing. She thought it might have fallen off in the front field when she was out with the cows.

"Oh dear," she sighed. "It was our first holiday together. And you gave it to me."

I thought it was worth a try, so the next evening after supper I did a grid-pattern search of the front field, following the route she took with the cows. I thought that if it had dropped in the grass somewhere it would probably stand out. The ground has been grazed practically bare, and the little patches of grass that are left crackle like potato chips under-foot. But I couldn't find it, and as the light started to fade I gave up and went to sit on the dock by the pond. It was so quiet you could hear the little gulp the trout make when they swallow a mayfly on the surface. And you could hear Don playing his trumpet in the distance. On still summer nights like this he often sits on an old couch in front of the milk house and runs through his entire repertoire. When I sat on the dock, he was halfway through "Danny Boy."

You would think from the sheer peacefulness of this scene that nothing is happening here or anywhere else. It's odd, but when I'm away from the firm for a few days and some crisis occurs, like the collapse of a big American bank, I don't even have to call in to know that the whole company will be turning itself inside out, everyone dashing about in a panic. And unless it's complete global meltdown, by the time I get back to the office, all the shouting and hand-wringing will be over, and you'd never know that anything had actually happened except for the wastebaskets full of Rolaids wrappers and discarded Valium blister packs. And that's because nothing really did happen.

But out here at the farm, it's just the opposite. Life appears to be perfectly tranquil and marching along just the way it always has, but in fact, real changes are happening everywhere you look. The water level in the pond is the lowest I've ever seen it.

Don had moved on to "You Made Me Love You."

There's only one happy-looking tree on the farm at the moment. It's actually a new species for us, a Carolinian cypress that somebody gave me the second year I was up here. I planted it beside the upper pond at the back of the farm, thinking it probably wouldn't survive because a cypress belongs about three climate zones south of us. Now the upper pond has completely dried up, but the cypress tree is flourishing. There's a pair of Kentucky warblers nesting in it. Normally, they live about five hundred miles south of us, too. And I now have possums making raids on the henhouse. At this rate, it won't be long before we're eating grits and playing banjos.

I can always tell when Don is done for the night. He plays . . . well, I can't tell you the name of it. But he always saves it for last. I think it's his favourite. But I can't tell you what it's called.

And in the middle of this drought, Pluto Township, just west of us, has approved an application for a water bottling plant. Anybody can see that the flora and fauna are changing. How can people just stand by and let them pump millions of gallons out of a pristine natural wetland like the Pluto Marsh?

The next morning at breakfast, I asked Maggie about the water bottling plant. She was standing at the dish sink, scrubbing a muffin pan.

"Do you think it's right that they should be doing this in the middle of a scorching drought?" I asked.

Maggie paused and wiped her brow with her wrist. "I don't know," she said. "At least it's not gin."

"Gin?"

"My grandmother ran the Women's Christian Temperance Union for about thirty years. She stitched a baby quilt for Freddy when he was born that said 'Water Is Best.' I think he still has it. Anyway, one of her missions during the Depression was to shut down all the stills operating up there in the Pluto Marsh. I think Gramma would be thrilled if she knew that the only thing coming out of that swamp today was water. Oh dear!"

She'd turned the faucet on into the kettle and the tap was spluttering and shuddering violently.

"No water," she said irritably. "There must be a problem with the pump."

We went down to the basement to check on the pump. It was running but the pressure was at zero, so I shut the switch off.

"That's odd," said Maggie. "It's always been a good, strong well. Maybe we should take the lid off and have a look."

We went outside to the well, fifty feet behind the house. I pried the concrete plug out of the well cap with a crowbar and peered down with a flashlight. I could see my reflection, so there seemed to be water down there.

Maggie called Freddy, and ten minutes later he was in the laneway. He must have called in some sort of alarm because the Squire, Willy and Dave also turned up a few minutes later. Freddy took the flashlight and stuck his head through the plughole.

"Well, I'll be dipped and battered," he said. "Yer water level's dropped away down and your foot valve is sucking air."

"Okay," I said. "So what do we do?"

"Generally, we just throw a tank of water in and hope she recovers. These dug wells get silted up and if you change the pressure sometimes they get goin' again. She was always a good well."

Willy and Dave brought a tanker truck with a thousand gallons of lake water. It went into the well like Niagara Falls. But the next morning, the pump was running dry again. On the way out the door to check the well I met the Squire, and while we were prying the plug out, Willy and Dave drove in with a thirty-foot extension ladder strapped to their pickup truck. The well was dry again, so they slid the ladder into the well, and the two of them descended with tools and pipe.

"Where does a thousand gallons of water go overnight?" I asked.

"Looks like the water table has dropped, all right," explained Freddy. "Throwing water in it ain't going to bring it back up. But we can still use what's there. So we're gonna splice another length of pipe to get down to it."

"But if the water table is dropping, what kind of a solution is this?"

Freddy shrugged. "Who knows? Just keep your fingers crossed, I guess, and pee outside."

There is a tradition in this community of making do and patching things, which normally I have a lot of respect for. But sometimes it becomes ridiculous. I've seen them tie a page wire fence together with grapevines, which works until the cows eat their way through the grapevines. There comes a point where you're better off to take control of a situation and fix it properly. It seemed pretty obvious to me that we were going to have to dig a new well.

I went back into the kitchen, where Maggie was handing off Hope to Gertrude Lynch, who is now spending three days a week with us while Maggie's at the store. Spike and Hope were doing laps around the kitchen table, playing Coyote and Road Runner, except in their version Road Runner chases the Coyote.

"Lovely morning," I said cheerily.

"Oh yes, lovely," said Gertrude irritably. "You sound like that dumb blonde that does the weather on the television every night. After sixty days with no rain she says 'another great day to go to the beach,' she says, as if we weren't trying to grow food to put on the table. Fine for her! She's so thin she probably just lives on hair gel. So, are you getting anywhere with the water?"

Maggie just smiled at me, and I excused myself to look up a well-drilling company in the phone book. The only local one is AAA Well Drillers. I called and told them I was thinking of drilling a new well. A woman on the desk told me they didn't have anyone available at the moment. I told them I had a two-year-old in the house and livestock to water, but she said there wasn't much she could do about it except put my name on their waiting list.

When I hung up I saw the Squire had followed me inside.

"Who's he on the phone to?" he asked.

"Well drillers," said Gertrude with pursed lips and that look she reserves for blonde weather forecasters and Internet poker.

The Squire's brow furrowed. "He wants to drill a well . . . on the Seventh Line?"

"Yes, I do," I said. "What's the matter with that?" There was no answer from either of them, and I looked to Maggie for enlightenment.

"It's just been so long since anyone dug a well on this road."

"Well it's going to be even longer, because they say they have no openings until October."

Gertrude snorted. "My goodness, you can get a heart surgeon before that!"

"Before you get a well driller," said the Squire, "you'll want to bring in a witch."

"A witch?" I asked.

"Yeah, it's always been hard to find water around here. And expensive. You know Wilf Smalley up on Short's Hill? He had to sell six cows every time the drillers drilled a hole, and they drilled six dry holes."

Gertrude nodded in agreement. "By the time the poor man found water for his cows, he had no cows to water," she said.

"But you're saying he finally did find water. Did he have a witch?"

"Yes, he did," said the Squire. "It was Delbert McNabb."

"You mean Don's father? He's a water witch?"

"Yeah. Water witch and well driller. One of the best. A lot of people say they can do it. But Delbert's the one who found water. He did it for Wilf, and he did it right here on this property. Nearly fifty years ago he witched and drilled that well of yours out there."

I remembered that Don's father had been in the Myra Connor Lodge, the nursing home in Larkspur, pretty much the whole time since I bought the farm. "Is he still . . . active?" I asked.

"Active is not a word I would use to describe anyone at the 'I'm a Goner Lodge,'" said Gertrude drily.

Five years ago they got a big donation from Frank Connor's widow, Myra, to renovate the nursing home. So they renamed it the Myra Connor Lodge. Of course, it's built on the municipally owned property out on the town line between the hospital and the cemetery, so when people aren't calling it the "I'm a Goner," they call it the "Halfway House."

Maggie had to go to work, so Gertrude took Hope across the road to the Squire's while we finished working on the well. I went behind the house to see how they were getting on. Freddy was leaning on a shovel and the two boys were still down the well. I told Freddy that I was going to slip into the nursing home and visit with Don's father about witching a new site.

"Drywell Delbert?" he said screwing up his face.

The nicknames they have for people up here are just brutal. Most of them draw attention to some prominent physical feature — Flatface, the Beak, Liver Lips, Square Ass. A man who was born with one leg shorter than the other is known as Skip. A lady who apparently blossomed in grade nine is still called Jersey.

"Drywell Delbert, huh?" I said. "The Squire and Gertrude both say he was a real water witch."

"Anybody can say they're a witch, Walt. It's not a highly regulated profession. Delbert also says he can diagnose cancer with a pendulum and bend spoons without touchin' them. He's as loony as a dollar coin. Nah, the old people believe in that water witch stuff, but you can get the same stuff off the back of a spreader."

Willy's head emerged from the wellhead.

"Did I hear you say Drywell Delbert? Don't go there, Walt. He's got a couple of raccoons loose in his attic."

Dave's voice was an echo from the well.

"Did I hear you say Drywell Delbert? Jeez, Walt, don't go talkin' to him. He'll grind yer ear off, but he won't tell you anything. He's just mashin' green strawberries with his bare gums."

"But how else am I supposed to know where to dig?" I asked.

"Water is where you find it, Walt," said Freddy. "It's all pretty much a matter of luck. You go see Drywell if you like. Just don't feed him or he'll move in with you."

Yours sincerely,

Walt

———— July 17

Dear Ed,

I have started to keep my own calendar on the drought. It is now seventy days with no rain.

The conversation about Delbert McNabb had piqued my curiosity. I decided to go and meet the man and decide for myself what sort of a character he might be. I drove in to the Myra Connor Lodge in Larkspur and pushed open the glass doors. A nurse looked up from her crossword on the desk.

"Delbert McNabb?" she said. "Why yes, he's right there." She raised one finger in the direction of the sitting room, where a rail-thin man with white hair sat in a chair reading a magazine.

"Delbert, you have a visitor," she said. "Imagine that!" She went back to her puzzle.

Delbert glanced up at me. It's impossible to estimate ages with a lot of the men around here. As Maggie says, they get a face when they're thirty and they seem to keep it until they're eighty. Delbert was probably in his late seventies but surprisingly fit-looking for someone in a nursing home. He put his magazine down and got out of his chair, moving like a much younger man.

"You've come to move the bed?" he asked quietly.

"No, my name is Walt Wingfield. We've never met. But I live next door to your son, Don."

"Oh," he said, with a slight frown. "Don sent you to move the bed?"

"If you need the bed moved, I guess I can help with that."

"It's in a bad place," he said shortly. He led me down a hallway to his room. It was about ten feet square and contained a bed, a chair and several piles of magazines. There was a window that looked out on the parking lot. On the wall there was a bulletin board with letters, notes and articles pinned to it. The bed sat along the wall with the head next to the doorway.

"Do you want the bed over closer to the window? Not much light where it is now."

"It's not the light," he said. "It's the electricity."

I pulled the bed away from the wall to see if there was an

outlet, and when I looked up, the nurse was looming in the doorway.

"Are you moving your bed again, Delbert?" If she had turned to me and told me to put on my snowsuit and go out and play, I probably would have done it.

"I told you it's in a bad place," said Delbert irritably.

She pushed the bed firmly back against the wall. "He does this all the time," she said to me. "Don't pay any attention to him. Now Delbert, why don't you take your guest down to the games room? You can watch baseball on TV. Wouldn't you like that?"

"They don't play baseball in the morning," he said sourly. "Any idiot knows that. And I'm not sleeping in that bed."

"That's fine," she said tightly. "You can sleep in the chair if that's what you want. Just don't be moving the bed again. We have enough to do around here without you moving the furniture all the time." She turned on her heel and clicked away down the hall. Delbert eyed her retreating figure coldly.

"She spends all morning not paying any attention to you, which frees up her whole afternoon to ignore you. That bed is in the wrong place. It's picking up pestiferous telluric emanations. Comes out of the faults in the ground where tectonic plates intersect. And it's making me sick."

"Pestiferous . . . emanations?"

Delbert gave a little nod and continued his report. "I know what you're going to say. Any emanation is pestiferous. But the telluric stuff is the worst, especially if you sleep over it. That's why I want the bed moved. We're on a disease point here. Ask them how long anyone's ever lasted in this room. Not very long."

"Well, it is an old age home. . . ." I ventured.

"And they won't let me move the bed. So I sleep in the chair."

"I see," I said, although I didn't really. There was a pause, and I decided to change the subject. "Pretty dry out there, wouldn't you say?"

Delbert nodded again. "She's a dry summer. But I guess we knew it was coming, eh?"

"We did? The weather people in Ottawa didn't say anything about it."

"Seemed pretty clear to me. I told them. There was the obvious stuff, like the tail end of El Niño and the long string of dry moons. But then you add in the stuff you can see and hear. Big jump in the aphid population and the way the crickets slow right down with their chirping. It's right up there on the board."

I looked at a curled and faded email pinned up on Delbert's bulletin board. It was addressed to the National Weather Office. It ran to three pages, showed tree ring spacing charts, El Niño patterns, and concluded: "This part of the country will be hit with a summer drought lasting at least seventy days . . . and possibly to the end of the lunar cycle in September." It was dated October of last year.

"So you actually predicted this?"

Delbert shrugged. "They never wrote back. I guess I should get my predictions in earlier. A year is a pretty tight turnaround for guys in the weather office. They often get run over by glaciers."

Apparently some of Delbert's emanations weren't so pestiferous.

"I understand you're a water witch."

Delbert looked at me with no expression. "I was at one time. I don't do it anymore."

"My well has gone dry and I'm trying to find a new source," I explained. "They say you found the spring fifty years ago . . . on the Fisher place on the Seventh Line."

"Oh, yeah. You don't forget a spring like that. Couldn't draw it down with a five-horse pump. Gone dry, you say? Mmmm-mmm. That's strange. Might be blocked somewhere." He lapsed into silence again.

"I know you're retired, but I was hoping I could persuade you to come out to the farm with me and find a better well."

Delbert looked at me impassively. "I'm not retired. I just don't do that anymore. Haven't done it for years."

"But, if it was blocked somewhere, could a witch find the spot?"

"Oh, yeah. A good witch can find water anywhere. Years ago there was a man by the name of MacLean. They say he could find coffins in the graveyard and tell you which ones died by drowning. A good witch can find anything . . . water, septic tanks, plugged tile drains, oil, gold."

"Gold, huh?" I smiled. "My wife just lost a gold bracelet. I think it's in the pasture somewhere."

"A good witch would find that for you. But I can't do it anymore."

"Why not?"

"I just can't," he said simply. "Either you have it or you don't. I've lost it. Tell you one thing, though. That spring of yours is still there. A flow like that doesn't just dry up and disappear."

I got up to go and shook his hand. He had long, graceful fingers and his grip was surprisingly gentle. The hand dropped quickly, he went back to his magazine and I left. He certainly was an odd duck.

When I got back to the house shortly before noon I found a phone message waiting for me from AAA Well Drillers saying that they had just had a cancellation and they could have a crew out to the farm this afternoon. I called them, and an hour later a big truck with a giant latticework steel tower lumbered down the lane and stopped in front of the house. The foreman opened the cab door and climbed down the steel ladder. He was a stout man with a smooth face and a tight smile.

"Where would you like your well, Mr. Wingfield?" he asked.

"I'm not sure. Do you have any method you use to find water?"

"Nooo," he chuckled mirthlessly. "We always leave that up to the property owner. Saves a lot of trouble all round. Here's the deal. We dig anywhere you tell us to, but you have to pick the spot."

This was unsettling. Just think if I took that approach with a client at the firm. Imagine how they'd react if I said, "You pay me to make money for you in the stock market, but I get you to pick the stocks. In other words, you take the risk and I get the reward."

"So where do you want me to dig?" he repeated.

I had no idea. I told him that this was always a really strong well and there hadn't been a problem with it before. It just suddenly stopped.

"Wells dry up," he said. "Springs move. If you had a good well before, chances are you'll find another one. Water is where you find it, Mr. Wingfield. Pretty much a matter of luck."

"Just luck, huh? That's what my wife's brother says." I didn't feel at all comfortable about this, but AAA had a waiting list and I had a baby in the house and livestock to water. "All right then," I said. "We'll do this the same way

I used to pick mining stocks. You see that old dog over there? That dog has always been my good luck charm. Let's put the well right where he is lying."

Spike got to his feet and looked at me sadly. The foreman climbed back into the cab, backed the truck into position and elevated the tower. The engine revved up, the drill sank into the ground and over the next three hours drilled a hole two hundred feet deep. When I heard the truck drop down to an idle, I went out and noticed a heavy sulphurous smell hanging on the air. The foreman came over to me, with a smile on his face that could have signified win, lose or draw.

"We hit gas," he said. "Don't happen very often, Mr. Wingfield, but it looks like we've got a dry hole. Sorry about that. What do you want us to do? Do you want to try another spot?"

"How much do I owe you so far?"

He drew out his calculator and tapped. "Let's see, two hundred feet at forty dollars a foot. . . ."

My heart sank. "Eight thousand dollars . . . ?" I winced.

"Oh, no, no . . . it's . . . let's see . . . yep, eight thousand. And then there's the tax."

I told him I'd have to think about it before I did any more digging. He smiled at my cheque and he smiled at my shoes and he assured me that they were in the neighbourhood all this week and even though they were very busy he was quite sure they could get back around to me. Before he turned to go, I asked him if he knew anyone who could find water.

"You mean a water witch? A dowser? A diviner? Oh, yeah. Lots of them around. You should try down at the Legion or the Myra Connor Lodge. Good luck to you."

The truck passed Maggie and Hope driving down the lane. Maggie had to put the 4×4 up against the rail fence to let them squeeze by.

"AAA Well Drillers has a brand-new truck," she said. "How much of that are we paying for?"

I went next door to see Don. I thought maybe he might help me persuade Delbert to come out here and witch a new spot to dig. I found him at the barn, where he was replacing the thermostat on the refrigerator unit of his milk tank. He glanced up at me and shook his head.

"No luck, huh?" he said.

"Is it that obvious?"

"Oh, yeah. A dry hole leaves its mark on a man's face. They say that when the drillers came to drill the seventh hole on Wilf Smalley's farm, he was sitting in his kitchen with a revolver on the table."

"Good heavens. Do you mean he was going to shoot himself?"

"Some folks said that. I reckon he was gonna shoot the well driller first, then maybe think about it. So, you gonna try again?"

I told him about my visit to the nursing home. Don looked away, back to the thermostat.

"And how is Dad today?" he asked.

"He seems to think his bed is in the wrong place. He thinks it's making him sick."

"Yeah. Emanations."

"So, he's done this before, has he?"

Don kept talking to the thermostat. "They call me every now and then. He has a problem anytime they lay new tiles or carpet. He decides they're crossing a magnetic field the wrong way. He frets about stray voltage from the microwaves and the computers and goes around pulling plugs. Yanks cell-phones away from people and warns them about brain cancer. Last year, he decided the windows should be triangles instead of square panes. He's a little different, you know."

"I asked him to witch a new well for me but he says he can't do that anymore."

Don turned to face me. "So, what do you want me to tell you?"

"The Squire and Gertrude both say they remember when he was really good at it."

"They remember a lot of stuff that didn't happen, Walt. If he was so good at it, why didn't he find a decent well on his own place? I've got two wells with the pumps suckin' air right now. And I'm wondering what's going to happen to the third one."

"Well, I have no water at all, and I have no idea where to dig. Would you talk to your father and see if he might help me?"

"No," said Don flatly. "I don't talk to him, Walt. It's better that way."

"Do you mind if I ask him out to the farm to look at the well?"

"Don't waste your time, Walt. I've been down that road and it's a dead end. The man is useless."

He shrugged in a half apology and went back to work.

Yours sincerely,

Walt

———— *July 24*

Dear Ed,

I lingered in the shade of the verandah after lunch today while Maggie put Hope down for her nap on the porch swing.

Maggie's ivies and hanging baskets provide lots of shade and still allow for some air movement. It's often the coolest place on the farm. As she tucked the bug netting around the cot and Hope settled, Maggie hummed gently to her.

And there it was, the same tune that Don plays on the trumpet.

"What is that song?" I asked her.

Maggie stopped and thought for a minute. "I don't know," she said. "Don's always played it. I asked Elma once and she said she didn't know either. She said even Don doesn't know where it came from. It's just always been in his head. It's a nice tune, isn't it? It's comforting."

Whatever it's called, it certainly is a comfort. Three bars of that tune act like a tranquilizer dart on Hope. We moved off to sit on the steps and talk, and before long Freddy appeared in the driveway in a small cloud of dust raised by his boots.

"G'day, fellow Israelites," he grinned. "Seventy-seven days in the Sinai Desert now, and where the hell is Moses? Jeez, she's hot out there! Nothin's growin'. I just saw a bunch of grasshoppers sittin' on the rail fence with tears in their eyes."

I handed him the *Hillhurst County Shopper* with the live-stock reports from the Pluto Sales Barn. "Prices are way down. I guess people are shipping out their animals."

"Sure they are," he agreed. "No pasture. You can't make money on livestock if you have to buy feed."

"We're running out of pasture, too," said Maggie. "We could fence off that low spot around the upper pond and put the sheep and goats in there for a couple of weeks."

"Do you really think we should pasture that spot?" I asked.

"It's still green," said Freddy. "Why wouldn't you?"

"It's a wetland," I said. "Wetlands are a carbon sink. They absorb the emissions that cause global warming."

"Oh," said Freddy. "Is that what they're for? I thought they were for dumping chesterfields and refrigerators."

"If we let the sheep and goats on it, it'll look like Afghanistan in a month."

"We could try it for a couple of weeks, Walt," said Maggie. "If the weather doesn't break by then we could work on an exit strategy. When Hope wakes up I'm taking her into town to set up the hall for the Institute bake sale tonight. We'll be home a little after dark. Why don't you and Freddy dig some postholes and string the electric fence?"

Freddy and I took shovels and a long crowbar out into the blistering sunshine and trooped up to the pond. Spike carried the water bottle. I still didn't feel right about disturbing this natural area, but we dug a few postholes. It was hot work. The sweat poured off us and we drained the water bottle within the hour. Finally we sat down in the shade of the cypress tree, and Freddy rolled a cigarette.

"Did you see that piece in the paper about the Pluto Marsh?" I asked. "The consulting engineer, some kind of hydrologist, claims the bottling plant can take a million litres of water out of the aquifer every day without any effect on the environment. How can he know that? He can't calculate a thing like that. He's obviously never heard of the butterfly effect."

"Neither have I," said Freddy. "What's that?"

"It's an idea that comes out of chaos theory. The concept is that nothing happens in isolation. Little things like a butterfly flapping its wings create tiny changes in the atmosphere that have a ripple effect that might ultimately alter the path of a tornado. Everything is connected. Anyway, the paper says they're taking the first truckload of water out on August 10th."

"That'll make it the first legal export out of the marsh since Confederation," Freddy chuckled. "And if the water guys can create a few jobs, what's the harm?"

"But that's just the point, Freddy," I protested. "We can't know what the harm is. Why can't we just come to a place and leave it as we find it?"

"And that is exactly the point I made with the township when they told me to clean up my front yard. I told them, some of those species out there are at risk and need protection. Chrysler . . . GM. . . ."

I stood up and we went back to work. I put my shovel into the ground at the next posthole position, stepped on the blade and felt a warm hum beneath my foot. I bent down to examine the earth turned over by the shovel. It was glistening with the little golden bodies of insects. They boiled out of the ground in biblical numbers. It was fascinating. This wetland wasn't just a carbon sink, it was teeming with biological diversity. I called to Freddy to come over and have a look, but Freddy wasn't there. He and Spike were thirty yards away, hurdling the rail fence like white-tailed deer. He turned to yell at me: "Run for your life, Walt! Those are yellow jackets!"

Back in the kitchen, we caught our breath. Surprisingly, there was no damage, but it was pretty clear that there wouldn't be any more fencing until we dealt with the yellow jackets. Freddy asked if I had any spray bombs in the house, but I wasn't keen on using insecticides.

Just the week before I had been reading a piece in the *Green Farmer* about how to get rid of a nest of bees without using a toxic chemical spray. They recommended that you wait for the sun to go down, get a pail of really hot water and pour it down the hole.

"Oooh, yeah?" said Freddy. "Never heard of that one. But I guess it's worth a try. Hey, what can go wrong?"

We worked on the other side of the pond for the rest of the afternoon. As soon as the sun went down, we boiled several pots of water, dumped them into a large plastic bucket and carried it out to the pasture. Spike trotted faithfully behind. The article in the magazine said that it didn't have to be pitch dark. As soon as the sun goes down all the bees return to base and become dormant. They won't fly or sting after sunset.

"I'm right behind you, Walt," said Freddy.

I carried the first bucket to the little hole I'd made earlier with the shovel, and tipped the hot water into the nest. It was bathtime for the buzzies!

Baking soda is something you should always have around the house for emergencies. Back in the kitchen, we smeared over the welts with baking soda plasters and ice packs. Spike soaked one ear in his water bowl.

"I never even saw them, Freddy," I said. "Did you see where they came from?"

"There was another hole, about ten feet behind us. That nest is huge. It goes way underground. There must be a gazillion of them down there."

"It's like science fiction. What are we going to do?"

"There was . . . another method we used to use years ago," said Freddy slowly.

"What was that?"

"Well, it's not anything you could do today. I mean, in those days we didn't have any idea of the terrible effect we had on the environment. We're much more sensitive to that sort of thing now."

"What did you do, Freddy? I want to know."

"Basically, we'd burn 'em out."

"Uh-huh? And how would you do that? Like you say, they're underground."

"A couple of pounds of triple-15 fertilizer and a can of gas."

"Good heavens, Freddy! That's what terrorists use."

"We thought of it first."

Sometimes the old ways are the best. We drove Freddy's truck out to the pasture this time. It was pitch dark now, and the northern lights lit up the sky like a supermarket opening. Spike decided to stay in the truck. We made our way over to the postholes, and Freddy shone a flashlight at the first hole and the second one, about ten feet away.

"Now here's how it goes," whispered Freddy. "I pour the stuff down the first hole, and as soon as I'm done, you take yer shovel and cover it over. Then we wait until we smell gas comin' out of the other hole and we just light a match and toss it in. Here we go."

Freddy leaned over and gingerly poured a little gas into the first hole. Then he grinned at me and poured a little more. I asked him if he thought maybe that was enough.

"Barely," he said. "When you're dealing with an insurgency this big, you gotta show them you mean business."

He emptied the can and tossed it away. Then I handed him the shovel and he covered the hole with dirt.

"She'll be a hot time in the old town tonight. Now, where was that other hole?"

I shone the light on it. "Freddy," I said. "I smell gas. It's really strong."

He struck a match, said, "Fire in the hole!" and tossed it in.

Baking soda is good for burns as well as bee stings. Back in the kitchen we used up the rest of our supply, and Freddy went up to his place to get some more. It turns out there was a third hole. We'd been standing on top of it. It was very much like the northern lights, only brighter and a lot hotter. Maggie arrived home a little while later with Hope asleep on her shoulder. She paused in the doorway and looked carefully at me.

"What happened to your eyebrows, Walt?"

She took my hand away from my forehead to look closer.

"Oh my!" she said. "Well, I suppose they'll grow back. I'm not sure about the nose hairs. They look like steel wool. Do you want to tell me what happened?"

Spike said it for both of us.

"WOOF!"

The sound of footsteps came from the verandah, and we looked around to see Don standing at the screen door. Maggie pushed it open and he came in.

"I saw the fireworks," he said. "Are you blasting for water now, Walt?"

"Would you like a cup of tea?" asked Maggie.

"Sure," he said. "I could use it. Looks like I'm out of water, too. My third well quit this morning."

I pulled out a chair for him. "That must be a shock," I sympathized.

"Not really. I figured it would eventually quit . . . since it's hooked up to your well."

I paused. "It is? How could that be?"

Don pushed the cap off his head and set it on the chair beside him.

"You didn't know that? Years ago, when they dug your well here they put a pipe across your front field to my place. It's kinda my backup. There was one really dry summer about ten years ago when your well was the only reason I could keep going."

"But I don't understand," I said. "A pipe crossing a property line should have been registered on the title to the property, shouldn't it?"

Don stroked his chin. "I guess maybe it should. But then again, if Fisher had mentioned the pipe to my place he would have had to explain about the other ones, too, wouldn't he?"

"Others?"

"Yeah. Your well feeds the Squire and me. And from my place it goes down to the three houses on the corner. And from the Squire's it goes back across the road to Freddy's."

"Maggie, did you know this?" I asked.

"I guess so," she shrugged. "Everybody kind of knows that. I thought you did, too."

I sat down. You know, Ed, if I found out about things at the brokerage as late as I do up here, I would be fired. Imagine! I've lived up here for six years and suddenly discover I have a network of underground pipes on my farm. But that's the way it goes in this neighbourhood. In government intelligence circles, they have three levels for classifying sensitive information: confidential, secret and top secret. Top secret is so sensitive you aren't even allowed to know who the people are who actually know the secret. Up here, they have one more category that's even more exclusive: it's for those things that everybody knows, so nobody ever talks about.

"Anyway, this all explains why everyone was so interested in my well. So, where do we go from here?"

Don picked up his cap again and balanced it with one finger. "I don't know about you," he said quietly, "but I'm done."

"Done?" I said. "What do you mean? We're going to put in a temporary holding tank and truck water and drill more holes until we get through this. Can't you do that?"

"Sure, I could live in a tent and eat grasshoppers. But it's not practical. You can't run a dairy herd on trucked water. It's pretty clear to me the whole Seventh Line is goin' dry. I've had enough. I called the milk board this morning and told them I'm putting the quota and cows up for sale while they're still worth something."

"Selling the cows?" cried Maggie. "But you'll still crop the farm, won't you, Don?"

"Nope, I think I'll go out west. There's a jazz band out on Vancouver Island. A bunch of retired dairy farmers. It's called the Cowlicks. I'm pretty sure they could use another trumpet."

He set his mug down, pulled on his cap and said good night. We watched him go, and it was long time before any of us spoke. Finally Maggie asked, "If Don is quitting, what hope is there for the rest of us?"

"It's just what people were saying about Montreal in 1976 when the PQ first got elected," I said.

"What were they saying?"

"Last one out turns out the lights."

Yours sincerely,

Walt

———— *July 28*

Dear Ed,

I've been thinking about my ecological footprint lately. When I first came to the farm, I had a dream. I was going to live in close harmony with nature on a little plot in the forest. I would take only what I needed from the land, and tread lightly in the sun-dappled meadows beside the softly lowing cows and gentle sheep.

When I lived in the city, I walked to work most days. If I went across town, I took the subway. I did own a car, but it sat in the basement parking lot of the apartment building for months at a time. Twice a year I inflated the tires and recharged the battery.

Fast-forward seven years. I now own a 4×4, a tractor, a lawn tractor, a lawn mower, a chainsaw, a rototiller, a Whipper Snipper and a diesel generator. None of these machines is particularly energy efficient. A lawn tractor is the only four-wheeled vehicle that gets worse mileage than a Hummer. A fleet of trucks handles my garbage, the mail, the firewood, snow removal, dead stock removal, appliance delivery, appliance repair, dead appliance removal. . . .

Ecologically, this decision to move to the country has been a catastrophe. In the city I was living like a Buddhist monk compared to what I'm doing now. I use enough fossil fuel to run a small Chinese village. When I meet someone at the firm who lives in a downtown high-rise condominium, I kneel and kiss the hem of his Armani suit and praise him for his deep commitment to future generations.

I do recycle. Every week, I set out my empty Scotch bottles, so I'm trying to do my bit. I have a compost pile, too. Mostly dead chickens. But it is clearly not enough. We must do more. I've done some calculations, and it's pretty clear to me that if we ordered every hobby farmer like myself back to the city and told them to stay put, we could meet our obligations under the Kyoto Accord in about two weeks.

I read another article in the *Green Farmer* about omega-3 eggs. Apparently North Americans aren't getting nearly enough linoleic acid in our diets; that's why we have such a high rate of stroke and heart disease. The article says I can produce my very own omega-3 eggs, just by feeding flaxseed to my hens.

So I picked up a bag of flax at Dry Cry's and added it to the lay mash. Then I sat back and waited for the health benefits to roll in. Of course, the effects aren't immediate. It takes about ninety days for the stuff to work its way through to the eggs. Ninety days is a long time in the life of a chicken around here. In mid-June, just as the eggs were reaching their maximum omega-3 potency, a family of skunks burrowed under the henhouse and started swiping the eggs. I plugged that hole, and some raccoons quickly made another one, ate several of the hens and traumatized the rest of the flock so badly that they stopped laying altogether. So the eggs didn't actually make it to the table. But we did notice a statistically significant reduction in the incidence of stroke and heart attack in the local skunk and raccoon populations. They appear to be healthier than ever.

This is often the way it goes up here. I have lost count of the number of failed enterprises that began with some *aha!* moment late at night in bed while I leafed through the *Green Farmer*. Maggie just sighs and shakes her head.

"Why can't you be like other husbands and read *Playboy*?"

On top of everything else, a great big hawk started bothering my hens. He comes around every morning at dawn. He drops out of the sky, scoops up one of the hens and takes it to a dead elm tree on the line fence, where he tears it to pieces. I showed Don a picture I took of the hawk eating one of my hens.

"For God's sake, Walt," he said. "Why don't you shoot the bugger?"

"It's a red-tailed hawk, Don. They're a protected species."

"Why don't you shoot the bugger?"

I went to consult Dr. George, an eminent ornithologist who sometimes rides the train with me on the way back from the city. He's the author of *Nesting Birds of Canada*, chairman of the local conservation council and a well-respected environmentalist.

"Well, it wouldn't be a red-tailed hawk, Walt," he said. "Red-tails don't eat chickens."

I showed him a photo of the hawk standing on a dead chicken on the henhouse roof. There were white feathers sticking out of his mouth.

"He seems to eat chickens just fine," I said.

Dr. George looked closer. "Good heavens! He shouldn't be doing that. Why don't you shoot the bugger?"

The next day, the hawk made off with a guinea hen. That was his big mistake. It's impossible to do anything quietly with guinea hens. If something upsets them they just explode and start shrieking. It's a sound that starts like a shriek and rises until you can't hear yourself think. And they don't stop. They go on for days. They're like the NDP when someone proposes a tax cut.

The noise didn't just wake me up; it woke up Maggie, and they're her guinea hens. I heard her speaking softly on the phone late one night and I haven't seen the hawk since. I asked Maggie about it but she just pursed her lips and said, "Guinea hens are a protected species, too."

Yours sincerely,

Walt

Dear Ed,

Day eighty-five and still no rain. The water truck comes every few days to fill the temporary tank we have sitting out by the lane, but there is just enough to keep the house and the barn going. In the vegetable garden, everything above ground is dead and rattles in the breeze. The ground itself is as hard as the road and riddled with cracks. Every afternoon the storm clouds pile up and blow over us without shedding a drop of water.

Yesterday after chores, I cut a Y-shaped branch from the cherry tree in the front yard, stripped all the leaves off it and left it on the wellhead. Then I went back to the Myra Connor and found Delbert in the sitting room, right where I left him, his face in a science journal. I sat down beside him, and he looked up. He didn't smile, but he didn't seem to be irritated by my presence either.

"I know you don't witch anymore," I said, "but I was wondering if you might come out to the farm anyway, just for a visit."

He looked at me with a tired frown, and I thought for a minute I was pushing him too far.

"Sure," he said. "You gotta keep moving around here. If you lie still too long, someone will put you in a box and start throwin' dirt on you."

We drove out to the farm together in silence. I stopped the 4×4 in front of the house and went around to the passenger side to open the door, but Delbert was ahead of me. He set off across the yard around to the back of the house. When he got to the wellhead he paused.

"This was the best well I ever drilled," he said. "Lots of water. Good water, too. Is that the hole there that your driller put down?" He gestured towards Spike's dry hole, over by the fence.

"Yes," I said. "He went down two hundred feet."

"Too bad. No water there."

"There isn't?"

"Nothing you could use," said Delbert, leaning over and picking up a clod of dirt from the pile left by the drilling rig. "Around here, the good water is at thirty feet. You go deeper and it gets brackish, you know, briny. And at fifty feet you're into the blue clay."

"And that's bad?"

Delbert nodded. "It's the aquitard. That's a layer of rock or clay that water won't pass through. The blue clay goes down for a hundred, maybe a hundred and fifty feet. And once you punch through that you hit gas."

"That's what the man said. He said he hit gas at two hundred feet."

"Well, there you go. So, if you don't find water at thirty feet or so, you might as well quit right there."

"I guess that's good to know."

Delbert shrugged. "Still doesn't help you much. The aquitard goes for miles back under these hills, all the way to Pluto Township. It dipsy-doodles and splits apart. The water channels run over it every which way. It's like me telling you that Larkspur is two miles away. Can you find it knowing that? You need someone to point to it. Same thing here. You need a witch."

I went over to the wellhead, picked up the cherry branch and held it up for him. "That's the wood you use for witching, isn't it?"

"Yeah, you can use cherry," he agreed. "Or apple. . . ."

"So fruitwood is best, is it?"

"No," Delbert said vaguely. "Willow is good, too . . . or maple. Some people use black wire or a coat hanger."

I must have looked pretty puzzled because Delbert came over to me and took the cherry branch from me. "The gift is not in the wand. It's in the hands. You've got to have it here, in your hands. And I don't have it anymore. You might be able to do it. Why don't you try it yourself?"

He turned my palms up and placed the two arms of the branch in my hand. Then he folded my fingers over, pointed me across the lawn and gave my elbow a little nudge. I took a few slow steps and looked back at him.

"How will I know?" I asked.

"Don't worry. You'll know. You'll feel it."

I walked slowly across the yard holding the branch and waiting for a tingle. I circled the old wellhead, went out past the corner of the house. I even went over to the temporary tank to see if it might give me a little jolt. I felt absolutely nothing. Finally, I gave up and tossed the stick back on the wellhead.

"You really can't do it?" I asked. Delbert shook his head.

"So I'm just supposed to keep drilling these expensive holes all over the farm like Wilf Smalley?"

"Well, no," said Delbert. "You don't have to do that. I remember where the spring went."

"You remember?"

"Oh yeah. You don't forget a cracker like that one. It went right by the corner of the house here and on between those two maples and then out yonder into that pasture. I followed it a long way."

"If it went right beside the house, why did Fisher dig the well way over here?"

"Oh, I warned him it was a strong spring. It might have taken the foundation right out of his house."

"Really? So if I were to dig another hole, say, twenty feet from the well on a line with the corner of the house I should hit the old spring." I picked up the cherry branch and walked to the centre of the yard.

"Yeah," said Delbert. "That's where it was. And the water is still there—somewhere. I'll guarantee you that."

I stuck the cherry branch in the ground to mark the spot and drove Delbert back to the nursing home. The outing seemed to have tired Delbert. He nodded off in the passenger seat beside me, his head tilted back, muttering to himself. Actually, he wasn't muttering, he was humming a tune. I couldn't place it for a minute, and then I realized that it was Don's tune. Delbert was humming the same tune that Don always plays last on his trumpet. Back at the nursing home, I helped Delbert out of the car and walked with him to the door of the lodge.

"It's the strangest thing," I said as he turned to go. "That tune you were humming. Do you know what it's called?"

Delbert looked at me blankly. "Sorry, I don't know what you're talking about." He raised one hand in a vague gesture of farewell and went into the lodge.

Back at the farm, I caught the AAA office a few minutes before it closed for the day and told them I had a new spot for them to drill. They were in my yard again the next morning, shortly after breakfast. I told the foreman that I wanted him to dig right where the branch was sticking out of the ground. But I made it very clear to him that I wanted him to tell me when the drill reached thirty feet.

I went in and sat at the kitchen table, listening to the

roar of the diesel engine running the compressor. Half an hour later I heard a shout and I trotted out to the yard. Shiny wet gravel was spilling out of the hole now, and they were putting a pump on it. A stream of muddy water poured out of the hose. After a few minutes the water cleared. The foreman's eyebrows went up and he grinned at me. "Just the stuff we're lookin' for, isn't it?" he shouted. Then the stream slowed and sputtered. The foreman shook his head, but he was still grinning.

"What a shame," he said. "There's water there. But not enough for a well. Probably just a little pool. But it's a good sign. You'll want us to go deeper, don't you think?"

"Go another few feet," I ordered.

The drill plunged into the ground again, and as it bit deeper the wet gravel was replaced by a brownish muck. At forty feet, a little more water poured out, clearer this time. I put my finger in it and tasted it. It was salty. Brine, just like Delbert said.

At fifty feet, the drill rig shuddered and the material turned an elephant shade of grey.

"We're into the blue clay!" announced the foreman cheerily. I put my hand on his arm and told him to stop the machine.

"Don't worry," he assured me. "This machine will go through blue clay like a hot knife through butter."

"I'm not worried about your machine. There's no water in blue clay. It's an aquitard."

The foreman's eyes narrowed and the grin faded. "You've been doing some reading, have you? I hate it when people do that! Well, it's your call, Mr. Wingfield."

I wrote him another cheque and walked heavily back inside, where I thought through the diminishing number of options left to me. Then I heard Freddy's cheerful voice at the screen door.

"We've come to gather up all the ropes and knives for your own safety, Walt." Maggie, Gertrude and the Squire followed him into the kitchen. It felt like an intervention.

Freddy went over to the sink. "Put that blender away, will ya Maggie? That's a messy way for a man to do himself in."

"Don't worry," I said, waving them off. "It was only two thousand dollars this time."

"Hmph!" said Maggie. "I would say it's like flushing money down the toilet, except of course we can't flush the toilet, can we?"

Gertrude pressed her knuckles on the counter and looked out the window to the backyard. "Delbert said the water was there, did he?" she asked.

"He said he 'guaranteed' it, whatever that means," I replied.

Gertrude shook her head slowly. "If Delbert said it was there, I'd keep looking for it."

"Really?" I said. "You mean, call the drillers back and make a pin cushion out of the lawn at two thousand dollars a pop? I'm beginning to understand what Wilf Smalley must have felt like."

The Squire walked stiffly over beside Gertrude. "Delbert's your man, Walt," he said. "If anybody knows where that water is, he does."

"But he doesn't," I cried. "He just remembers where it used to be. And he won't even search for it. He says he's lost the gift."

"Probably left it the same place he put his marbles," chortled Freddy. "Would there be enough water left in the house for a cup of tea?"

It seemed to me there must surely be other people in the neighbourhood who could witch for water. So I put a little classified ad in the *Free Press* and got three replies the same day the paper came out. I invited them all out to the farm.

Maggie watched me do this and raised one eyebrow. "Consulting three witches? Didn't someone write a play about that? A tragedy, as I recall?"

Talking to witches is not that unusual for me. We just have a different name for them at the firm. We call them strategic planning consultants. We plot each of their projections on a graph and where the lines intersect, that's where we put our money. Or, in the case of the water, that's where we dig.

The first witch arrived after breakfast. I left Maggie and Freddy on the verandah and went out to the lane to meet him. He was a short, stocky man with a haunted look and a habit of suddenly turning as if someone might be listening to the conversation.

"The wells are all going dry around here," he said. "You know why that is, don't you?"

"Something to do with three months of drought, I would have thought."

"That's what they want you to think," he said and whirled around as if he'd heard someone in the shrubbery.

"They?" I asked.

"And I guess you think this is all because of global warming, don't you? Hmm? That's what they want you to think."

"Wait a minute," I interrupted. "Who is 'they'?"

He lowered his voice and leaned in again. "Water is the new oil, right? And how do they jack up the price of oil?"

"They limit the supply."

"Exactly. And the same thing is happening with the water. Do you really think that's a coincidence?"

"Oh, come on. There's a shortage of water because the climate is changing. They don't have any control over that."

"That's what they want you to think!"

"How do you know any of this?" I sighed.

"I hear 'em," he muttered. "I hear 'em in my head. They chatter. They talk about world events all the time. They talk about an attack on an embassy and the next day, there it is in the paper. Then they started on the weather. Tornadoes in the Midwest. And it happens. They're going to let something slip about the water pretty soon."

Now, Ed, some people who have two or more different kinds of fillings in their teeth are able to hear high-powered AM broadcast stations. The radio waves act on the teeth fillings the same way they do on a crystal radio set. The electromagnetic oscillations get transformed into mechanical vibrations in the person's head, and these are heard as sounds.

"So you hear these world events . . . and the weather. Do they ever do traffic reports?"

His eyes widened. "You hear them, too?"

"Yes," I said. "I have a portable radio on the tractor I keep tuned to CKNX All- News Radio."

I gave the poor man twenty bucks and a referral to a dentist south of Highway 13. Then I went into the house to await the next candidate. About half an hour later, a taxi from Ace Cab in Larkspur came up the lane and dispensed a bug-eyed character with a pattern of gin veins on his nose that put me in mind of a map of the London underground system. He lurched to the verandah and looked at me uncertainly.

"Have we met somewhere?" he wheezed. His breath could have preserved a tray of peaches. He raised a finger as if he had just remembered the answer to a skill-testing question.

"Oh," he said. "I know you. You're that stockbroker."

"I'm still with my company, but I don't actually trade securities myself anymore."

"Course you don't. Securities Commission pulled your licence, didn't they?"

"I'm sorry. What are you talking about?"

He gave me a conspiratorial grin and pointed the finger at me. "Didn't you do that stretch in Millhaven Penitentiary for insider trading? Oh, excuse me! You probably tell everybody it was a 'short stay with the government.'"

"Oh, for Pete's sake," I interrupted him. "You're thinking of Wingspread Developments. My name is Wingfield. Nothing to do with Wingspread."

"Oh," he said, pausing for a moment and working his eyebrows. Then the finger came back up. "But aren't you the one that runs those vulture funds? Bunch of predators take over a sick company and strip the assets and leave the employees and the shareholders holding the bag."

"That's Wingate, not Wingfield. Listen, I haven't had so much as a query audit in twenty-five years in the business."

"Really?" he said, genuinely puzzled now. "Not even a little hotel hot tub rodeo on your expense account?"

I shook my head. "No. I have not."

He spread his arms in a gesture of surrender. "Oh," he said. "Well then, I'm sorry. I can't help you."

"Why not?"

"The water aquifer in this township has a mind of its own. And it is perverse. It punishes the clean-living and rewards the wicked. The tax evaders and the pyramid sales promoters always get fifteen gallons a minute with a posthole digger. A Quaker who contributes a fifth of his income to Save the Children comes up dry after a thousand feet. You sure you haven't fiddled the books somewhere? Got some bank accounts in the Caymans?"

"I'm afraid I just have a chequing account here in Larkspur," I said.

"I'm really very sorry," he said, patting my shoulder and turning back to the cab. "I thought I could do something for you, but it appears I have been misinformed." As he opened the door he turned. "If things change . . . you know, if your company goes belly up and you take the big performance bonus, just give me a call."

He decanted himself into the cab and was gone. Maggie looked at me from the screen door.

"Do you have any idea who that man was?" I asked.

"Yes, it's sad really," she said. "I believe he had a bad experience with water as a child and hasn't touched a drop since."

I did recognize the third witch. He used to work at the dump, helping people pull the trash off the back of their trailers and pickups. He lost his right hand many years ago in a farm accident, so the neighbours call him Lefty, of course. When he arrived he unscrewed the hook from his prosthesis and replaced it with what looked to be part of an old-fashioned TV antenna. Then he set off on a trek around the old wellhead. Suddenly he stopped and touched his forehead as if he were communing with the spirit world.

"The water has moved away from this well," he announced. "I've seen it happen time and again. A good spring will just suddenly stop for no reason and then you find it's only a few feet away."

"So can you find it?"

"Oh sure," he said and took two steps forward. "It's right here now."

"So, do you think I should dig right there?"

"No, no. I can move it for you."

He made an impressive pantomime of a weightlifter struggling against several hundred pounds of fresh air. After several moments of exertion he stopped, panting for breath.

"There," he said. "It's back where it should be."

I pried the plug out of the wellhead and we both peered down. There was no water.

"Sometimes it takes a couple of treatments to make it stay put," he assured me. "That'll be twenty dollars."

I told the well chiropractor that I would call him if I needed another adjustment to my wallet and sent him on his way. I went back to Maggie and Freddy, who had been watching this performance from the verandah.

"How did that guy lose his hand, anyway?" I fumed.

Freddy scratched his ear. "I don't remember exactly what happened to him, but I'll tell ya, it made him about fifty percent more honest."

Yours sincerely,
Walt

—— *August 8*

Dear Ed,

I found myself on the verandah the other day staring at the clouds like some desperate homesteader during the Dust Bowl. It is now ninety-two days of drought, and the forecast says it's going to be another great week at the beach. It's also one day closer to our wedding anniversary, and I suddenly had an idea for the perfect gift.

I remembered the name of the jewellery shop in Tuscany where we bought the carnelian bracelet, and it took me just a few minutes online to find their website. I scrolled through their list of products to see if they were still making the same one. There was no email address, but there was a telephone number. So I snuck into town and went to see Mariella, who was minding the dress shop for Maggie that morning. She not only knew the town, she remembered the jewellery shop.

"How *romantico!*" she sighed. "Of course I will do this. Maggie will love it!"

I dialled the thirteen-digit number and handed her the phone. There followed a brisk conversation in Italian. I recognized the words *braccialetto* and *meraviglioso*, which sounded promising. Finally, Mariella turned to me and smiled.

"They say they have the bracelet and they can send it to you today. It will be simple."

I handed Mariella my credit card and waited for her to complete the transaction. But she put her hand over the phone.

"They don't take credit cards," she said. "They have a bank number you send the money to. *Aspetta!*" I gave her my pen and she wrote down a series of numbers that looked like the VIN on the 4×4. I went down the street to the bank to arrange a wire transfer. The bank officer asked me to take a seat.

"We put the account number together with the IBAN, that's the international branch account number, and I can do a transfer right here. It's very simple. It won't take a minute."

She tapped away at her keyboard and studied the screen

for the next ten minutes, before she took a deep breath and frowned. She consulted the bank specialist in the city who said that Italy might be one of the countries that now requires a SWIFT code. It contains the same information as the IBAN as well as a multiple-digit national code number.

"I suppose it might be simpler to just call the bank in Italy and find out." She looked at her watch. "We'll just catch them before their closing time." She dialled and sat for a moment tapping her pencil on the mousepad.

"'Pronto'?" she said.

"That's 'hello' in Italian," I offered.

"Oh, right . . . hello!" she said into the phone and listened. "He does speak English . . . sort of," she whispered to me. She explained what we were trying to do and listened for a few moments.

"She turned to me again and said, "He says 'sarah sempleechay.' What does that mean?"

"He is saying it will be simple."

Well, it wasn't simple. There may have been a SWIFT code and an IBAN but they weren't called that in Italian. We tried every different combination with the Italian banker still on the line, but nothing would go through. While I was sitting there, it occurred to me that just last week at the firm, we managed a hundred-million-dollar foreign exchange global transfer with a country that fifteen years ago didn't even have typewriters. But I could not pay that jewellery shop for the bracelet. I walked back up the street to break the news to Mariella. She seemed just as disappointed as I was.

"So sad you lose the bracelet," she sighed. "To find it you need a *rabdomante* . . . how do you say . . . a witch. In Italy, lotsa good witches. In Canada, I think. . . ."

"No, there's no good witches here," I said flatly. "Believe me, I've been looking for one. It seems to be a lost art."

Mariella thought for a moment. "There was one, here, when I first come to Canada. I can't remember names so well . . . Nabb . . . ?"

"McNabb?" I said. "You don't mean Delbert McNabb?"

"*Si, si!* Diberto." She tapped her finger on my chest three times. "Now that man . . . he was a witch!"

On the way out of Larkspur, I found myself coasting slowly past the Myra Connor nursing home. On impulse, I steered into the parking lot and went into the building. I was about to ask for Delbert, when I saw Gertrude Lynch at the piano in the . . . well, I don't know what it's called. It's the room where they hold all the events. Freddy calls it the "cafetoriafundraisium."

"Hello, Walt," said Gertrude. "Are you coming to my concert on Sunday?"

"Your concert? Ah, yes, the benefit . . . what will you be playing?"

"Schubert's 'The Trout.' I thought it should be something to do with water. And there's a lady coming down from Port Petunia to sing."

"Oh," I said. "Does she have a nice voice?"

"Not particularly. She has what I call a church voice. It carries over the organ."

I wasn't that anxious to spend my Sunday afternoon trapped in the Myra Connor listening to some ironclad soprano with a church voice. I mumbled an excuse about the well business. Gertrude didn't press me to buy tickets, as she usually does.

"I still think Delbert could help you," she said.

"So does the Squire. You know, there's something that puzzles me about this. Anybody over sixty-five thinks Delbert is a genius, and anybody under sixty-five thinks he's an idiot. It's as if they're talking about two different people."

"In a way they are talking about two people," she said. "Delbert used to be quite different. He had a golden touch about finding water. But more than that, he was a very out-going man, the life of the party. He played at all the dances."

"Really? What instrument?"

"Why, the piano, of course. It was Delbert who taught me to play the piano. I'm just a church organist, but Delbert was a real talent."

"So, that's where Don gets his music. What happened to Delbert, then? What changed him?"

"His wife died. That was Don's mother, Melissa. It was cancer, and Delbert just went to pieces. I was one of her nurses, and I can tell you the whole thing was really quite awful. After she died, Delbert never played the piano again. He started drinking, left the farm to run into the ground. It was Don's older sisters who kept food on the table. Don stepped in when he was twelve years old and took over the barn and the field-work. He quit school. The poor boy grew up much too fast. He had no childhood. I don't think Don has ever forgiven his father for that."

Oh dear, I thought. How sad. Gertrude sighed and put her hands back on the keys. She closed her eyes and began to play, a gentle melody in a haunting major-minor key. With a start, I realized she was playing Don's tune. Here it was again.

"I keep hearing that tune," I said. "Everybody seems to know it except me. But nobody knows what it's called or where it comes from. Even Delbert knows it. He was humming it in his sleep in the car just the other day."

Gertrude opened her eyes. "Of course Delbert knows it," she said. "He wrote it."

"He wrote it?"

"Yes. It's called 'Melissa.' Pretty tune, isn't it?"

"Why doesn't Don know this?"

"Oh, surely he must know. But then, he was just a toddler when his mother died . . . perhaps he doesn't know."

"Don really should know where that tune comes from, don't you think?"

Gertrude stopped playing and folded her hands in her lap. "Yes, Walt," she said. "You're right. I think he should. And, if you can get Don to come to my concert on Sunday, I think I know how to do it. So, let me know how many tickets you need." Her eyes twinkled and she went back to her Schubert.

Two nights later, Don turned up at our place just as I was closing up the barn. He looked very weary, and there was a heaviness about him that I hadn't seen before. He sat down at the kitchen table and waved away my offer of tea.

"I just got an offer in for the cows and the quota. It's a good offer, and I think I'm going to take it."

"Well, I guess if it's what you want to do. . . ."

Don was not looking for advice or consolation. "My dad's name is still on all the quota documents. The milk board wants a letter saying that he wishes to transfer his share to me because he is inactive as a farmer. I've written it up here. You've been visiting with him lately. I was wondering if maybe you could get him to sign it for me?"

I hesitated. "I'm not sure, Don. I suppose I could. But isn't that something you should ask him yourself?"

"I told you, Walt, I don't talk to him."

"Well, I can do the talking if you like, but I really think you should be there in the room with us. It's a big step, selling the cows after all these years."

Don nodded slowly. "Yeah, I guess I see your point. Okay, I'll go down there with you. But I'm not askin' him for anything. I haven't asked him for anything since I was twelve years old and I'm not going to start now."

"We're going down to the concert at the Myra Connor the day after tomorrow. We could get together with your dad there, if you like."

Don said he thought that would be fine.

First light came to the township like dawn in those desert scenes from *Lawrence of Arabia*. The sun rose like a fiery chariot and blazed down on the withered corn stubble. It was actually a relief to seek shelter in the air-conditioned comfort of the nursing home. When Maggie and I arrived at the lodge, we found the residents of the Myra Connor assembled in front of the stage in three rows of soft chairs, wheelchairs and hospital beds. Gertrude Lynch was at the piano, administering no-nonsense treatment to a 1920s Ivor Novello ditty as if it were a difficult patient. People drifted in from the parking lot, grateful to be out of the heat and the dust. As usual for these events, Freddy served as master of ceremonies. He hopped up on the raised platform that held the piano and glanced at the program notes in his hand. He tapped the microphone.

"Can you hear me at the back?" he asked. "Jeez, can you hear me at the front? Welcome to concert number four in the I'm a Goner Concert Series. Today we have a selection of music from the great German lieder. Did they spell that right, Gertrude? Jeez, I hope they don't mean Hitler . . . anyway, as usual, it is a real treat to have Gertrude Lynch playing for us today. She's just burnin' the carbon off the plugs on that piano right now, but in a few minutes she's gonna perform a work by the composer Frank Sherbert. Which reminds me: the ladies of the church are gonna be serving ice cream with the pie later on, or just ice cream in case you left your teeth in your room. And Gertrude will be accompanied by soprano Brenda Pargeter, the Lark of Port Petunia. So you're in for a real treat here. The proceeds from this series go towards helpin' our dear friends in the I'm a Goner. They got a real strong lawn darts team here, and today's concert will help cover the team's travel and first aid costs when they go to the county finals in September. Although 'finals' is not a word we use around here. Let's just call it the next game. It's all for a good cause, so crank your oxygen up to nine, sit back and enjoy the show. We're going to get underway in about fifteen minutes . . . which around here is like almost immediately."

Delbert came in the door of the hall and took a seat not far from the piano. Gertrude saw him and stopped playing.

"Oh, there you are, Delbert. Come over here with me. I've been trying to remember this tune all morning. Can you help me out?"

She played the first line of Don's tune, but it wasn't quite right. Delbert spoke up.

"The fifth note goes up a fourth," he said.

"Oh," said Gertrude. "Like this?" She tried again but it still wasn't right.

"No," said Delbert. "That's not it."

"Oh, just come here and play it for me," she said, shifting on the piano bench and patting the seat.

"I haven't played for so long. I don't think I can do it."

"Of course you can, Delbert. Just come over here and pick out the melody for me."

Delbert shrugged and sat down beside her. His long, graceful fingers hovered over the keys as if he were reaching for something. "It goes something like this," he said. With a slight hesitation, his fingers found the keys and the piano came to life. As the top line of "Melissa" sang in his right hand, heads turned and the hall fell silent. I felt as if I were hearing something that had been hidden away in a dark place for a very long time.

The front door of the lodge opened, and I saw Don and Elma coming in the door of the hall. I walked quickly over to them.

"There you are," I said. "Have you . . . ?"

Don stood motionless, his eyes adjusting to the lower light after the glare of the parking lot. "Who's playing that?" he asked. He blinked hard at the piano. "I've never heard anybody else play that."

He walked across the room and stood beside the piano. Delbert continued to play.

"How the hell would you know that tune?" asked Don warily. Delbert didn't answer him. His eyes were closed and he was lost in the music. Gertrude spoke for him.

"He knows it because he wrote it, Donald. He wrote it for your mother. It's called 'Melissa.' When she was so sick, your father would play it for her, and at times it was the only thing that would give her any comfort, poor soul. You didn't know that about your father, did you?"

"No, I didn't know that," he said. "I had no idea."

Delbert broke off playing. He was looking at his hands. They were still stretched out over the keyboard but they were motionless.

"What's the matter, Dad?" asked Don.

Slowly, Delbert turned his hands over, palms up, and stared at them. He closed his fingers, opened them again and slowly turned his palms down over the keys.

"I can feel it," he said. "The feeling is back in my hands."

That was it for the concert. Don took his father by the elbow and walked him straight out to the parking lot to his truck. Gertrude and Freddy took one look at each other and left Brenda Pargeter to sing the Schubert concert a cappella. Maggie and I followed them. Four vehicles driving down the Seventh Line together is like a big sign in the midway saying, "This way to the three-headed chicken." The Squire, Willy and Dave soon joined the crowd in the yard behind our house next to the old well. We watched as Delbert took the cherry branch in his hands and held it out in front of him. He closed his eyes and slowly circled the well.

"It's dry, all right," he said. He looked across the fence into the pasture and pointed. "The old channel went this way."

We helped him over the fence. He set off across the pasture in a straight line towards the hill at the back of the farm, the rest of us following silently. He stopped once and took several deep breaths, blinking in the scalding sun.

Don took his elbow. "You okay, Dad?" he asked.

Delbert nodded. "Oh yeah."

"Do you want to keep going?"

"Oh yeah."

He straightened up and continued across the pasture. Then he stumbled down into the dry pond bed and we helped him up the bank beside the cypress tree, the only bit of green on the Seventh Line. As Delbert approached the tree he hesitated and nearly went down on his knees. He suddenly let go of the branch and spread his hands apart.

"It's here," he said. "Thirty feet. The roots of this tree have blocked it."

"Is it strong?" asked Don.

"Yeah, very strong. You'll have to go careful and you'll need some way to cap it.

"All right," I said. "Should I call AAA Well Drillers again?"

Freddy stepped in. "Don't have to do that, Walt. Delbert's old percussion drill rig is still sittin' over there in Don's side of the bush."

"Is that what that big tower is for?" said Willy. "And here I always thought it was a hunting stand for the deer season."

"If we use the belt pulley on Walt's old tractor to run the cable winch, I'll bet you dollars to donuts she'll still dig a well," said Freddy.

Delbert looked at Don. "They told me you were gonna pull that thing apart and sell it for scrap."

"I guess I never got around to it," said Don quietly.

We found the old drill rig, gaunt and rusting, standing beside a pile of moss-covered steel pipe, and we hauled it with three lengths of steel pipe across the field. Using my old AR tractor to power the winch, we drilled a hole just uphill of the cypress tree, dropping lengths of pipe into the hole as the drill bit punched its way down. As the third length of pipe sank into place, the water came, shooting up through the pipe with the force of a broken fire hydrant.

"Holy dambusters! Thar she blows!"

"Call me Ishmael!" I said to myself as the air filled with a fine spray. The air soaked up the water like an April rain, and Willy and Dave began to dance arm in arm, one singing

"Raindrops Keep Fallin' on My Head" and the other "Singin' in the Rain."

The Squire licked his lips and grinned. "It's the sweet water, too."

After a few minutes, Don cranked the valve shut and turned to Delbert. The two men looked each other in the eye for the first time in many years.

"I just want to say, Dad . . ." There was a long pause and Delbert waited expectantly. " . . . it was twenty-eight and a half feet."

Delbert nodded. "Yeah. Well . . . I haven't done this for a while. I may be a bit out of practice."

We drilled a second hole on the dry side of the cypress and piped around the tree, forcing the spring back into its old channel. Within twenty-four hours, my well was full again. The day after that, Don drove down my lane in his pickup and jumped out. I asked him what the news was.

"I got water this morning. And the Squire and the three families down on 25 Sideroad did, too. Freddy should have his by tomorrow."

There was a bed and a mattress in the back of Don's truck. "What's that?" I asked.

"Oh, that's my dad's bed from the nursing home. Dad kept wanting it moved. So we're moving it."

"Okay. And where are you moving it?"

"We got lots of room now that young Donny's moved out. And Elma never thought Dad belonged in the Myra Connor anyway. We're moving him back into the house."

On a pipe in the ground behind some bushes at the base of a cypress tree at the back of my farm, there's a valve that effectively regulates the entire water supply of the Seventh Line of

Persephone Township. You wouldn't know it's there unless you went looking for it. And you can't see it from the air. It's just one more of those obscure little bits of information you find salted away in the dry hills of Persephone Township. It's one of those things that everybody knows, so, of course, nobody ever talks about it.

A few days after my well filled up, I was sitting on the verandah steps with Maggie enjoying a mid-morning coffee and a muffin. Spike was lying on the verandah with Hope pulling on his ears. I was picking absently at the dead blossoms that had fallen into a pot of geraniums beside me. My eye caught a glint of something in the pot. Maggie's eye followed mine and we both saw it at the same time.

"The farm on the arm!" cried Maggie. "My bracelet! It must have fallen off when I was watering the hanging baskets."

"Isn't that amazing?" I said. "You know, I tried to surprise you with a new one from that shop in Tuscany. Now I don't have an anniversary present for you."

"It doesn't matter, Walt," she said, putting her arms around me. "It was lost and now it's found, and that's like having the gift given to me all over again."

Yours sincerely,

Walt

A FINAL NOTE FROM THE EDITOR

So that's how it went.

It never did rain that summer. But Delbert was right. The drought ended with the end of the lunar cycle in September. And, just in time for the fall fair, it snowed.

Willy and Dave decided that AAA needed some competition and asked Don if they could borrow the drill rig and take Delbert out as a pilot. Don reminded them they needed a licence to drill wells the same as they do to fish and hunt. And Willy said, "We'll do it the way we hunt and fish then. We'll only do it at night."

I drove out along the Seventh Line the other day past Don's place, and I noticed he'd made some changes. All the square barn windows had been replaced by triangles. Don says the cows are happier now.

On August 10, two days after Delbert found the spring, the water bottling company held a news conference and production launch up in the Pluto Marsh. They asked me to drive up and take a picture of the first tanker truck to take a load of water to the city. When I arrived, there was a big crowd of municipal people and engineers and water experts all in a flap. Seems that overnight, the water level in the marsh had dropped a foot and a half, and the township was talking about an injunction to revoke the company's permits.

The company manager practically shouted at me that he had taken out only one truckload. He insisted it wasn't his fault.

I said, "It appears you have upset the fragile ecosystem of our township. When a butterfly flaps its wings on the Seventh Line, a water bottling company goes bankrupt in the Pluto Marsh."

A NOTE TO THE READER FROM DAN NEEDLES

I like farmers. I like the way they talk and I like the way they think. I've been listening to farmers ever since I was a kid, and they have helped to shape the way I look at the world. I hear their voices every time I pick up a shovel or try to start one of my ancient tractors.

In 1955, my family took up residence on an exhausted hundred-acre farm in the sand hills of Mono Township, an hour north of Toronto. My parents were both artists: my father was a Shakespearean actor and my mother wrote children's plays. About the only thing they agreed about in their chaotic marriage was that children needed vast amounts of unsupervised time to develop properly. Every summer, I was set free with my brothers to range the creeks and cedar swamps of the Seventh Line with a fishing rod and a .22 rifle.

Each of the farms on that dusty road was owned by a family that could trace its ownership of the land back to the Crown deed. It was a tightly knit community that revolved around the activities of two churches and the Orange Hall. At the age of twelve, I was handed into the care of a handful of windbroke cattle farmers who introduced me to the world of work. Those men were a terrific source of practical information. They showed me how to use an axe, and how to chop chickens. The last words a chicken heard were, "Pull yer nose back a little, Danny." They gave me driving lessons on the little orange Case tractor with the jumpy hand clutch. Then they showed me how to put the boards back on the drive shed after I'd gone through it with the tractor. They taught me how to tighten black wire around a fencepost, how to hoe turnips and how to keep hoeing turnips once you thought you'd got the hang of that job. They were authorities on the rhythm and the pace of work.

"We don't have to do it fast, Danny," they would say, "but we do have to do it all day."

My adopted uncles and grandfathers treated me like the rarest form of crystal until they were certain I understood just how many ways there were to kill yourself on a working farm. They also led very hard lives. Many of them drank heavily, and the rest were alcoholics. The only escape from farm work for the women was church functions and what one of the farmers called the "Women's Artillery."

By all of this I mean to say that the Seventh Line was no paradise, and I have been careful in my writing never to pretend that it was. The fences were flimsy, the machinery was ancient and the weather was brutal. But I came to feel a great affection for that community. I loved the way it worked together and played together. It had a marvellous talent for making its own fun, and it had a terrific way of pulling together in a serious crisis, like a fire or a death or a defeat in the Conservative party.

After studying economics long enough to realize I had no future as an economist, I returned to the farm in 1974 and went to work for the local newspaper, where I created the character of Walt, the stockbroker-turned-farmer who writes a weekly letter to the editor of the local paper. The column ran for three years, and when I went south to the city again, to work as a speechwriter at Queen's Park, my friend Rod Beattie's mother presented me with a scrapbook in which she had pasted every single column. She placed it in my hands and said very firmly, "Do something with this."

I finally did something with it in 1984. Rod and his brother Doug helped me put Walt on stage for the first time on a hot August night in the Rosemont Orange Hall, in front of a small audience of Seventh Line farmers sitting on squeaky folding chairs. Within two years, Rod had taken the play on as a full-time project. Not very long after that, I married a beautiful shepherdess from further up the Seventh Line, where it crosses the Boyne River. Then I made my own escape from the city to a thirty-seven acre farm in the Pretty River Valley, where we settled down with a small flock of sheep and began to raise a family.

It's been twenty-seven years since that tropical night in the Orange Hall in front of the neighbours. There are now seven Wingfield plays in the series, and Rod has given more than four thousand performances, in just about every English-speaking theatre in Canada as well as on national radio and television.

I wrote the first Wingfield play as a hymn to a lost world. The slow death spiral of the family farm and the unravelling of the old rural community saddened me. But as I travelled with the Beattie brothers to perform the plays in other parts of rural Canada, I began to realize that, although the family farm was in trouble, the rural community was rapidly transforming itself. Many farmers had accepted that the universe had changed for good and turned their hand to trades that paid better and encouraged shallower breathing. The voices I loved and the thinking I admired were alive and well. Very reluctantly, I had to concede the possibility that change wasn't entirely a bad thing.

Farmer thinking is a combination of relentless practicality, healthy scepticism, humility in the face of awe-inspiring natural forces, a dry sense of humour and a cosmic sense of what is enough. There isn't nearly enough of it in our public life. As a writer I feel that I have been charged with the safekeeping of all the little nuggets of farmer thinking that come my way. I fear that I would be held accountable to a higher authority if I were to misplace a single one of them.

Farmers are trained instinctively to get out of bed in the morning and start looking after the life around them. That's what a farmer does. And when you take responsibility for the life around you, it gives you a sense of purpose and makes you feel important. Not the kind of importance that comes from seeing your picture in the newspaper. It's the feeling you get knowing that living things depend on you. As the old farmer once said to me, even a chicken can be glad to see you. And this helps to explain why so many of them carry on so long after any financial incentive has disappeared and the accountant has begged them to give it up. It still *feels* like the right thing to do.

Some years ago, my neighbour and close friend Hughie, the last mixed farmer in Nottawasaga Township, was leaning on the box of his pickup truck listening as I did a cost-benefit analysis to explain why I keep my little flock of sheep.

"Danny," he said finally, "stop trying to justify what you're doing with that calculator. Put that thing away before you hurt yourself. The fact is you keep sheep because you like them. That's the only reason you ever have to give me for anything that you do."

I believe Hughie was right. Affection is the one human emotion that the economists cannot understand, and I have come to believe that anything that confuses an economist usually makes the community a better place to live.

Since I began the Wingfield series, the stream of city dwellers moving out into the countryside has turned into a flood. Just a few years ago, my township finally recovered the population it lost during the Depression and passed the peak that it last reached in 1870. The number of full-time farmers has dropped to where it was in 1834, the first year of settlement. Five families probably account for eighty percent of the food produced here. And yet, despite all the neo-colonial ski chalets and cookie-cutter subdivisions, more land is under cultivation and the value of total agricultural output is higher than ever before.

Biologists tell us that edge communities, where the savannah meets the rainforest or the meadow meets the woodlot, produce the greatest diversity of species. These junction zones often contain species of each of the overlapping communities, as well as some species that have adapted specifically for living in these zones. Persephone Township is one of these edge communities. In the old farmsteads that dot the concession roads you will still find a wide assortment of farmers, from cash-croppers on Battlestar-sized combines to the part-timers with twenty-five cows and a job on the township road crew. There are lots of hobbyists like myself, with a henhouse, a dozen sheep and a big garden, who will never be caught up in the butterfly net and classified properly by Statistics Canada. But more likely you will find a retired captain of industry, an airline pilot or a young couple who telecommute from a home office in the old summer kitchen and make stained glass in a shed behind the house. They have taken over the old listening posts at the mailbox, at the counter in the village store or in a booth in the diner. They may even take a position on the agricultural society and help put on the fair.

We all like to step back and look affectionately at the earnest naiveté of these newcomers and marvel at how otherwise capable and talented people can be reduced to stammering helplessness by a power outage or an escaped cow. But we are laughing with them, because we know the learning curve in country life is a steep one and, if we're honest, we can't help but see a little bit of ourselves in them.

Northrop Frye once wrote that Canada is a land of ruins. Our history is a procession of leave-takings. We find a place, use it up and move on. I, too, come from a long line of wanderers. But it appears the great migration has paused, at least in my own immediate family. My sister and two brothers also live in old farmhouses, and we share a common bond. We are the first of our direct ancestors to stay in one place for thirty years since the American Revolution.

The theatre can be a wonderful community, but it has always fostered a certain rootlessness. Actors and directors are always on the road, always looking for work. Plays must travel and seek out new audiences in order to live. Everyone's life alternates between "When will this show be over?" and "Will I ever work again?" I recoiled from this way of life at an early age and resisted my parents' attempts to draft me into their theatre ventures. As my father always said, "Dan ran away from the circus and joined a farm."

Persephone Township, on the other hand, has always

fostered permanent residence, work at home, respect for the land, memories, stories and the ancient art of neighbouring. These are all things that give us a sense of place and help us protect that place from the forces that would otherwise destroy it. But let us not forget that Persephone is a very peculiar community; if you would like to know how it got to be that way, consult my guidebook *With Axe and Flask: The History of Persephone Township from Pre-Cambrian Times to the Present.* Everything will become clear.

Apart from all this, my advice to you about country life will have to be of a very general nature. I would say to you, as my father-in-law used to say, go to bed early, and rise with the rooster. It always gives you a wonderful reputation in the community when you can say that you rise with a rooster. And if you get the right kind of rooster, and you work at him, you can easily train him to get up at half past nine, like mine does. It's the easiest thing in the world.

DAN NEEDLES 2011

DAN NEEDLES is the creator of the Wingfield Farm series of stage comedies, seven full-length pieces starring actor Rod Beattie that have been performed continuously in theatres across Canada and the United States since 1984. Beattie has given over 4,000 performances in every English language theatre in the country, including appearances on CBC radio and television and the Bravo channel. Dan is a regular columnist for *Harrowsmith Country Life* and *Country Guide* magazines. He lives with his wife and family on a small farm near Collingwood, Ontario.

A NOTE ABOUT THE TYPE

Wingfield's World is set in Monotype Dante, a modern font family designed by Giovanni Mardersteig in the late 1940s. Based on the classic book faces of Bembo and Centaur, Dante features an italic which harmonizes extremely well with its roman partner. The digital version of Dante was issued in 1993, in three weights and including a set of titling capitals.